MW01641712

ENDORSEMENTS

"Wow! This book stands out among the many deconstruction books I've read. The number of insights and pearls of wisdom per page is well above average. Hicks writes in interesting and winsome ways while being honest and helpful. *The Quest for Thin Places* is hopeful without being pollyannish. I highly recommend this book!"

THOMAS JAY OORD, Ph.D., Co-Author of
God After Deconstruction and many other books

The Quest for Thin Places is my new go-to recommendation for people on the deconstruction/reconstruction journey. It's an honest, humorous, and intelligent way forward; something that many of us Christians or post-Christians or Jesus-followers or whatever it is we call ourselves these days will benefit from."

JONATHAN J. FOSTER, Ph.D.,
Author of *Indigo: The Color of Grief*

"Filled with meticulous research and poignant illustrations, *The Quest for Thin Places* skillfully explores the challenging journey of spiritual deconstruction and reconstruction with urgency yet humility. Hicks not only honors the complexities of spiritual evolution but also offers a compassionate roadmap for navigating both the difficulties and rewards of rediscovering meaning and truth. This book deserves wide and repeated reading."

WM. CURTIS HOLTZEN, D.Th.,
Author of *The God Who Trusts*

"If you're looking for a book to help explain why people deconstruct, this is the book for you! It's one of the best books I've read explaining the process, helping understand why people deconstruct and giving deep psychological insights into what deconstruction actually looks like from the inside, out. Dana does an amazing job of connecting the dots in a way that is easy to read, but also challenging to the status quo. I highly recommend The Quest for Thin Places: How to Find Spirituality After Deconstruction to anyone looking for a deeper insight into deconstructing and reconstructing one's religious beliefs."

LESLIE NEASE, Speaker, Writer, and
Honoring the Journey Podcast Host

"Dana Hicks provides a well-researched smorgasbord of powerful, interesting research; authenticity in personal vulnerabilities; and insights. Always so honest…I appreciate his candor about painful experiences. This book provides many moments of thought-provoking explorations. I loved the many stories!"

KARA HUDSON, LCPC,
counselor and author of *Who am I?*

THE QUEST FOR THIN PLACES

How to Find Spirituality after Deconstruction

DANA ROBERT HICKS

Nampa, Idaho

Print: 978-1-958670-57-6
Ebook: 978-1-958670-56-9

Printed in the United States of America

Library of Congress Cataloguing-in-Publication Data
The Quest for Thin Places: How to Find Spirituality after Deconstruction /
Dana Robert Hicks

FOR JENNA

"I fell in love the way you fall asleep:
slowly, and then all at once."

—John Green—
(American author from *The Fault in Our Stars*)

Deconstruct

When You Find Yourself in That Space between Falling Apart and What's Next.

1

Clarify

What We Often Think We Want Is Not What We Really Want.

2

Remove

Spirituality Is More About Removing Barriers than Adding More Stuff.

3

Quest

The Pursuit of Truth and Spirituality Requires a Mindset of Humility and Courage.

4

Re-Construct

Re-Building It Right This Time.

5

Cultivate

Establishing Sustaining Habits for a Life of Spirituality.

6

CONTENTS

REMOVE

Spirituality Is More About Removing Your Barriers than Adding More Stuff.

QUEST

Your Pursuit of Truth and Spirituality Requires a Mindset of Humility and Courage.

RE-CONSTRUCT

Re-Building Your Spirituality with New Tools.

CULTIVATE

Sustaining Habits for a Life of Spirituality.

ACKNOWLEDGMENTS

This book was written with the premise that rugged individualism is a carefully crafted illusion and that everything in the universe is ultimately connected to everything else. In arranging these words into a book, I could not be more cognizant of that reality. This book did not arrive in a vacuum: too many people to mention have influenced my thoughts and ideas. Here is a small sampling of some of them:

Jenna Beck is my girlfriend, but that seems to be too trivial of a word for our relationship. She is a constant stream of encouragement and hopeful optimism. In almost every instance, intimate partners are not good editors – it's a dual role that almost nobody can handle well. But Jenna is far from ordinary. I have never met anyone able to speak the truth with as much kindness. She constantly reminded me of Mark Twain's famous quip, "I would have written a shorter letter, but I didn't have the time." Thousands of words did not make this book because Jenna was able to help me pull the trigger and, in the words of Stephen King's advice on writing, "kill my darlings." To top it off, she is really cute.

Thomas J. Oord was another constant source of encouragement for this project. Tom and I have been close friends for about 40 years and have seen many ups and downs along the way. As this book was going to press, Tom was in the process of being defrocked by the denomination he has served his entire adult life because his boundaries of inclusion and love were way too broad for them. I couldn't be prouder of him. His brilliant mind is only surpassed by his kindness.

Two people who profoundly influenced my life died within three months of each other in 2022: **Christina Gage** and **Reg Watson**. While not overt, their spirits permeate many of the thoughts and ideas in this book. The aftermath of their enormous wake continues to hold me beyond the grave. I miss both of you every day. ("I know better, but I still feel you all around." IYKYK)

Debbie Coutts, **Jenna Barnes**, **Amanda Oster**, **Susan Rasmussen**, **Teri Whilden**, and **Bob Hunter** all gave feedback to early drafts of this book that made it much, much better. Thank you for your friendship and for taking the time to improve this book.

Joe Bell and I attended McMinnville High School together in the 1980s. Knowing how we behaved then, it blows my mind that we both became responsible adults! Joe gave me great feedback and encouragement on early drafts, especially on the Twelve-Steps of AA and its integration with spirituality.

When it came to the nuts and bolts of publishing, I am indebted to those who helped me out along the way:

- **Jonathan Foster** and the good people of SacraSage Press (https://sacrasagepress.com/) have been a delight to work with and have provided much-needed advice, insight, and encouragement.

- **Kevin Scott** took a rough manuscript and edited it to make me sound much smarter and more polished than I am. His feedback was an invaluable asset in making this book what it is. https://kevinrscott.com/

- **Meredith Messinger** created a mind-blowing cover design. I couldn't recommend her more highly if you need freelance graphic work: https://meredithfernillustration.com.

- **Josh Gilbert** edited and produced the audiobook version of this book. He made me sound much better than I am. I hope others will also use him because he is really good at what he does: https://joshgilbertmedia.com/.

INTRODUCTION

Paleolithic Emotions, Medieval Institutions, and Godlike Technology

"To see a world in a grain of sand
and a heaven in a wildflower
hold infinity in the palm of your hand
and eternity in an hour."

–William Blake–
(18th century English poet)

"There is nothing to writing.
All you do is sit down at a typewriter and bleed."

— **Ernest Hemingway–**
(20th century American author)

A decade ago, Edward O. Wilson, the Harvard professor and renowned father of sociobiology, was asked whether humans could solve the crises that would confront them over the next 100 years. "Yes, if we are honest and smart," he replied. "The real problem of humanity is the following: We have Paleolithic emotions, medieval institutions and godlike technology."[1]

1. Tristian Harris, "Our Brains are No Match for Our Technology." New York Times. December 5, 2019. https://www.nytimes.com/2019/12/05/opinion/digital-technology-brain.html, accessed October 13, 2023

I cannot think of a better summary of our experience with spirituality in the West. The internet age facilitated the democratization of thoughts and ideas, and cryptocurrencies the democratization of economics. Now, spirituality is being democratized and made independent from religious professionals. Stanislav Grof reflected in his work on human consciousness:

> Organized religion, bereft of its experiential component, has largely lost the connection to its deep spiritual source and as a result has become empty, meaningless, and increasingly irrelevant in our life. In many instances, live and lived spirituality based on profound personal experience has been replace by dogmatism, ritualism, and moralism.[2]

However, abandoning medieval institutions is not enough to guarantee a clear, compelling spirituality for modern people. Moore's Law states that the number of transistors on a microchip doubles approximately every two years, while the cost of computers is halved during the same period.[3] The exponential growth of information and computing power gives a small insight as to why homo sapiens are in uncharted waters. It remains difficult to be a spiritual person in the 21st century because our paleolithic minds are interfacing with rapidly evolving technologies that our ancestors would have considered godlike. I will discuss these things in detail in the third section of this book.

What we do have in common with our ancestors is that it still takes enormous reflection and self-awareness to understand our souls' deepest desires. And, like our ancestors, it still takes great courage to unlearn the unhealthy thoughts and ideas from our past (deconstruct) and start over (reconstruct).

2. Stanislav Grof, *The Cosmic Game: Explorations of the Frontiers of Human Consciousness* (Albany: State University of New York Press, 1998), 245–246.

3. Moore's Law is derived from an article written by Gordon Moore, the co-founder Intel in 1965. Cf. Gordon E. Moore, "Cramming More Components onto Integrated Circuits," Electronics, vol. 38, no. 8, April 19, 1965.

American singer-songwriter and podcast host Michael Gungor shared some thoughts about the process of religious deconstruction on X (formerly Twitter):

He described a process in which the stages of deconstruction are linear and look something like this:

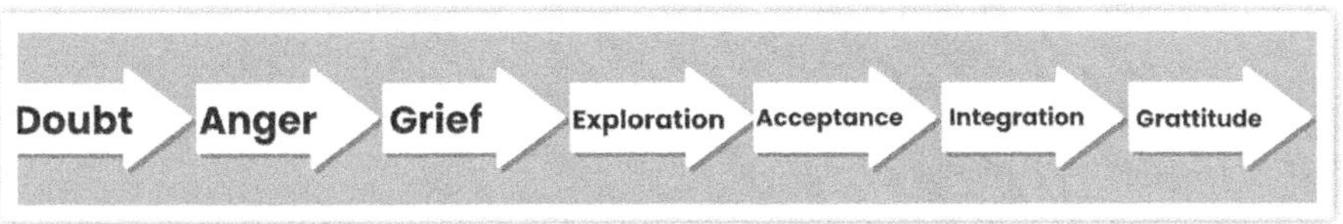

Michael probably meant for this Tweet to be nothing more than an anecdotal observation, but how we view the process of religious deconstruction is important. In *my* anecdotal observation, many people who deconstruct from an unhealthy form of dogmatic fundamentalism adopt a *new* form of dogmatic fundamentalism that is just as toxic. The problem with describing deconstruction as a linear process is that it suggests we will one day "arrive" and figure it all out. But there is no "end" to this process.

If we do it right, we remain in a never-ending cycle of deconstructing and reconstructing. During the Reformation, the Protestants declared they were "*ecclesia reformata, semper reformanda*" or "reformed and always reforming."[4] In other words, the process of deconstructing, clarifying,

4. Cf. Jaroslav Pelikan, *Reformation of Church and Dogma (1300-1700), vol. 4 of The Christian Tradition: A History of the Development of Doctrine* (Chicago: University of Chicago Press, 1984).

reconstructing, and cultivating was an ongoing cycle and never-ending process of growth for them.

In the Christian tradition, Jesus was the deconstructor/reconstructer par excellence. Six times during his Sermon on the Mount, Jesus said, "You have heard it said [deconstructed idea], but I say to you [reconstructed idea]…"[5]

So, what does the deconstruction/reconstruction cycle look like? The statistician George Box famously observed, "All models are wrong, but some are useful." With that in mind, here is my humble attempt at a model that may be useful:

1. **Deconstruct**: When You Find Yourself in That Space between Falling Apart and What's Next.
2. **Clarify**: What You Often Think You Want is Not What You Really Want.
3. **Remove**: Spirituality Is More About Removing Your Barriers than Adding More Stuff.
4. **Quest**: Your Pursuit of Truth and Spirituality Requires a Mindset of Humility and Courage.
5. **Re-Construct**: Re-Building Your Spirituality with New Tools.
6. **Cultivate**: Sustaining Habits for a Life of Spirituality.

This is a cyclical model, so here is what it looks like as a cycle:

5. Cf. Matthew 5:21–38.

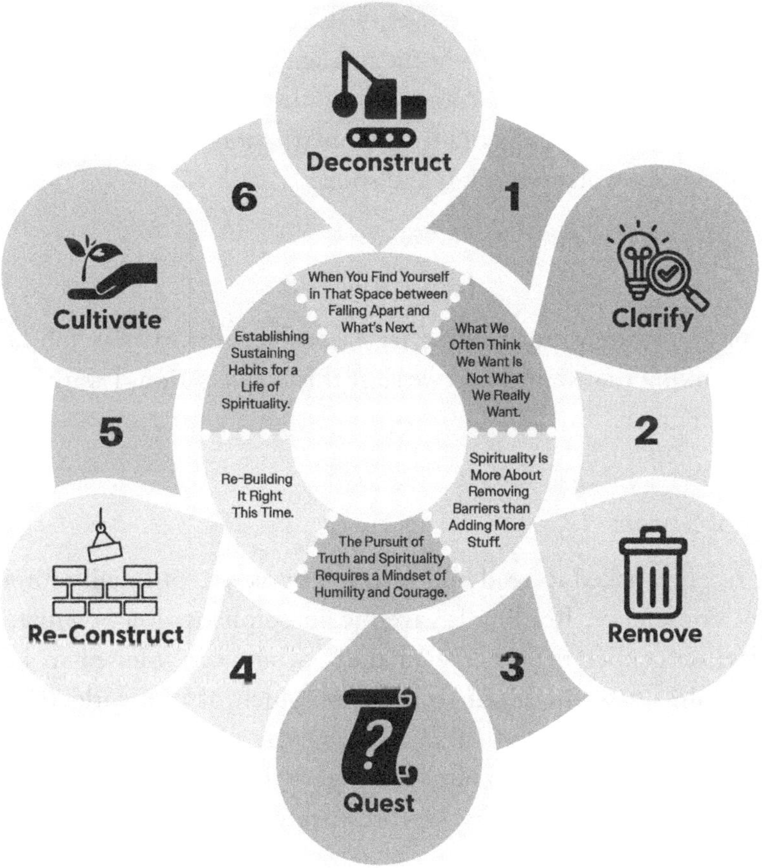

Deconstruct

1

When You Find Yourself in That Space between Falling Apart and What's Next.

Clarify

2

What We Often Think We Want Is Not What We Really Want.

Remove

3

Spirituality Is More About Removing Barriers than Adding More Stuff.

Quest

4

The Pursuit of Truth and Spirituality Requires a Mindset of Humility and Courage.

Re-Construct

5

Re-Building It Right This Time.

Cultivate

6

Establishing Sustaining Habits for a Life of Spirituality.

Alcoholics Anonymous famously uses the "Twelve Steps" of recovery for healing from addiction. However, contrary to popular belief, the steps are not a linear checklist process but an ongoing, never-ending cycle of growth. After a person "works the steps, " they return to the first step and start over. They emphasize that healing our minds and souls is similar to healing our bodies. When we have a deep physical wound, cleaning it once is insufficient. As each layer heals, we must remove the dressing, clean it again, and redress it—again and again.

Not unlike Alcoholics Anonymous, this book shows you how to "work the steps" of deconstruction/reconstruction repeatedly to facilitate the healing of a wounded mind and soul.

DISCLAIMERS

I'm not an attorney, but reading legal contracts for my day job has my mind thinking that way! So, as we start this conversation, I want to make a few disclaimers.

Spiritual Quests

I was recently asked to read and review a book on spirituality for an academic conference. Reading it gave me an epiphany: I, as a white, middle-class, cisgender male living in the US, am very blessed to be able to entertain questions about spirituality. Much of the world (probably most?) is too far down on Maslow's hierarchy of needs (pursuing food, shelter, safety, etc.) or is too busy picking up the kids and fixing dinner to think much about spirituality. Unfortunately, if you are in that boat, this book can't fix that.

However, if you are like me and have the capacity to reflect deeply on the ultimate questions, I hope you will join me in feeling a deep sense of gratitude that we can have this conversation together.

God Language

Any book about spirituality must discuss ultimate reality, even though it is beyond mere words and phrases. By "ultimate reality," I mean the most fundamental, absolute, or ultimate nature of life from which everything else arises. In the tradition I grew up in, our word for ultimate reality was *God*. I recognize that for many, the word *God* is problematic or even triggering. In the spirit of twelve-step groups like Alcoholics Anonymous, this book's intention is not to convince you to believe anything about "God." I would much rather you engage with and experience ultimate reality than argue about its definition.

In this book, I will almost always use the phrase "The Divine" to speak of ultimate reality. When I use the phrase "The Divine," I am referring to the notion that our lives matter, that everything in the universe is ultimately connected to everything else, and that history seems to be slowly enticed toward better outcomes. Perhaps you can appreciate why this would be too cumbersome to write every time and why instead I choose to say, "The Divine."[6]

My Memory

In talking about my experiences, I strive to be as accurate as possible, but the frailty of human memory limits me. So, I ask for understanding where my memory may deviate from others' memories. Where I speak of specific people in this book, I have either received their permission to use their story, created composite characters to represent a variety of conversations, or changed the details enough to obfuscate their identity.

6. Many gallons of ink have been spilled in arguments about how to talk about God and/or ultimate reality. It is beyond the scope of this book to be a theological treatise on language. However, if this discussion triggers some curiosity for you, I recommend to you as an accessible introduction Rob Bell's book, *What We Talk about When We Talk about God* (New York: HarperOne, 2013).

Evangelicals

As an X (I still say Twitter) aficionado, I see a lot of online vitriol about Christian Evangelicalism and its destructive force on the world. I understand and appreciate the backlash. Evangelicalism may be the greatest existential threat to the future of humanity.[7] However, I want to clarify that I am not bitter toward my Evangelical friends or resentful about my Evangelical upbringing. I gleaned treasures from my upbringing that I still cling to today. I'll mention some of them in this book. Writing off all Evangelicalism as wholly false or with no redeeming qualities is way too simplistic and binary.

In *Catching Fire*, the second book of The Hunger Games trilogy, the hero, Katniss Everdeen, is forced to compete a second time in the Hunger Games. During her preparation, one of her advisors tells her, "Always remember who you are really fighting against." Katniss's ostensible opponents are the other tributes in the arena, but her real enemies are the Capitol and President Snow's totalitarian regime—the oppressive forces that instituted the Hunger Games in the first place.[8]

I sometimes think about that scene from *Catching Fire* when arguing or disagreeing with someone else. We are not fighting against evangelicalism but against systems, institutions, and stories that try to define and control us. The author Jonathan Foster has helped me see that I sometimes scapegoat Evangelicals as if they are the problem and not a symptom of a more significant problem. I want to avoid that temptation in this book.

MY INTENTION

Several people have asked me why I wrote this book, so let me be direct: I wrote it for myself. I recently heard an interview with the author Morgan Housel in which he recalled a conversation with Jason Zweig from The

---

7. In Brian McLaren's new book, he makes a compelling argument that Evangelical beliefs have unintentionally put the world as we know it in existential crisis. Cf. Brian D. McLaren, *Life after Doom: Wisdom and Courage for A World Falling Apart* (New York: St. Martin's Essentials, 2024).

8. Suzanne Collins, *Catching Fire* (New York: Scholastic Press, 2009), chapter 12.

Wall Street Journal. Zweig mused that a person should only write a book if, in their mind, they *have* to do it. Not, "Oh, I should do it." Or "Oh, that's a lot of money I could get for doing it." Instead, "I can't sleep until I get these ideas on paper." That is how I have felt during the writing process of the last two years. Verlyn Klinkenborg's reflections on writing capture a lot of my own sentiments:

> Writing doesn't prove anything.
> And it only rarely persuades.
> It does something much better.
> It attests.
> It witnesses.
> It shares your interest in what you've noticed.
> It reports on the nature of your attention.
> It suggests the possibilities of the world around you.
> The evidence of the world as it presents itself to you.
>
> Proof is for mathematicians.
> Logic is for philosophers.
> We have testimony.[9]

This book is my testimony.

I'm delighted you could join me on the ride, but I do not intend to try to convince you what to believe about ultimate reality. I will, however, try to convince you to become more open to unexpected moments of ineffable transcendence, because I think that is what we all really want.

I wrote this book because I needed to process my own deconstruction and reconstruction and consider its meaning. As such, it contains some personal things, but it is not meant to be a memoir per se.

Stephen King set the scene for his novel *The Body* with the following words that I also find a fitting beginning to this book on spirituality:

9. Verlyn Klinkenborg, *Several Short Sentences about Writing.* (New York: Knopf, 2012), p. 117.

The most important things are the hardest to say. They are the things you get ashamed of, because words diminish them—words shrink things that seemed limitless when they were in your head to no more than living size when they're brought out. But it's more than that, isn't it? The most important things lie too close to wherever your secret heart is buried, like landmarks to a treasure your enemies would love to steal away. And you may make revelations that cost you dearly only to have people look at you in a funny way, not understanding what you've said at all, or why you thought it was so important that you almost cried while you were saying it. That's the worst, I think. When the secret stays locked within not for want of a teller but for want of an understanding ear.[10]

10. Stephen King, *The Body* (New York: Scribner, 2018), 1. Many will recognize this story from the 1986 film adaptation, "Stand by Me." (Rob Reiner, dir. 1986. *Stand by Me.* Columbia Pictures.)

Deconstruct
Clarify
Remove
Quest
Re-Construct
Cultivate

DECONSTRUCT

When You Find Yourself in That Space between Falling Apart and What's Next.

Few people set out to deconstruct their religious beliefs. Most of us prefer doing Olympic-level mental gymnastics rather than address any cognitive dissonance we experience. When we do finally surrender to deconstruction, deconstruction is often frightening and disorienting before it becomes liberating.

1

Please Tell Me All Your Thoughts on God

Welcome to the "Nones"

"One of our most common temptations is to turn the way into a place, to turn the adventure into a status, to trade the runway for the hangar, to turn the holy path into a sitting room—even if we call it a sanctuary. When the movement becomes an institution, those whose hearts call them to pilgrimage get restless."

—Brian McLaren—
(Author, speaker, activist, and public theologian)

"The important thing is this:
to be able at any moment to sacrifice what
we are for what we could become."

—Charles Frédéric Dubois—
(19th century Belgian naturalist)

Sometimes I reflect on a story that Will Willimon told me about a conversation he struck up with a man while flying on a commercial flight. Will asked him what he did for a living.

"I am an astrophysicist with NASA," the man replied. "What do you do?"

"I am a United Methodist minister," Will responded.

The astrophysicist thought for a minute and said, "I've thought a lot about it, and I think all the world's religions can be summed up with: 'Just love each other.'"

Will Willamon

Will told the man, "That's ironic. I fancy myself an amateur astrophysicist. I think all of astrophysics can be summed up with: 'Twinkle, twinkle, little star. How I wonder what you are.'"

I resonated with Will's story, because I often don't know what to say in such situations. It seems people want me to agree with them on their thoughts and beliefs about God, the world, or morality—thoughts I recognize as re-hashed from some famous preacher or spiritual guru. I don't like to argue or disagree with people, so I usually acquiesce and nod politely, at a loss for words. Despite my aversion to spiritual conversations, I often find myself embroiled in them, as if there is a sign on me that says, "Please tell me your thoughts about God."

Recently, a couple of friends I met for happy hour at The Fat Ox, a trendy restaurant in North Scottsdale, asked me, "Have you always been in social services?" I knew that if I told them I had spent 30 years as a pastor, it would change the conversation and probably the trajectory of our relationship. Nonetheless, I took a deep breath and told them about my journey in and out of professional ministry.

"I grew up Catholic," one of my friends responded. "I don't go to church anymore. I haven't been to mass in years. I guess you could say I'm agnostic, but I pray. I pray almost every day during my morning run. I'm not sure why."

"It sounds like you are a spiritual person despite your religious background, not because of it," I replied.

She thought briefly and said, "Yes, I guess so."

This book started with a phone conversation with an old friend and former parishioner. "I have a friend I want you to talk to," Marie said.

"She grew up in a conservative Christian home but left all that behind. Now she is in a place where she wants spirituality in her life but doesn't know how to move forward." I began sketching how to answer this question in anticipation of the phone conversation. That sketch turned into an outline; before I knew it, it had become this book.

While the question takes different forms, it is by far the most common question people ask me. I first met Kacy about a decade ago at a restaurant where a mutual friend's band was playing. When Kacy learned I was a pastor, she shared an unsolicited description of her spiritual past. She grew up in a tiny, very exclusive house church in a small town. They believed that their small movement was the only group that was going to make it to Heaven; the rest of us were doomed to eternal damnation. Kacy's childhood was full of rigid legalistic practices.

When Kacy hit her late teens, she began to wonder about her family's church. She had many questions for the leaders of her church, but questions were strongly discouraged in their sect. At some point, shortly after high school, the cognitive dissonance of her life became overwhelming. If her church was so amazing, she wondered why it made people worse, not better, human beings.

Kacy, like many people I know, became one of what social science researchers call the "nones": people with no religious affiliation at all. It is, by far, the fastest-growing segment of religious affiliation in our country: "none of the above." The group is estimated to be around 30 percent of the US population.[1] This trend's impact on the religious lives of

---

1. Jessica Grose, "Why Do People Lose Their Religion? More Than 7,000 Readers Shared Their Stories" The New York Times (online). June 7, 2023. https://www.nytimes.com/2023/06/07/opinion/religion-nones.html, accessed July 12, 2023.

Americans can't be overstated. Jim Davis and Michael Graham call it "the largest and fastest religious shift in the history of our country."[2]

The reasons are nuanced and multifaceted, but the perfect storm of the dawn of the information age, Christianity's association with Donald Trump, and the social acceptability of not being religious have all been factors. A former parishioner of mine who spent years serving Evangelical and Pentecostal churches said to me recently, "The Christians' embrace of Donald Trump after all their pearl-clutching about Bill Clinton and talk about 'character matters' proved to me that it was all bullshit. It was all a ruse for political power."

Jia Tolentino

Another friend, Andrew, began his journey into the "None Tribe" during the COVID-19 pandemic. When churches were forced to temporarily close, Andrew quit attending and never returned. He said, "I realized that I don't really need or want that kind of religious experience anymore. I discovered that I was much happier without it. My wife agreed. So, for the first time in our lives, we don't have a church we belong to. Our parents are alarmed, but we are much better off."

2. As quoted in Jessica Grose, "The Largest and Fastest Religious Shift in America is Well Underway" The New York Times (online). June 21, 2023. https://www.nytimes.com/2023/06/21/opinion/religion-dechurching.html, accessed July 12, 2023.

I recognize that different social scientists use different terms to describe those who no longer affiliate with religious organizations. "Dones" is another more nuanced term that some people prefer—those who have been there but are now "done with all the religious stuff." Pew Research and Gallup Consulting have done a lot of research on this. Authors like Stephen Aisthorpe, Josh Packard with Ashleigh Hope, David Kinnamon, and Alan Jamieson have also written extensively on Nones, Dones, and The Deep Shift.

I can relate to Jia Tolentino's memoir where she reflects on her deconstruction after growing up in a Dallas megachurch she nicknamed "The Repentagon.":

> I read the Gospel to be constantly preaching economic redistribution—John the Baptist commands, in the book of Luke, "Let him who has two tunics share with him who has none," et cetera—but everyone around me seemed mainly to believe in low taxes and the unconditional righteousness of war. The fear of sin often seemed to conjure and perpetuate it: abstinence education led to abortions, for rich people, and for poor people to children who would be loved and supported until the day they were born. There was so much beatific kindness, and it was so often undergirded by brittle cruelty.[3]

It's not only Evangelical Christians who are driving this trend. Buddhists, Jews, Mormons, and Orthodox Christians are also deconstructing from toxic religion and are flooding the internet with their heartbreaking stories. If you are reading this, you are very likely one of them.

Those who remain inside the institutional religious structures often criticize those who deconstruct as people who abandon the teachings and practices of their religion for an "easier" life. However, most people I know who have deconstructed did so out of *fidelity* to what their religion's founders taught them, despite it being much more challenging to leave the comfort and ease of their support systems. In the Evangelical tradition in which I was raised, for example, I have noticed that most people deconstruct not because they reject Jesus' teachings but because they take Jesus' teachings so seriously. Evangelicals sanctimoniously emphasize opposition to things like abortion, women in leadership, and all kinds of sexual conduct about which Jesus says little or nothing. Yet, in the words

3. Jia Tolentino, *Trick Mirror: Reflections on Self-Delusion* (New York: Random House, 2019), 140–141.

of Richard Rohr, they "live in comfortable doubt about God's will in regard to war, riches, and non-violence (about which Jesus is absolutely clear)."[4]

My friend Kacy's deconstruction story is also eerily like many others in this way: she still considered herself a spiritual person. She realized a lot of the religious baggage from her childhood church was, as she described it, "pure bullshit." Yet, she also knew that beneath that baggage was something real. So, in a noisy concert hall late one Friday night, Kacy spoke over the music and asked me, "How can you separate those things? How do you get around the baggage of religion to what is really real?" That is the million-dollar question.

4. Richard Rohr, *Simplicity: The Freedom of Letting Go* (New York: Crossroad Publishing, 2015), 18.

2

Jenga and Divorceañera

That Liminal Space between Falling Apart and What's Next

"When I let go of what I am, I become what I might be."

–Lao Tzu–
(Ancient Chinese philosopher)

"Re-examine all you have been told in school or church or in any book, and dismiss whatever insults your soul."

–Walt Whitman–
(American poet)

A person's process of moving toward a deeper, richer, more authentic spirituality doesn't happen incrementally. It usually occurs through disruption: we have experiences that allow us to see the world differently than we had ever seen it before. Human beings are sleepwalkers. That is why religious teachers recognize that people don't naturally see spiritually; we must be taught *how* to see. The Buddha's name means "I am awake" in Sanskrit. Jesus often talks about "staying watchful,"[1] and if one's eye is healthy, "your whole body is full of light."[2] So you travel, you taste,

1. Matthew 25:13, Luke 12:37, Mark 13:33–37

2. Luke 11:34

you meet people from other tribes, you read new things, you hear new perspectives, you see data or research you hadn't seen before, and you discover that your previous ways of categorizing and labeling and believing don't align with what you are now experiencing. Or you experience some traumatic experience that rocks you to your core: an accident, the death of someone close to you, an illness, or a heartbreak.

Disruptive experiences present a choice: We can ignore, deny, or minimize our experiences, or we can open ourselves to the pain of leaving that way of understanding behind. The hardest thing about seeing and hearing is having to do something about what you have seen and heard. Disruptive events can be exciting and liberating, but they can also be traumatic—like the pieces of your life are crashing down.

It reminds me of the board game Jenga—the game made up of a bunch of precariously stacked blocks. The object is to remove one block after another without having the entire tower collapse. As we begin pulling out antiquated beliefs or ways of seeing the world, we may wonder, "How many blocks can I pull out before the whole thing comes crashing down?" But more than that, we wonder, "What will happen to *me* when it all comes crashing down?"

But once you've tasted it, you can't un-taste it. Once you've seen it, you can't unsee it. Maybe you received a way of seeing God and the world that once seemed to fit neatly together, but now it doesn't work for you anymore. Yet your old way of seeing things still has a gravitational pull on you. Maybe important people said you would suffer if you believed anything else. Or maybe you grew up in a calm, cool, rational world of evidence and data where only facts can be trusted. Maybe physics and complex equations make sense, but you've had experiences that don't fit into your nice, neat, modern categories.

In my journey, I was deeply influenced during the 1990s and early 2000s by the life and teachings of Bill Hybels, a megachurch pastor from

Chicago's Willow Creek Community Church. Hybels was famous for repeating the mantra, "The church is the hope of the world." When people would ask me during that season why I was a pastor, I would tell them, "I evaluated all the ways I thought I could make a difference in the world and decided that the best way to make the world a better place was through the church."

But things changed. Maybe it is more accurate to say that I changed. All I know is that, at some point, enough Jenga pieces had been removed that I realized American Christianity is not very helpful in making the world a better place, and often, it is actively making the world much *worse*. In this regard, my story is like countless others: we left the church *because* of our fidelity to what is good, true, and beautiful, not because of our abandonment of it. I found freedom in reading Richard Rohr's observation: "God is always bigger than the boxes we build for God, so we should not waste too much time protecting those boxes."[3]

Unless a person has experienced it firsthand, the existential angst and destabilizing effect of watching your Jenga pieces crumble to the ground is difficult to describe. Judgment by people in the communities that formed you is often the most challenging aspect.

And so many of us are in that in-between space where the Jenga pieces have fallen, but we have not put a new framework together. It creates what some spiritual writers call "liminal space"—a place between what was and what can be. It is a transitional state that is soaked in ambiguity and uncertainty. It is a space neither here nor there, where the old structures and identities have been left behind, and the new has not yet fully emerged.

Deconstruction allows us to surrender control and open ourselves to new possibilities and more profound truths. Liminal space becomes

3. Richard Rohr, *Everything Belongs* (New York: Crossroad Publishing, 1999), 25.

essential to our personal growth, our spiritual awakening, and our encounter with the divine. It is a space where we experience profound transformation, increased self-awareness, expanded consciousness, and a deepening of our connection to the divine, ourselves, and others. But to get there, we must take the pain and wear it like a shirt rather than trying to get rid of it before we have learned what it must teach us.

Anthropologists also describe "liminality" when explaining how boys become men in most cultures. In most cultures, men are not born; they are made. Certain things must be said to boys because they cannot figure these things out on their own. They must be shocked and displaced to learn that the world is much bigger than they imagined. So, the boys experience initiation rites to move from boyhood into a liminal space and later emerge as men.

We in the West have few rites of passage.[4] So, the rhythm of deconstruction and reconstruction, death and rebirth, or Jenga-crashing and Jenga-restacking, is mostly unfamiliar. We disdain a space of vulnerability, openness, and receptivity, where we are stripped of familiar patterns, certainties, and attachments.

Recently, I had lunch with a friend who had just completed a long and arduous divorce process with his wife of over 25 years. The Jenga pieces of his life were strewn all over the ground as he was grappling with what his next steps would be. It reminded me of a conversation with a parishioner many years ago. She had suddenly lost her husband, when he left home one Saturday afternoon to take his car to the car wash. While there, he was assaulted by a group of thugs. A struggle ensued; they shot him and ran away with the six dollars in his wallet. Years after the event, she reflected to me:

> Yes, the whole thing was unbearably painful and difficult. But here is the thing I noticed: my family surrounded me and loved me in ways that I didn't know were possible. My in-laws showed

---

4. I have been haunted by Richard Rohr's observation that the failure in the West to have meaningful male initiation rites into manhood leaves boys to initiate each other through domination and violence.

> up and cried with me; people checked in on me, they brought me flowers, they cooked me meals, and we had a beautiful funeral in which people laughed and cried and told amazing stories about my late husband. Meanwhile, I have watched some friends of mine go through divorces. But there is no ritual for a divorce. There is no ceremony. You lose all your in-laws, and your family isn't sure what to do with you. People stop talking to you because it is awkward. 'Couple friends' don't want to take sides. It's incredibly isolating and destabilizing. I think it is easier to be a widow than to be a divorcee.

I told my friend this story and then said, "Let's send out invitations to all your friends to a party to come and grieve your loss and celebrate your future! It will be like a quinceañera for a middle-aged, divorced dude. We'll have it at a Mexican restaurant, people can bring gifts, we'll have a piñata that looks like your ex-wife, and we'll call it "Divorceañera."

He hasn't taken me up on the offer yet.

Part of the reason why deconstruction and reconstruction are so difficult is that we have yet to build a ritual around them in which, after we deconstruct, we naturally emerge into something new, meaningful, and beautiful. I'm not sure what it would look like, but I hope people smarter and more creative than me will come up with something.

3

Rising from The Ashes

Endings are Beginnings

"There is no coming to consciousness without pain. People will do anything, no matter how absurd, in order to avoid facing their own soul. One does not become enlightened by imagining figures of light, but by making the darkness conscious."

–Carl Jung–
(Swiss psychologist and founder of Analytical Psychology)

"Behind every beautiful thing, there is some kind of pain."

–Bob Dylan–
(American musician and songwriter)

It may be my own journey that makes people so quickly feel safe baring their souls to me about their spiritual journeys and deconstruction. I, too, grew up in a very toxic version of evangelical Christianity. My adult life has been an attempt to, as Kacy framed it, separate the baggage of religion from what is really real.

A piece of the Jenga puzzle got pulled out of my world when my heart was crushed in college by a young woman I thought I was going to marry. Another piece was pulled when the professors at the small Christian liberal arts university I attended taught me how to learn, think, and question what I assumed to be true. Another piece was pulled during my graduate studies and by friends who asked hard questions for which the pre-packed answers I was taught were woefully inadequate. But nothing prepared me for the Jenga pieces that would be removed during the Covid-19 pandemic. A new church, for which I had risked and sacrificed way too much, crumbled to pieces as the pandemic shutdowns took hold, and a mainline Christian denomination left me holding the bag on thousands of dollars of debt. Meanwhile, one of my children was going through a potentially life-or-death mental health crisis. The stress from all of this, among other things, brought a very painful end to my relationship with the woman to whom I was married.

As I reflect on the last days of my marriage, I find it curious how snapshots of emotionally intense experiences can accentuate a long sequence of events. She asked me to find somewhere else to stay for a while. I assumed this meant that we would work on things, but while I was gone, she changed the locks on our home. I had made mistakes, but in my mind, they were not the kind that should be a deal-breaker for a marriage. When I told her, "I'm going through a shame spiral," she contemptuously rolled her eyes. At that moment, I knew we had reached a point of no return.

I filled up a U-Haul in the alley of our Northend Boise home and slowly loaded half of everything that we owned. I was still in denial that it was over. Is this how it would end? As I pulled the truck out of the alley and around to the front of the house, the memories came flooding back of all we had sacrificed to build this house and this home together. The moment is seared in my memory. I grabbed my cell phone and called her. Could we talk? We've always been able to talk through things.

"I'm too tired. I don't want to talk tonight," she told me. It would be the last conversation I had with her.

The following day, I left Boise for Phoenix. I stopped overnight in Las Vegas, where cheap and nice hotels were the charm. I woke early the following day and drove South on Interstate 11 toward Hoover Dam. The freeway turned West as the sun came up, and I crossed the Colorado River into Arizona. The timing was impeccable; the sun was rising on a new era of my life in a new place. I was no longer "pastor" or "husband" or any of the other identities or stories from which I had created my sense of self. It was painful and destabilizing, but it was also freeing. I sensed the first pieces of the Jenga puzzle being put back together into a new and different shape. I felt the emotion welling in my chest and tightening my throat as I pushed down on the accelerator.

Entering Arizona from Nevada on Interstate 11

Years later, the symbolism of that journey dawned on me. My new home, Phoenix, was settled in 1867 as an agricultural community near the intersection of the Salt and Gila Rivers. When they incorporated the city in 1881, they chose the name "Phoenix" because the town had sprung from the ruins of a former civilization that had vanished into history. In Greek mythology, the phoenix is a mythical bird known for its ability to be reborn from its ashes. As I arrived in Phoenix from Boise 153 years after the European settlers arrived here, my life, too, was being reborn from the ashes.

I met Christina not long after arriving in Phoenix. Although Christina grew up Roman Catholic, she no longer identified as Christian. That meant I didn't have to wear any of my tired, old identities around her. Christina was a Buddhist, but not one of those jack-buddhists who occasionally does a mindfulness exercise at work and now identifies as Buddhist. Christina was a Mahayana Buddhist who spent her 20s and 30s meditating on average three to four hours a day and studying under teachers in Tibet and around the world. She had written several books on Buddhism.

Through hours-long conversations, Christina inspired me to push beyond the superficial identities I had created for myself to ask, "Who am

I?" She coached me through my meditation practice, which became the most powerful spiritual discipline I had ever experienced. I now know that the neuropathways my previous spiritual experiences had established in my brain allowed me to transition to new varieties of spirituality quickly.

What was most uncomfortable for me, however, was Christina's desire to talk about Jesus. For months, I refused to engage in her attempts to bait me into that conversation. But when the dam finally broke, I connected to my former spirituality in a new way and began to envision what it might become.

Reading people like Richard Rohr, Peter Rollins, Rob Bell, and Brian McLaren helped me begin to put pieces of the Jenga puzzle in place. Long and deep conversations with wise people, like my former college roommate, Tom, gave me a new framework for seeing God and the world. My reconstruction gained steam when I met people from other religious traditions, like Robert Wright, Tara Brach, and Adyashanti, who taught me practices and showed me ways of seeing the world I could never have imagined.

A couple of years ago, my spiritual reimagination took a new direction when I had a profound religious experience while in the Mexican state of Quintana Roo, in the middle of a jungle, miles away from other human beings. A Mayan shaman introduced me to their traditional plant medicine in a ceremony that shifted how I see the world. I still occasionally have flashbacks to that experience in my meditation practice. I find myself overwhelmed with emotion, and it reminds me of the closing scene of the 1999 film *American Beauty*, in which Lester Burnham lies dying in his suburban home:

Somewhere in the Jungle in Quintana Roo, Mexico

> It's hard to stay mad when there's so much beauty in the world. Sometimes I feel like I'm seeing it all at once, and it's too much;

> my heart fills up like a balloon that's about to burst. And then I remember to relax and stop trying to hold onto it. And then it flows through me like rain, and I can't feel anything but gratitude—for every single moment of my stupid, little life. You have no idea what I'm talking about, I'm sure. But don't worry, you will someday.[1]

I tell you this story, dear reader, not to garner sympathy or empathy for my experiences. I sincerely don't need that. But I hope my story in some way sheds light on your own journey of pain, hurt, disappointment, and even trauma. Many of us discover that what initially looks like destruction may be the necessary death of our spirituality before its resurrection or re-building. We can wait expectantly for new possibilities to rise from the ashes, not unlike the mythical phoenix. As my friend Jonathan Foster is fond of saying, "Endings are beginnings."

By no means do I think I have "arrived." I'm not sure what that would look like or what it even means. And I don't think I am an "expert" on world religions; my formal education is focused on Christian theology. But I have seen a thing or two and spoken with many people about spirituality in my 30 years as a Christian pastor. I have been fortunate to have experiences that may prove helpful to others. To borrow a phrase from my inherited religious tradition, I'm just one beggar showing another beggar where to find bread. In that spiritual tradition, the Divine reveals themselves to humanity through the embodiment of love, grace, and beauty in a human being. Several people in my life have fit that description. I hope to be one of those people for you.

---

1. Sam Mendes, dir. 1999. *American Beauty*. DreamWorks Pictures.

I am aware that quoting a scene that Kevin Spacey performed is distracting at best and problematic at worst. I am also aware that the film's portrayal of certain issues, particularly its treatment of sexuality and gender, is, by today's standards, problematic. Despite that, I hope you can see past these legitimate critiques and feel the weight of what the writer, Alan Ball, was trying to convey.

To see the clip in its entirety, click here: https://www.youtube.com/watch?v=VGiI-MuTWf0&ab_channel=rjun67

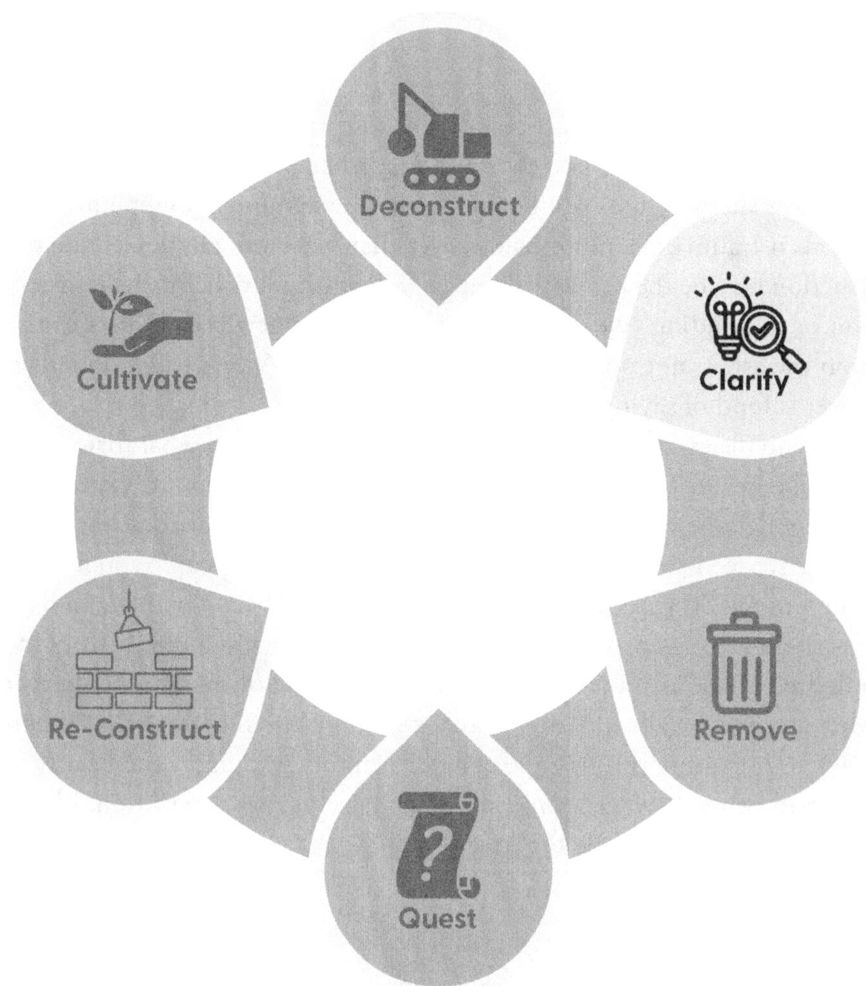
Deconstruct
Clarify
Remove
Quest
Re-Construct
Cultivate

CLARIFY

What You Often Think You Want is Not What You Really Want.

The deepest longing of our souls is the search for awe, wonder, beauty, and being fully alive. People often mean this when they say they are "spiritual but not religious." But many of us fall for cheap imitations rather than authentic spirituality.

4

The Five Why's

What You Really Want

"I did not ask for success, I asked for wonder."

—Abraham Heschel—
(20th Century Jewish theologian)

"People say that what we're all seeking is a meaning for life. I don't think that's what we're really seeking. I think that what we're seeking is an experience of being alive, so that our life experiences on the purely physical plane will have resonances with our own innermost being and reality, so that we actually feel the rapture of being alive."

—Joseph Campbell—
(American writer and professor)

In Matthew McConaughey's memoir, *Greenlights*, he recalled wrestling with the trappings of success. McConaughey had achieved some accomplishments in movies, and his life and lifestyle were beginning to change. He writes:

> One Friday night after work, a friend of mine, Beth, came over for dinner and drinks. Like a kid on Christmas morning, I was telling her all the things I was so happy about in my new digs—the

> mud-brick architecture, the national park as my backyard, the fact that it came with a maid. Especially the maid.
>
> "She cleans the place *after* I go to work, *washes* my clothes, *does* the dishes, puts fresh water *by my bed*, leaves me *cooked* meals—and, *she even presses my jeans!*" I told Beth, holding up my Levi's to show her the crisp, starched-white line running down the legs. Beth smiled at my enthusiasm, then said something I hadn't ever thought to ask myself, and haven't forgotten to since.
>
> "That's great, Matthew, *if you want your jeans pressed.*"
>
> I'd never had my jeans pressed before.
>
> I'd never had anyone to press my jeans before.
>
> I'd never thought to ask myself *if* I wanted my jeans pressed before because for the first time in my life I *could* have them pressed.
>
> The never-before-offered opulent option now being a reality, *of course* I wanted my jeans pressed.
>
> Or did I?
>
> No, actually, I didn't.
>
> When you *can*, ask yourself if you *want* to before you do. [1]

After reading this story, I couldn't help but think of a story in the Christian Scriptures about Jesus's life. The New Testament records that Jesus was leaving the town of Jericho with his entourage when a blind beggar named Bartimaeus began to cry out to him. He yelled, "Jesus, Son of David, have mercy on me!"

Jesus's handlers tried to shut the guy up, but Bartimaeus yelled all the louder and created a big scene. So, Jesus called him over and asked him, "What do you want me to do for you?"[2]

(Uh…duh. He was blind. What do you think he wanted?)

But I think Jesus was asking this question to probe at something more profound. His query showed great insight into the human condition and

1. Matthew McConaughey, *Greenlights*, (New York: Crown, 2020), 133, original emphasis.

2. Mark 10:46–52

the heart of spirituality. *It is not always obvious what people want.* Being cured of blindness may have seemed like the answer to all of Bartimaeus' problems, but facing one's disabilities means taking responsibility for oneself instead of begging. I once had a wise friend tell me: "There are two things people can't stand: 1. The way things are and 2. Change."

Do we really want our jeans pressed? Do we really want to be cured of blindness? Or do we want something else?

And just because we *do* want something or *can* have something doesn't necessarily mean that is the deepest desire of our souls. One spiritual thinker framed it like this: "We are half-hearted creatures, fooling about with drink and sex and ambition when infinite joy is offered us, like an ignorant child who wants to go on making mud pies in a slum because he cannot imagine what is meant by the offer of a holiday at the sea. We are far too easily pleased."[3] Our obsession with "drink and sex" remains mostly because we don't know how to obtain what our soul truly wants.

"I mean, I can throw it a third time."

Many years ago, I made a living as a youth pastor in a small town in southern Idaho. A critical aspect of my job was to discourage the teenagers in our church from having sex with each other.[4] Even though the kids knew the church's expectations about sex, like all teenagers, they loved to talk about it. On one occasion, I took the kids to see Josh McDowell, an evangelical apologist who was known for giving moving abstinence-only talks to teenagers.

3. CS Lewis, *The Weight of Glory and Other Addresses* (New York: HarperOne, 1949), 27.

4. The virtues of abstinence education I view very differently today. However, it was all I knew at the time. An in-depth discussion on deconstructing the evangelical view of human sexuality is beyond the scope of this book; but I go into detail on how my thinking has changed in my book, "The Knot" (SacraSage Press, 2022).

What was memorable to me was a throw-away line that Mr. McDowell used in the middle of his talk. He looked at the kids and said, "I know something about you guys. Here is the truth about you: you don't really want sex." Of course, the kids laughed, and some of them booed. Josh interrupted their boos and said, "No, deep down, what you really want is not sex; you want intimacy." A stunned silence came over the hormone-filled adolescents as they contemplated this observation.

I've known a few teenagers in my day, and contrary to Josh McDowell's generalization, some really *do* want sex. But his observation stuck with me because it's true that sometimes what we think we want is not really what we want. In our better moments, in our wise minds, what most people want more than a physical encounter with another person is a holistic sexual intimacy that includes mind, body, and soul. It reminds me of the D.H. Lawrence quote, "[People] are not free when they are doing just what they like…[People] are only free when they are doing what the deepest self likes. And there is getting down to the deepest self. It takes some diving."[5]

This is not just true about our sexuality; it's true in other areas of our lives. I sometimes wonder: Do we really want money, or is it security and stability that we crave? Do we really want power, or to feel as if our lives are not out of control? What is the "thing underneath the thing?" What is the "why" underneath what we think we want? What presents as what we desire is often a proxy war for something deeper.

In organizational leadership studies, there is a concept that Six Sigma adopted[6] called "The Five Whys." The inspiration for this concept was stolen from Sakichi Toyoda, who started the Toyota Motor Company. The idea is to find the root cause of a problem by repeating the question, "Why?" five times. The answer to the fifth "why?" should reveal the root of the problem.

---

5. D.H. Lawrence, *Studies in Classic American Literature* (New York: Thomas Seltzer, 1928), 10.

6. Lean Six Sigma is a set of methodologies and tools used by managers and consultants to improve organizational processes by reducing defects and errors, minimizing variation, and increasing quality and efficiency. For more information, see: https://asq.org/quality-resources/six-sigma

For example, a few years back, the National Parks Service discovered that the Lincoln Memorial's stone exterior was deteriorating and showing significant signs of wear. Replacing the stone or painting over it frequently proved to be very expensive, so the managers asked the maintenance crew, "*Why* is the stone deteriorating?" The maintenance crew explained that the pressure washers used every two weeks to wash the memorial were eroding the stone exterior.

This seemed like an excessive amount of washing. So the managers asked, "*Why* are you washing the memorial so often?" The maintenance crew explained that birds loved the Lincoln Memorial and consequently left their droppings all over it.

The managers instructed the maintenance crew to put up nets to keep the birds out. But the nets were ineffective and unsightly. So, the managers asked again, "*Why* do the birds love the Lincoln Memorial so much?" The maintenance crew explained that the birds came, not because they were fans of Abraham Lincoln, but because the Lincoln Memorial had lots of delicious insects for them to eat.

So, the managers hired a pest control company to spray the memorial. However, the treatments were largely ineffective, and the guests complained about the toxic smell. The managers returned to the maintenance crew and asked, "*Why* are there so many insects at the Lincoln Memorial?" The maintenance guys rolled their eyes and said, "Have you ever been to the memorial at night? The bright lights that shine on the memorial attract billions of bugs."

So, the managers adjusted the lighting schedule. Instead of having the lights come on at sunset, they waited 30 minutes, while the bugs found other lights in Washington, DC. This reduced the number of bugs at the Lincoln Memorial by 90 percent.

Fewer bugs meant fewer birds.

Fewer birds meant fewer droppings.

Fewer droppings meant fewer washings.

Fewer washings meant less deterioration of the stone outside the memorial.

Often, the presenting problem is only a symptom of the real problem.

When it comes to spirituality, what we think we desire is often merely a proxy for our deepest desires. We sometimes miss knowing what we really want because we fail to ask enough "Whys?"

So, I'll ask again the question that Jesus and Matthew McConaughey alluded to—what do you *really* want? When you get to that thing beneath the thing, you will find the pursuit of spirituality. If you dig even deeper, you will find things like transcendence, intimacy, and meaning. If you dig even deeper than that, you will find the divine.

5

Spiritual but Not Religious

The Quest for Awe, Beauty, and Transcendence

"The world is full of magic things,
patiently waiting for our senses to grow sharper."

—William Butler Yeats—
(20th Century Irish poet)

"There are in life a few moments so beautiful,
that even words are a sort of profanity."

—Diana Palmer—
(American writer)

During my years as a pastor, I often helped host an Alcoholics Anonymous meeting at our church building. Sometimes, I would be there in person to support the program and its participants. A kind and gracious guy named Dave would always set up the chairs in our building for the meeting. Dave's face carried the grooves of someone who had been through a lot of heartache in his life—some from his self-destructive decisions and some from the bad cards he had been dealt. Dave attended our church on Sundays, but like many who participate in 12-step programs, he found the experience rather superficial and empty. Dave was kind enough to put up with us anyway. When I asked him about his spiritual journey, Dave told me: "Religion is for people who don't want to go to hell. Spirituality is for people who have already been there."[1]

I've thought a lot about the distinction Dave made between religion and spirituality. I've also noticed that people have increasingly adopted the moniker "spiritual but not religious." I like to think that what they mean is that their spiritual pursuit is not "fire insurance" from eternal conscious torment but a way to find transcendence, connection, and meaning in the darkness of life. Diana Butler Bass's book, *Grounded,* helps unpack this shift.[2] Dr. Bass explains that for most of human history, people in monotheistic religions viewed the universe as a three-tiered universe. According to the Bible, the world is flat, and God is in Heaven above. Earth is in the middle, and the Underworld is below. This had been the dominant worldview for most of history.

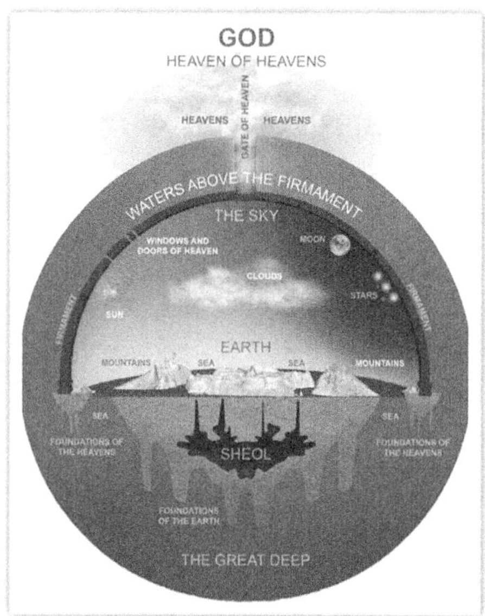

Illustration of The Three-Tiered Universe worldview

From this point of view, religious professionals mediated the space between Heaven and Earth. They were a kind of holy elevator in which God, who was distant and elusive, sent down directions. The training and expertise of the religious professional helped bridge the gap. Therefore, to disobey a religious professional was to disobey God.

---

1. Years later I learned that this saying was an appropriation from Richard Rohr's book: *Breathing Under Water: Spirituality and the Twelve Steps.* (Albuquerque: Franciscan Media, 2011).

2. Diana Butler Bass, *Grounded: Finding God in The World. A Spiritual Revolution* (New York: HarperOne, 2015).

While people no longer think of the world as flat,[3] some continue to believe that religious professionals are necessary to bridge the gap between Heaven and Earth. Most religious organizations continue to ordain clergy and give them special powers to administer sacraments. Like the believers in a flat earth, their numbers and influence dwindle.

If we believe our planet is a tiny spec in a vast universe, it is a small step to acknowledge that God is not found in some heavenly realm directly above us. Nor is God found exclusively in a church, mosque, synagogue, or other setting mediated by professional clergy. Instead, we can find The Divine everywhere in the universe—in nature, art, our children, the homeless guy we encounter on the streets, or quiet silence. In the words of Rob Bell, "Everything is spiritual."[4] I love the way Wendell Berry poetically described it in his novel, *Jayber Crow*:

> As I have read the Gospels over the years, the belief has grown in me that Christ did not come to found an organized religion but came instead to found an unorganized one. He seems to have come to carry religion out of the temples into the fields and sheep pastures, onto the roadsides and the banks of the rivers, into the houses of sinners and publicans, into the town and the wilderness, toward the membership of all that is here.[5]

So, many people are abandoning the three-tiered universe and recognizing that The Divine is with us everywhere. People are turning toward the aspects of our world that the German theologian Rudolf Otto called

3. A tip of the hat to the small (but growing) group of people in our modern world who, despite the evidence, continue to believe the world is flat. Cf.: Steve Mirsky, "Flat Earthers: Whey They Believe and Why." Scientific American. March 27. 2020. https://www.scientificamerican.com/podcast/episode/flat-earthers-what-they-believe-and-why/, accessed May 19, 2023.

4. Rob Bell, *Everything is Spiritual: Who We Are and What We're Doing Here* (New York: St. Martin's Publishing Group, 2020).

5. Wendell Berry, *Jayber Crow* (Washington, DC: Counterpoint, 2000), 321.

"the Holy"[6] with a very down-to-earth kind of spirituality. Diana Butler Bass notes:

> At the same moment when massive global institutions seem to rule the world, there is an equally strong countermovement among regular people to claim personal agency in our own lives. We grow food in backyards. We brew beer. We weave cloth and knit blankets. We shop local. We create our own playlists. We tailor delivery of news and entertainment. In every arena, we customize and personalize our lives, creating material environments to make meaning, express a sense of uniqueness, and engage causes that matter to us and the world.
>
> It makes perfect sense that we are making our spiritual lives as well, crafting a new theology. And that [The Divine] is far more personal and close at hand than once imagined.[7]

Ironically, the spiritual evolves into the religious, not vice versa. Nearly every religious movement began *not* with a desire to control or escape the fear of eternal torment but with someone having some kind of mystical experience. The philosopher and psychologist William James wrote longingly at the beginning of the twentieth century about spiritual experiences that take us "into the depths of truth unplumbed by the discursive intellect."[8]

The Jewish faith begins when Yahweh appears to Moses as a burning bush. Moses's experiences were so overwhelming that at one point, Yahweh warned him, "You cannot see My face; for no man can see Me and live."[9]

---

6. Rudolf Otto, *The Idea of the Holy: An Inquiry into the Non-rational Factor in the Idea of the Divine and Its Relation to the Rational,* trans. John W. Harvey. (New York: Pantianos Classics, 1917).

7. Diana Butler Bass, *Grounded,* 21.

8. William James, *The Varieties of Religious Experience* (London: Longmans, Green Co., 1917), 381.

9. Exodus 33:20

The turn of the Jesus Movement in the first century hinges on the experience of Saul of Tarsus, who had a mystical experience so profound that he was struck blind for three days and had auditory hallucinations of Jesus.[10] Saul was so profoundly transformed by the experience that he renamed himself "Paul" and became the first century's most effective missionary.

"Moses before the Burning Bush" by Domenico Feti (1613-14)

The existence of the Qur'an is due to the mystical trances of its prophet, Mohammad. The Prophet dictated the Scriptures word for word from the angel Gabriel during "ecstatic seizures," for which modern scholars say that he was prone.[11]

In the Protestant tradition I was raised in, the now stuffy-shirt Methodists owe their origins to a mystical experience that its founder, John Wesley, experienced on May 24, 1738. While attending a meeting on Aldersgate Street in London, someone read aloud from Martin Luther's *Preface to the Epistle to the Romans.*[12] Wesley experienced a profound spiritual revolution. Later, he wrote in his journal that God had "strangely warmed" his heart.[13]

---

10. Acts 9:1–19

11. Ahmad Shameem, *The Fascinating Story of Muhammad* (Bloomington, IN: AuthorHouse, 104), 11.

12. I have read part of Luther's *Preface to the Epistle to The Romans.* How someone could have a mystical experience listening to it is beyond me!

13. John Wesley, *The Journal of John Wesley* (New York: F.H. Revell, 1903), 56ff.

The Benedictine Monk David Steindl-Rast observed, "There is no other way to start a religion. Every religion has a mystical core. The challenge is to find access to it and to live in its power."[14] The Jesuit theologian Karl Rahner famously observed, "The Christian of the future will be a mystic or will not exist."

There is an adage in the political sphere that a conservative is someone who admires a dead liberal. Perhaps an appropriate corollary in the religious world is that religious institutional professionals are people who admire a dead mystic.

While we "ordinary" folks may not have these kinds of life-altering mystical experiences, we all have milder experiences of awe in our daily lives: beauty, transcendence, and virtue. New psychological research shows that these simple experiences of awe can change us because they force us to step outside the confines of our egos and reconsider our ways of knowing, our role in society, and even our place in the universe.[15] The sociologist and writer Anthony Campolo explained it well in his book *Carpe Diem*:

> "How long have you lived?"
>
> I posed the question to the students on the first day of a special seminar course on existentialism. No one answered. It may have been that my manner was intimidating. But then again, maybe it was because the question had a certain ambiguity to it. So I picked out one of the students on the front row of the lecture hall and, riveting my attention on him, I asked the question again, this time with an intensely personal emphasis.

---

14. Bokara Legendre, "The Monk and the Rabbi - Mysticism & the Peak Experience." YouTube, May 5, 2009. https://www.youtube.com/watch?v=4egjKZe4wJs&ab_channel=GratefulLiving, accessed September 1, 2023.

15. Emma Stone, "The Emerging Science of Awe and Its Benefits." Psychology Today, April 27, 2017. https://www.psychologytoday.com/us/blog/understanding-awe/201704/the-emerging-science-awe-and-its-benefits, accessed August 26, 2023.

See also: Jo Marchant, "Awesome Awe: The Emotion that Gives us Superpowers." Scientific American. July 26, 2017, https://www.newscientist.com/article/mg23531360-400-awesome-awe-the-emotion-that-gives-us-superpowers, accessed August 26, 2023.

"How long have you lived?" I asked.

My inquiry must have seemed like an attack on him. I could see that he was taken aback. The question seemed to pull him out of a time of private reverie. Instinctively he answered, "Twenty-four years!"

"No! No!" I responded. "I didn't ask you how long you have existed as a breathing, functioning member of the human race. I wanted you to tell me how long you have been really alive."

The Empire State Building

I could tell that this poor, besieged student was befuddled. I sensed he had some inkling of what I was getting at. But he wasn't sure. I knew he needed some help.

"When I was twelve years old," I told him, "I was taken to New York. It was one of those cultural enrichment trips that was designed to broaden the experiences of the sixth-grade class. There must have been close to forty of us in the group, although I don't remember enough about it to say for sure. What I do remember was being on the observation deck near the top of the Empire State Building. I had been running around chasing somebody just for the fun of it, as kids on a school trip are prone to do, when I stopped, went over to the guardrail, took hold of it, and gazed over the city.

"I remember that moment vividly. Everything around me seemed to drop away. A strange stillness drowned out the noise of the other kids. For me that moment belonged to another dimension of time and space. And I took it in—that incredible city, sprawled out before me with its towers of concrete and glass.

> There was an awesome expanse of what seemed to be a vast, miniaturized, make-believe, toy world. It was like looking at one of those model railroad displays you see in department stores at Christmas, only infinitely larger. I was awestruck! Full of wonder! And I remember saying these simple words to myself: Tony! You are on top of the Empire State Building. It was with a heightened awareness, a hyper-intensive consciousness, that I held that moment far too wonderful to describe. In a mystical way, I stepped outside of myself at that moment and reflected upon myself experiencing it.
>
> "I do not know how long I will live," I told my student, "But if I were to live a million years, I would remember that moment, because I truly lived it."
>
> "Now, let me ask you the question again," I said. "How long have you lived?"
>
> The young man had been moved to serious reflection, and he responded very slowly, as though he were carefully weighing each word of his answer: "When you talk about living like you lived that particular moment in New York, maybe a minute. Maybe two! I mean, if I were to add up all those times when I experienced life with that kind of heightened awareness, they are not likely to come out to much more than that!"
>
> Then he added a regretful afterthought. "When I stop to think about it, most of my life has been the meaningless passage of time between all too few moments when I have really been alive."[16]

Recently, I spoke to a friend who grew up evangelical but is now somewhere on the border between agnostic and atheist. While Luci is adamantly opposed to talking about "God," when I pressed her, she admitted having profound experiences of awe and wonder while experiencing yoga in a group context and while at a rave hosted by her favorite DJ. "I

16. Tony Campolo, *Carpe Diem: Seize the Day* (Nashville: Thomas Nelson, 1995), 12–13.

don't want to label it," she told me, "but these experiences linger with me and have changed how I see myself and the world."

Like Tony and Luci, I've also had profound experiences of awe and wonder—like quietly watching the sunset over the ocean in Canon Beach, Oregon, a few years ago. It happened again when I saw U2 at Lumen Field in Seattle, as Bono counted down to the song "Vertigo." ("Unos, dos, tres, catorce!")[17] I also feel a profound movement in the center of my being when I see amazing art or have a deep connection with another human being. I'm sure you have had similar experiences. Last month, I stepped outside myself into an experience that transcended me as Coldplay sang "A Sky Full of Stars" to 60,000 fans at the Rose Bowl.[18]

U2 Live in London in 2018

One of the consequences of the Enlightenment on Western Christianity was making "belief" central to defining faith. Intellectual ascent to propositions about God, Jesus, and human nature remains important for modern Western Christians to discern who is "in" and who is "out" of their religious systems. I don't find those kinds of intellectual exercises helpful or interesting. If you are reading this book, I imagine you don't either.

Instead, I think most people's quest for being "spiritual but not religious" is about asking a different set of questions and pursuing a different set of goals. It is about seeing the same old world with fresh eyes to encounter the beauty, awe, and transcendence that was there all along. William Butler Yeats was right; the world is full of magic things, patiently waiting for our senses to grow sharper. The Zen Buddhists call it *shoshin*

17. For a similar video version of this live experience, check out this YouTube video from Milan in 2007: https://www.youtube.com/watch?v=YmjVgqZ21tU&ab_channel=U2.

18. For a similar video version of my live experience, check out this YouTube video from one Buenos Aries in 2022: https://www.youtube.com/watch?v=Fpn1imb9qZg&ab_channel=Coldplay.

or "beginners mind": approaching life with an open and fresh perspective, free from preconceptions, judgments, and preconceived notions. Jesus called it "becoming like a child"[19] because, as anyone who has been around a toddler knows, children don't need to be instructed on how to experience transcendence—their days are loaded with awe, beauty, and wonder. The nineteenth century philosopher and writer G.K. Chesterton famously elaborated on Jesus' idea from his Christian worldview:

> Because children have abounding vitality, because they are in spirit fierce and free, therefore they want things repeated and unchanged. They always say, "Do it again"; and the grown-up person does it again until he is nearly dead. For grown-up people are not strong enough to exult in monotony. But perhaps God is strong enough to exult in monotony. It is possible that God says every morning, "Do it again" to the sun; and every evening, "Do it again" to the moon. It may not be automatic necessity that makes all daisies alike; it may be that God makes every daisy separately, but has never got tired of making them. It may be that He has the eternal appetite of infancy; for we have sinned and grown old, and our Father is younger than we.[20]

The writer John Green says that seeing beauty "is as much about how and whether you look as what you see. From the quark to the supernova, the wonders do not cease. It is our attentiveness that is in short supply, our ability and willingness to do the work that awe requires.[21] It is true - spirituality is about the attentiveness to see The Divine in the elusive moments of beauty: in the sound of a baby crying, in an amazing novel, in the fall leaves, in a sunset, and in a gut-wrenching film.

---

19. Matthew 18:3, Luke 18:17

20. G. K. Chesterton, *Orthodoxy* (London: House of Stratus, 2001), 41.

21. John Green, *The Anthropocene Reviewed: Essays on a Human Centered Planet* (New York: Dutton, 2021), 33.

But it is also about the attentiveness to see The Divine in the ordinary and mundane moments: in the ICU, in the quiet silence when the kids finally go to sleep, in the commute to work, in the middle of doing the laundry, in the changing of the diapers, in the doing of the dishes, and while you are on hold listening to a robot tell you that "your call is important to us." The English poet Elizabeth Barrett Browning frames it much more eloquently than I ever could:

Earth's crammed with heaven,
And every common bush afire with God,
But only he who sees takes off his shoes;
The rest sit round it and pluck blackberries.[22]

22. Elizabeth Barrett Browning, *Elizabeth Barret Browning: Aurora Leigh and Other Poems.* John Robert Glorney Bolton and Julia Bolton Holloway, Eds. (London: Penguin Classics, 1996), 232.

6

Chasing Shadows

Why We Settle for Cheap Imitations

"Many people buy confidence when they're really shopping for truth."

—Donald Miller—
(American author)

"As our eyes grow accustomed to sight, they armor themselves against wonder."

—Leonard Cohen—
(Canadian singer/songwriter)

Around 375 BC, the Greek philosopher Plato wrote what we now refer to as "The Republic"—a dialogue in which Socrates engaged with his interlocutors to investigate the nature of justice and the ideal society. In Book 7 of their discussions, Plato introduced the "Parable of the Cave." In the parable, Plato described a group of people imprisoned in a cave since birth, with their heads fixed so they can only see the wall in front of them. Behind them is a fire, and between the prisoners and the fire, there is a walkway where people pass by carrying objects. The prisoners can only see the shadows of these objects projected onto the cave wall, and they mistakenly believe that these shadows are the only reality they have ever known.

1-Plato's Cave

One day, one of the prisoners is freed and forced to turn around and look at the fire, which initially blinds him. As he adjusts to the light, he begins to see the objects that are casting shadows on the cave wall. This prisoner is then dragged out of the cave and into the outside world, where he experiences the sunlight and sees the reality of the world, realizing that the cave's shadows were mere illusions.[1]

MORALITY AND PUNISHMENT

I often think about this parable and how human beings usually approach spirituality. As I write these words, the state of Texas is embroiled in a debate about whether to mandate that the Ten Commandments be placed in every public school classroom. I understand the impulse. It seems so simple—if people were just aware that a god out there would punish them for doing bad things, they would do fewer bad things. Morality and Western religion have had a tight relationship over the years. For most evangelical Christians, their god is an all-power being in the sky who is so disgusted by human beings that he wants to destroy them. Luckily, as the narrative goes, Jesus came along, and God took out his anger and repulsion on Jesus (on the cross) as our proxy so that God wouldn't take it out on us. We humans are still disgusting, of course, but now, thanks to Jesus, God looks past our hideousness.

The Reformed Christian belief in the total depravity of humanity is good for drawing in people desperate for guilt and shame relief, but it carries with it unintended consequences and collateral damage. My friend Bob confided in me once, "When I believed that there was nothing good

1. Plato, *The Republic* (Trans. Desmond Lee) (London: Penguin Classics, 2007), 240ff.

in me, it came out in the way I treated other people. If Jesus said to 'love your neighbor as yourself,' it was easy to treat them like crap, because that is how I felt about myself."

Most Western religions are structured so that God is the big stick-carrying authority in the sky, ensuring law and order and that people's social contracts are fulfilled. As the Enlightenment philosopher Jean-Jacques Rousseau famously observed, "God created man in his own image. And man, being a gentleman, returned the favor."[2]

Avoiding eternal conscious torment from a vengeful deity by not doing bad things is not a very inspirational or exciting way to live. However, if you are the person or institution in power, this kind of religious manipulation is an excellent way to maintain social control.

One of the critiques made by religious people about those who identify as "spiritual but not religious" is that this worldview does not have an ethical imperative. If people aren't afraid of eternal torment in Hell, why would they want to act with love or kindness?[3] But research is showing just the opposite: people who can see the illusion of rugged individualism, have experiences of the world as a unified whole, and have experiences of being bathed in the love of The Divine are much more inclined to live ethical lives than those who are driven by fear and guilt. Dacher Keltner summarized his extensive research into "awe" at the University of California at Berkley by writing:

2- Dacher Keltner

2. Theodore Besterman, ed., *Voltaire's Notebooks*, (Paris: Institut et Musee Voltaire, 1952). Translated from the phrase, "*Si Dieu nous a faits à son image, nous le lui avons bien rendu.*"

3. In my humble experience, this "concern" seems to reveal more about the questioner and what motivates them than the person in question.

> We have found that awe—more so than emotions like pride or amusement—leads people to cooperate, share resources, and sacrifice for others, all of which are requirements for our collective life. And still other studies have explained the awe-altruism link: being in the presence of vast things calls forth a more modest, less narcissistic self, which enables greater kindness toward others.[4]

People who have deep spiritual experiences, see themselves as interconnected with the entire human race, and are concerned about the future of our planet are more motivated to live ethical lives than people who can recite the Ten Commandments.

Morality can be a tricky thing when it gets entangled in spirituality. As difficult as it is to believe, most people are doing the best they can, given their circumstances. While bad behavior is usually the presenting issue, it is rarely (if ever) the real issue. People act in entirely rational ways given their circumstances, experiences, chemical makeup, and the stories they believe about themselves and the world. If we focus our conversations solely on a moral compass, we will not ask better and deeper questions about our lives, society, or spirituality. Lacking better tools, some people try to display the Ten Commandments in school classrooms because that is the best they've got.

Of course, morality is, by definition, good for society. To be clear, I don't think we should murder each other, lie to each other, and so on. My point is that morality should not be the goal of our spiritual pursuits, but the byproduct of the paradigm shifts we gain from awe, wonder, and beauty. What is tragic is that many people think they are on a spiritual quest but are, in fact, only pursuing guilt alleviation or the resolution of their cognitive dissonance. The deepest desire of our souls is for beauty, transcendence, or The Divine. Morality is, at best, a shadow of these things, but it is often the best that Western religion offers.

---

4. Dacher Keltner, "Why Do We Feel Awe?" Mindful. July 14, 2023.https://www.mindful.org/why-do-we-feel-awe/, accessed September 1, 2023.

That being said, I don't think all religion is bad. For many people, finding a group that agrees with their worldview, practices the same rituals, and shares the same moral code provides some psychological comfort. As discussed in the last chapter, most (if not all) religious groups started as a spiritual movement, examining questions about love, meaning, connection, and identity. Over time, however, movements naturally evolve to become institutions, and the energies of an institution naturally focus on preserving the gains of the past rather than asking difficult questions about how things are or what the future should look like.[5]

Replying to @alexandrosM

any sufficiently large organization/institution, if pressed, will almost invariably pursue its own existence at the expense of its founding principles, stated goals, morality, or any other consideration you can imagine. As such, a certain amount of distrust vs them is healthy

5:59 PM · 08 Jun 23 · **264** Views

With the possible exception of those who derive their paychecks from an institution, I would be willing to bet that what most people want is not to preserve an institution but to experience a deep sense of connection with themselves, others, nature, and the universe. In our better moments, most people long for beauty and transcendence more than conformity. People inclined to spirituality are less interested in "being right" as they are wrestling with questions of meaning, purpose, and identity. I love how my friend Jonathan Foster frames it:

> Beauty isn't concerned with "getting" truth. It's not a thing, an object, a rightness one possesses, a sword one swings. I imagine beauty enjoys rightness only when it resonates with goodness... Beauty is uninterested in such powerful objects, though I suspect this is the source of its own irrepressible power. "With beauty like

---

5. I discuss this concept in detail in my essay, "Allowing Good Thing to Run Wild" in the book, *Open and Relational Leadership: Leading with Love* (Roland Hearn, Sheri D. Kling, and Thomas Jay Oord, eds.) (Nampa, ID: SacraSage, 2020), 51ff.

that," Adelaida told his mother in Dostoevsky's *The Idiot*, "one might turn the world upside down."[6]

This pursuit of beauty sounds much simpler than it is. Many people, convinced they are pursuing goodness, beauty, truth, and The Divine, often chase shadows. The Divine can most easily be lost by being thought found. If you are inclined to believe the teachings of Jesus, there is nothing more dangerous than religious people who presume that they already "get it." [7]

RELIGION AND MAGIC

I have a friend named Andrea who self-identifies as a new-age, crystal-brandishing hippie. Recently, she has been strongly influenced by the book, "The Secret."[8] The heart of the book is what Rhonda Byrne calls the Law of Attraction—use your thoughts to attract the things you want.[9] The power of your mind is akin to the power of a magnet. Your life reflects your thoughts, and you can use them to create your future self that the Universe will bring your way.

I know many people in the Christian tradition who may change their labels and methods but approach their spirituality in a similar way. Prayer to God, for many Christians, is a way to name and claim what they desire so that God can bring it their way. "Prayer" is not about connecting with God but about giving God our list of what to do and how to do it.

I first became aware of this approach to spirituality when I took a Sociology of Religion course many years ago. Dr. Richard Stellway introduced me to the French sociologist Emile Durkheim and his distinction

6. Jonathan J. Foster, *Theology of Consent: Mimetic Theory in an Open and Relational Universe.* (Nampa, ID: SacraSage Press, 2022), 180.

7. John, the Beloved Disciple, tells the story of a man born blind in John 9: which illustrates this concept beautifully.

8. Rhonda Byren, *The Secret* (New York: Atria Books, 2006).

9. Later in this book, I will talk about the secret behind "The Secret" and, as my friend Andy likes to say (with his Louisiana drawl), "Take the spooky out of it."

between "magic" and "religion." Other sociologists have since built on his theories, but to simplify, magic is what humans do to manipulate powers or deities for immediate goals (the technical phrase is "instrumental coercive manipulation"). We use magic *not* to have a transcendent experience with The Divine or to allow ourselves to be altered by it but to get ahead of our neighbors by controlling spirits or deities.

In contrast, according to Durkheim, religion is about "personal and supplicative negotiation." Or, in layperson's terms, it's about allowing ourselves to experience and be altered by something bigger than us. These experiences will enable us to have generous and positive outcomes for ourselves and others. In other words, it is about allowing The Divine to change us rather than us trying to manipulate The Divine.[10] Many people think they are pursuing spirituality when, in fact, they are pursuing magic, hoping to manipulate or control spiritual forces for their own well-being. The practice of "magic" looks like spirituality, but it is a shadow of what is real.

As Plato lamented in 375 BC, it isn't easy to convince people that they see a shadow of reality rather than the reality itself. So, the difficult question is this: how do we remove the barriers that prevent us from seeing reality rather than the shadows?

10. H.S. Versnel, "Some Reflections on the Relationship Magic-Religion." Numen 38 (2), 1991, 177–95.

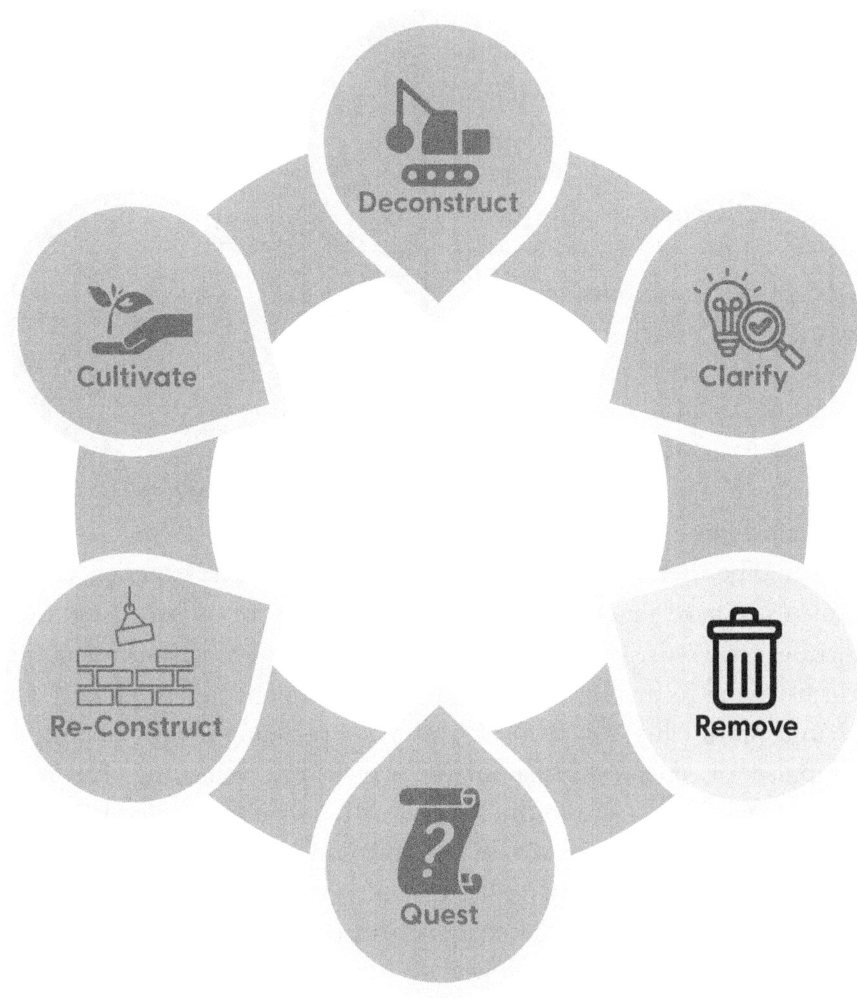
Deconstruct
Clarify
Remove
Quest
Re-Construct
Cultivate

REMOVE

Spirituality Is More About Removing Your Barriers than Adding More Stuff.

Spirituality, in stark contrast to the complexities of our modern lives, is a journey of subtraction rather than addition. It's about acknowledging and releasing what no longer brings us joy. Busyness, noise, social media, and 24-hour news cycles often cloud our perception of the world, making the need for subtraction even more crucial.

7

Michaelangelo's David

The Art of Removal

"Maybe the journey isn't so much about becoming anything. Maybe it's about unbecoming everything that isn't really you, so you can be who you were meant to be in the first place."

—Paulo Coelho—
(Brazilian Author)

"The moment of surrender is the moment you choose to lose control of your life, the split second of powerlessness where you trust that some kind of 'higher power' better be in charge, because you certainly aren't."

—Bono—
(Irish Rock Star, from "Surrender: 40 Songs, One Story")

In 1463, members of the City Council of Firenze (Florence), Italy, decided they needed a monument to enhance their city. They commissioned a sculptor to carve a giant statue to stand in front of the city hall. Someone suggested a biblical character wrought in the neoclassical style, an expression of beauty and strength. They approached an artist named Agostino di Duccio, who agreed to their terms.

Duccio went to the quarry near Carrara and marked off a 19-foot slab to be cut from the white marble. However, he had the slab cut too thin.

When the block was removed, it fell, leaving a deep fracture down one side. The sculptor declared the stone useless and demanded another, but the city council refused. As a result, the gleaming block of marble lay on its side for the next 38 years, a source of embarrassment for all concerned.

Michaelangelo's "David"

Then, in 1501, the council approached another citizen, the son of a local official, asking him if he would complete this ambitious project using the broken slab. Fortunately for them, the young man was Michelangelo Buonarroti. Michaelangelo was 26 years old and filled with energy, skill, and imagination. He locked himself inside the workshop behind the cathedral to chisel and polish away on the stone for more than three years.

When the statue was finished, it was so large that it took 49 men five days to bring it to rest before the city hall. Archways were torn down, and narrow streets were widened. People from across Europe came to see the enormous 14-foot statue of David relaxing after defeating Goliath. The statue far exceeded anything the city fathers had envisioned. The giant stone had been transformed from the massive, fractured waste of rock to a masterpiece surpassing the art of either Greece or Rome.

I saw the sculpture in Florence for the first time a few years back. If you have seen it in person, you know it is impossible to describe the size, beauty, and amazing amount of detail that Michelangelo incorporated into his masterpiece. The muscles, tendons, and veins are incredibly realistic.

Legend has it that when someone asked Michelangelo how he was able to create this statue of David, he is reported to have said, "It is easy. You just chip away all the stone that isn't David."

Yes, he shaped, formed, and rearranged the marble, but at its essence, Michelangelo removed everything that was unnecessary.

LESS IS MORE

Here is the best-kept secret of spiritual growth: Spiritual growth is usually not about learning new information and new techniques but about unlearning lousy thought processes and bad habits. The fourteenth-century German mystic Meister Eckhart said, "[The Divine] is not found in the soul by adding anything but by a process of subtraction."[1] As Jesus would say, the Kingdom of God is inside of you.[2] It's not that The Divine is trying to hide from us; it's just that there is so much marble to chip away to get to the beauty inside.

Meister Eckhart

In Western religions, there is an underlying assumption that people are born into original sin. That is, we are born a mess, and our task is to remove all the obstacles that hinder us from becoming better and better versions of ourselves. That is one way to view it.

1. Wayne Muller, *How, Then, Shall We Live?: Four Simple Questions That Reveal The Beauty and Meaning of Our Lives* (New York: Bantam Books, 1997), 56.

2. Luke 17:21. Some modern translations of the New Testament translate the phrase, –"βασιλεία τοῦ θεοῦ ἐντὸς ὑμῶν ἑστινas" as "the Kingdom of God is *among* you" instead of the literal and plain meaning "*inside* you." This obvious theological bias in some modern translations is troubling to me.

In Eastern religions, the vantage point is the opposite: people are born perfect, but we accumulate illusions as we grow up. In Taoism, Lao Tzu writes,

> In pursuit of knowledge,
> every day something is added.
> In the practice of the Tao,
> every day something is dropped.
> Less and less do you need to force things,
> until finally you arrive at non-action.
> When nothing is done,
> nothing is left undone.[3]

From either the Western or Eastern point of view, spirituality is about removal.

MARIE KONDO IT

It reminds me of the Netflix series that became popular a few years ago—"Tidying Up with Marie Kondo." In the series, a petite and soft-spoken Japanese woman named Marie Kondo visited various American families' homes full of clutter and demonstrated how to tidy up their homes through her Kon Mari method.[4] What I remember most about the series was how to let go of the objects in my life that may have served an important purpose at one point but now have become clutter and need to be let go. Her website describes it as follows: "your feelings are the standard for decision making—specifically, knowing what sparks joy. To determine

3. Lao-tzu, *Tao Te Ching*, trans. Steven Mitchell, (New York: Harper Perennial Modern Classics, 2006), verse 48.

4. I find it interesting that the spiritual foundation for Marie Kondo's work comes from her commitment to the Shinto religion. The spiritual practice is concerned with the energy or divine spirit of things (*kami*)—that is, treasuring what you own; treating the objects one owns as not disposable, but valuable, despite their monetary worth; and creating displays so one can value each individual object. Cf. Danielle Demetriou, "Japan's decluttering guru says she is on a mission to 'organize the world,'" *Daily Telegraph*, Jan. 16, 2016, accessed January 13, 2024.

Marie Kondo

this when tidying, the key is to pick up each object one at a time and ask yourself quietly, 'Does this spark joy?' Pay attention to how your body responds."[5]

If something no longer sparks joy or is no longer helpful or valuable, it is time to let it go and chisel it away from our lives through the art of removal. But what I love about her method is that we also take time to appreciate the purpose it once served and thank it for its service before we let it go.

I've taken this principle to my spiritual journey by learning to "Marie Kondo" those ideas, people, beliefs, and values that have served me in the past, but I need to let go. This process allows me to be kind to my past self as I deconstruct all the parts I have accumulated that aren't truly "me." I recognize that there was a purpose at one time for these ideas, people, beliefs, and values, but I can feel that they are no longer helpful. As a result, they will not be part of my life in the future.

For example, a few weeks ago, I was having dinner with a friend who is also an ex-vangelical. I recounted some good fortune that had come my way, and he commented, "Good for you. You deserve that." After a brief pause, I confessed to him, "I

5. "What is the KonMari Method?" KonMari. https://konmari.com/about-the-konmari-method, accessed January 13, 2024.

still get a twinge of dissonance in my mind when I hear someone say, 'You deserve that.' I still have that Reformed sense of human depravity seared deep in my soul. My first instinct is to think, 'No, I don't deserve anything. I am a miserable, lowly creature deserving of nothing but the cruel, torturous death that Jesus received.'" Then we both laughed, ordered another round of drinks, and drank a toast to Martin Luther, John Calvin, and the other theo-bros of the Reformation. I told my friend, "Thank you, Reformed doctrine of total depravity, for your service in my life. As a young person, it probably kept my younger self away from self-destructive behaviors and got me thinking about what divine grace looks like. I won't miss you, total depravity. Goodbye."

THE DEATH OF "SELF"

The art of removal is much more difficult than it sounds. We hold on to ideas, identities, stories, and nostalgia of the past that define our sense of "self," it feels like we are losing part of ourselves when we chisel them away. As I write today, a close friend is staying with me because he is going through a professional transition he did not choose. The transition has challenged his perception of himself and the stories he tells himself about himself. As a result, it has been extremely destabilizing and challenging for him.

It is easy to see how it can be very threatening when our sense of self is challenged. Yet, removing all the unhelpful peripheral aspects of "self" is the path by which the divine reveals itself to us. This chiseling away at our false selves is what mystics from many traditions have advocated for centuries. For my friend, this meant learning that his core identity is not what brings him a paycheck or a job title and letting it go.

When we have transcendent moments, like the viewing of a sunset, we get a tiny sliver of what the death of our selves is like. It is a realization of how small we are and yet how much a part of all of it we are. When we can dissolve our sense of self, we can begin to see illusions like rugged individualism and control and become more comfortable with things like mystery and paradox.

There is an old joke about mysticism: Atheists and mystics both believe in nothing. The only difference is that mystics spell it with a capital N.

Less is more when it comes to spirituality. Consequently, the rhythm of Christian spirituality is *death and resurrection*—a rhythm of constant removal and rebirth.

In Buddhism, enlightenment is not an achievement we attain but a continual removal process. The Buddhist teacher Adyashanti explains, "Enlightenment is the crumbling away of untruth. It's seeing through the facade of pretense. It's completely eradicating everything we imagined to be true—from ourselves to the world."[6]

In Hinduism, the Sanskrit phrase "Neti Neti", which means "not this, not that," is a meditation used to recognize the non-duality of reality and the removal of all that is not *Brahman* or ultimate reality.

The Islamic Sufi poet Rumi mused, "If you could get rid of yourself just once, the secret of secrets would open to you. The face of the unknown, hidden beyond the universe, would appear on the mirror of your perception."[7]

St. Paul's Monastery on Mt. Athos

Visitors to one of the most important sites in Greek Orthodox Christianity, Saint Paul's Monastery on Mt. Athos, will see a Greek saying mounted on the wall of the reception area: "αν πεθάνεις πριν πεθάνεις δεν θα πεθάνεις όταν πεθάνεις" which translates, "If you die before you die, you won't die when you die." Through the death of our false selves, we can be open to spiritual experiences that connect us to the divine in ways we never imagined.

6. Adyashanti, *The End of Your World: Uncensored Straight Talk on the Nature of Enlightenment* (Boulder, CO: Sounds True, 2010), 25.

7. As quoted in Brian C. Muraresku, *The Immortality Key* (New York: St. Martin's Press, 2020), 10.

Less is more in Michelangelo's and Marie Kondo's worlds. However, the idea of "less is more" is especially true in spirituality. In a consumeristic world like the one we live in, it is natural to think that if we get more—more learning, more attainment, more achievement, more performance, more success—then we will find the spirituality we seek. While this has a definite appeal to our egos, recognizing the divine and responding to The Divine is, in fact, more about removing the debris we have accumulated to make room for The Divine to take root and blossom.

8

A Hedge Against the Emptiness

The Reduction of Hurry and Noise

"Hurry is not of the Devil; it is the Devil."

—Carl Jung—
(Swiss psychiatrist and founder of analytical psychology)

"Be still. The quieter you become, the more you can hear."

—Ram Daas—
(American spiritual teacher)

Spirituality has never been "easy," but I think there are unique challenges in our modern world that human beings from previous eras of human history did not have to worry about. We have made many technological developments in recent years, but when it comes to the experience of awe and wonder, we are quickly regressing. Dacher Keltner observed from his research:

> Attendance at arts events—live music, theater, museums and galleries—has dropped in recent years. This goes for children, too: Arts and music programs in schools are being dismantled; time spent outdoors and for unstructured exploration are being sacrificed for résumé-building activities. At the same time, our

> culture has become more individualistic, more narcissistic, more materialistic, and less connected to others. [1]

Our intentions are good; we are just busy. Every day, as I drive the freeway system in my hometown of Phoenix, I am reminded that everyone is in a perpetual hurry.

During my years as a pastor, I adopted a "Hurry Sickness" quiz that I would give to people to help them recognize how their pace of life was affecting their spirituality. I would ask them to rate their symptoms of "Hurry Sickness" on a scale of one to ten—one being "not at all" and ten being "all the time":

> **Symptom #1 — Speeding Up.** You are haunted by the fear that you don't have enough time to do what needs to be done. You try to do everything faster and more efficiently. You chafe whenever you have to wait. At a stoplight, if there are two lanes and each contains one car, you read each car's year, make, and model to guess which will pull away most quickly. If you choose between two checkout lines at a grocery store, you note the number of people in each line and multiply that by the number of items in each cart. If the person who takes your place in the other line leaves the store while you are still in line, you feel depressed.

> **Symptom #2 — Multiple-tasking.** You find yourself doing or thinking more than one thing at a time. The car is a favorite place for this. Hurry-sick people may drive, eat, drink coffee, listen to music, shave or apply make-up, and direct business on their cell

1. Dacher Keltner, "Why Do We Feel Awe?" Mindful. https://www.mindful.org/why-do-we-feel-awe/, accessed September 1, 2023.

phones—all at the same time. Or they may try to watch TV, scroll social media, and eat dinner simultaneously.

Symptom #3 — Clutter. You can often measure how "Hurry Sick" a person is by the clutter on their desk or computer desktop or how messy their car is. The hurry-sick lack simplicity. Hurry-sick people often subscribe to several streaming services and then feel guilty because they don't use them enough. They often buy time-saving devices or apps and then fail to use them because they don't have the time to learn how to use them.

Symptom #4 — Sunset Fatigue. When those with hurry sickness come home after a long day at work, those to whom they are most committed end up getting their leftovers. At the end of the day, their behaviors show how fatigued they are:

- They rush around at home even when there is no reason to.
- They use sharp words to their partner and children, even when they have done nothing to deserve them.
- They hurry their children along. They set up mock races ("Let's see who can take a bath the fastest!") that are really about their own need to get through it.
- They tell their family everything will be okay in a week or two.
- They indulge in escapes from the emptiness—watching too much TV, abusing alcohol, or spending unreasonable amounts of time on social media.
- They flop into bed each night with no sense of gratitude or wonder for the day, just fatigue.

Symptom #5 — Love Impaired. The most serious sign of hurry sickness is a diminished capacity to love. Love and hurry are

> fundamentally incompatible. Love always takes time, and time is the one thing hurried people don't have. Hurry-sick people begin to resent the people they are supposed to love because they demand so much time and energy.[2]

Years ago, I had the privilege of hearing the spiritual sage Dallas Willard speak at an event. During the Q&A time, someone asked him, "What advice would you give someone who wants to be spiritually healthy?" After a long pause, Dr. Willard said, "You must ruthlessly eliminate hurry from your life." The questioner thought for a minute and said, "That is good. Anything else?" Dr. Willard said, "There is nothing else. That is everything."

Dr. Dallas Willard

If you have traveled to another country, you may have experienced the "reverse culture shock" of recognizing how hurried and noisy we Americans can be. While traveling to Africa for a nonprofit organization I was part of, I once mused to one of our hosts about the plodding pace at which our African friends would walk. "They call it at 'African pace,'" he told me. It makes Americans crazy in the head!" he laughed with his thick Burundian accent.

He then related a story he heard on the radio a few months earlier. The Puerto Rican pop star Ricky Martin had been touring in Africa. Ricky was slated to appear at a local venue, and a local radio station had him on air to promote the concert. The DJ asked Ricky, "You repeatedly use the Spanish word *mañana* in one of your songs. What does that word mean?" Ricky Martin replied, "It means 'tomorrow,' but it sums up our laid-back Latin culture. In other words, nothing is so important that it can't wait

2. Adapted from John Ortberg, "Diagnosing Hurry Sickness," *Leadership Journal,* Fall, 1998, 31.

until tomorrow!" The African DJ replied, "We don't have a word in our language that conveys that kind of urgency."[3]

Like me, you might also find it hard to wrap your mind around this pace of living. Our harried, frazzled lives find a physical incarnation in how Americans fill our days with more and more noise and visual distractions. It's hard to find a restaurant or bar that doesn't have a hundred TV screens blasting every conceivable sporting contest in the world. Many of us have confused being happy with being distracted from sadness. We have used hurry and noise to numb us from the emptiness. We modern Americans are working more, stressed out more, more disconnected from the natural world and other people, and spending more time with our faces on our smartphones.

Some of you will write off my reflections as the rantings of a grumpy old man, and maybe some of that is true. But I've experienced the other side of hurry, busyness, and noise and can tell you there is another way to live.

HOW HURRY AND NOISE SHORT-CIRCUIT SPIRITUALITY

When we are caught up in the urgency of hurry, our minds go into fight or flight mode, and our focus narrows. This would be great if a shark were chasing us or if our well-being were at risk. But most of us find ourselves in fight or flight mode because we tried to cram too much into a limited amount of time. Hurry makes it impossible to be aware of or reflect on anything other than the crisis at hand. In perpetual "survival mode," we focus on the things that appear most pressing, not necessarily on the most important things.

There is an analogy that is often used in organizational leadership circles about lions and field mice. Because lions are essentially giant, playful cats, they sometimes chase after field mice and eat them. But unbeknownst to lions, the energy required to act like a big housecat and catch

3. To be fair, after going through customs a few times in Africa, I have grown to deeply appreciate American's low toleration for inefficient systems!

mice exceeds the caloric content provided by consuming the mouse. A lion that spends its days only hunting and eating mice will slowly starve. It begs the question: what are the seemingly pressing things that you and I are focusing our time and energy on that might give us a rewarding feeling but, ultimately, will slowly kill us because they are not that important?

Of course, there are times when life demands our urgent focus, and we need to get things done. But when this pattern becomes chronic, we find the years passing without any sense of joy or wonder, and we become confused about how the kids grew up so fast. We skim over our lives, half-asleep, without actually living it. It reminds me of the film *Joe Verses the Volcano,* in which Patricia tells Joe, "My father says that almost the whole world is asleep. Everybody you know, everybody you see, everybody you talk to. He says that only a few people are awake, and they live in a state of constant total amazement."[4]

"Dear God, whose name I do not know, thank you for my life. I forgot how big... Thank you for my life" -Joe

THE THING BENEATH THE THING

Maybe you are convinced you need to put down your phone more and clear your calendar from all the craziness. This would enable many of us to "slow down and smell the roses" and make room for transcendent and beautiful experiences. But in the spirit of the "Five Whys" of chapter 4, if we keep asking more questions, we may see some patterns as to *why* so many of us are driven to fill our lives beyond capacity. Learning to clear your schedule may not slow down your life if you don't deal with the root issue: why do we take on more than we can?

4. John Patrick Shanley, dir. 1990. *Joe Versus the Volcano.* Warner Bros.

The Conflation of "Busy" and "Important"

Some people make a funny logical leap: important people are always busy; therefore, if I am busy, I must be important. Sometimes, we pack our schedule so full because it makes us feel valued. We may complain about how busy we are, but secretly, we love the adrenaline rush. Our insecurity can be one of the biggest motivations for being busy. In his thoughtful *New York Times* Op-ed, Tim Kreider reflected that in our world, "Busyness serves as a kind of existential reassurance, a hedge against emptiness; obviously your life cannot possibly be silly or trivial or meaningless if you are so busy, completely booked, in demand every hour of the day."[5]

Dysfunctional Ambition

Sometimes, our addiction to hurry and noise comes from a warped sense of ambition. The dream of doing something great or becoming admirable is a noble human goal. But when ambition is out of control, or we are ambitious for the wrong values or motivations, ambition can be one of the most destructive forces in the world. Dysfunctional ambition can destroy relationships, families, organizations, companies, and even countries. Dysfunctional ambition can be driven by guilt, resentment, fear, narcissism, revenge, or even by anger.

In American culture, men seem more susceptible than women to confusing their sense of self-worth with their work or conflating their identities with their professions. As one writer put it, "The Puritans turned work into a virtue, evidently forgetting that God invented it as a punishment."[6] For many people, their work becomes so tied to their identities that slowing down and quieting down can feel like an assault on their selves.

5. Tim Kreider, "The 'Busy' Trap." The New York Times, June 30, 2012. https://archive.nytimes.com/opinionator.blogs.nytimes.com/2012/06/30/the-busy-trap/, accessed October 17, 2023.

6. Ibid.

The Shadow Side of Capitalism

Ticks, like mosquitos, are tiny insects that grab onto mammals and suck their blood for nourishment. Ticks are known as the overeaters of the insect world. When they latch on, they can't stop. This picture is what a tick looks like before it lands on its host. Ticks can't jump, so they usually drop on their victims from a bush or a thicket and engorge themselves with the host's blood. They gorge themselves so much that they can balloon up to 7-10 times their normal size. The photograph shows a "before" and "after" comparison.

Before and After Feeding

A tick that has fully engorged itself automatically drops off its host. At that point, it literally cannot move because all its energy is working on digesting what it has consumed. For the next couple of hours, the tick is at the mercy of predators because it has eaten so much it cannot move.

The tick life is an absurd way to live. It boggles the mind to imagine a creature always wanting more to the detriment of its life. Yet for us homo sapiens, living in a capitalist society means that we are constantly bombarded with messages of our inadequacy. Advertisers in our capitalistic world know that people who are discontent are quick to add more to their lives with the promise of contentment ("own me", "wear me", "eat me", "put me in your hair"). For many, the promise of contentment becomes the path to living a tick-like existence—a frantic existence pursuing more and more and never being content with enough.

STILLNESS AND QUIET

For most of us, especially the extroverts among us, being still and quiet is not just tricky; it can feel painful. Eliminating hurry and noise often means doing "shadow work"—dealing with the parts of ourselves that we repress or deny[7]—to eliminate the "thing beneath the thing" that draws us to hurry.

On the other side of this work, however, is where we begin to experience our true selves and the most profound kinds of connection with The Divine. I love how the Franciscan Priest Richard Rohr described it: "We don't save our soul; we *discover* it. We don't go there and try to make ourselves holy; we wake our souls up. We're already united with [The Divine]; the problem is, we don't believe it."[8]

One of my favorite films is the 2019 movie, "The Sound of Metal." The film follows the story of Ruben Stone, a heavy metal drummer who begins to lose his hearing. As his condition worsens, Ruben's life is thrown into disarray, affecting all that he holds dear, including his relationships and his music career. Ruben reluctantly accepts an invitation to join a small deaf community overseen by Joe, a compassionate Vietnam War veteran. As Ruben tries to process his hearing loss, he laments to Joe:

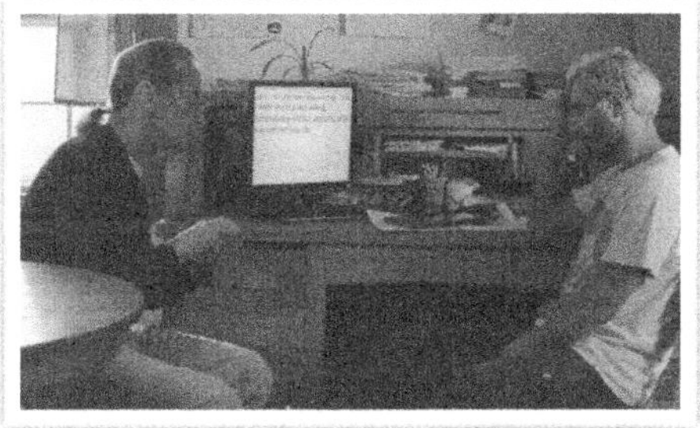

The Sound of Metal

> **Ruben Stone:** Like, what does it matter? What does it matter? It just passes. Yo. If I disappear, like, who cares? Nobody cares, man. Seriously. Yo, and that's okay. That's life. That's life. No, for real. Okay? It just passes. It just fucking…fucking passes.

---

7. The idea of Shadow Work comes from Jungian psychology which recognizes that "we all have metaphorical masks that we wear and images—our personas—that we seek to put forth in the world for how we'd like to be seen and known for. Yet, the more we focus on those idealized images, the more we repress and the opposites of whatever our preferred images may open up in our lives…when we try to minimize those shadows, we actually increase and magnify their power in our lives." Roger Wayne Wolsey, *Discovering Fire: Spiritual Practices That Transform Lives* (Chico, CA: Quoir, 2023), 89.

8. Richard Rohr, *Simplicity: The Freedom of Letting Go* (New York: CrossRoad Books, 2015), 93.

> **Joe :** I wonder, uh, all these mornings you've been sitting in my study, sitting, have you had any moments of stillness? Because you're right, Ruben. The world does keep moving, and it can be a damn cruel place. But for me, those moments of stillness, that place, that's the kingdom of God.[9]

Whether we choose it, or it chooses us, those moments of quiet—those unhurried moments of stillness—are the place where we encounter our true selves. It is the realm of The Divine.

For those of us who have been trapped in the headspace of hurry, noise, dysfunctional ambition, and the shadow side of capitalism, the poet John O'Donahue's poem "For One Who is Exhausted" has been a balm to my soul:

You have travelled too fast over false ground;
Now your soul has come to take you back.

Take refuge in your senses, open up
To all the small miracles you rushed through.

Become inclined to watch the way of rain
When it falls slow and free.

Imitate the habit of twilight,
Taking time to open the well of color
That fostered the brightness of day.

Draw alongside the silence of stone
Until its calmness can claim you.
Be excessively gentle with yourself.

---

9. Darius Marder, director. 2019. *The Sound of Metal.* Amazon Studios.

To view this scene in context, see: https://www.youtube.com/watch?v=3fQ3zy8iYtk&t=175s&ab_channel=LetsCrashThisParade.

Stay clear of those vexed in spirit.
Learn to linger around someone of ease
Who feels they have all the time in the world.

Gradually, you will return to yourself,
Having learned a new respect for your heart
And the joy that dwells far within slow time.[10]

10. John O'Donohue, *To Bless the Space Between Us: A Book of Blessings.* (New York: Doubleday, 2008), 126.

9

Drinking from the Fire Hose

Living in the Middle of the Internet

"The world is too much with us; late and soon."

—William Wordsworth—
(American poet)

"You...live in the world that this internet has created, a world in which selfhood has become capitalism's last natural resource, a world whose terms are set by centralized platforms that have deliberately established themselves as near-impossible to regulate or control."

—Jia Tolentino—
(American author, from *Trick Mirror*)

There are rare moments in history in which technology makes a quantum leap and expands and extends human being's capacity. They are easy to recognize in hindsight: The wheel was invented around 3500 BCE, and it revolutionized transportation and facilitated the movement of goods and people, leading to advancements in trade, agriculture, and communication. When Johannes Gutenberg invented the Printing Press in the 15th century, it allowed for the mass production of books and other printed materials, democratizing knowledge and facilitating the spread of ideas, leading to the Renaissance, Reformation, and Scientific

Revolution. In the early twentieth century, starting with the invention of penicillin by Alexander Fleming, antibiotics revolutionized medicine by providing effective treatments for bacterial infections, saving countless lives and extending human longevity.

We are likewise in the middle of another technological quantum leap in which human civilization will be forever changed: the advent of the internet. Information dissemination has democratized society, empowering individuals with access to vast knowledge repositories and educational resources. E-commerce, now a $4.2 trillion worldwide, has reshaped commerce, enabling global trade from the comfort of our homes. Over 4.48 billion people are using social media, changing social dynamics by fostering connections based on shared interests rather than geographic proximity. The internet has catalyzed innovation, propelling technological advancements, healthcare, and various industries.

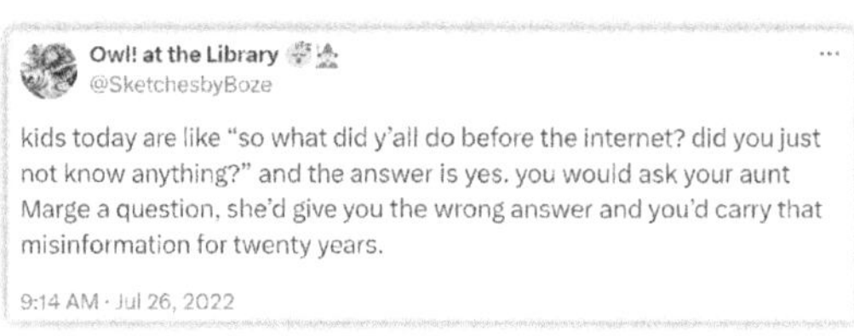

THE PROBLEM WITH NEW TECHNOLOGIES

Whenever a new technology arrives, there are skeptics and cynics of the innovation. In ancient Greece, Socrates warned against writing because it would create forgetfulness among the people, and they would be unable to use their memories. People lamented the invention of the printing press, saying it would overload the world with data and information that would harm our brains. A medical journal in 1883 argued that schools "exhaust the children's brains and nervous systems with complex and multiple studies and ruined their bodies by protracted imprisonment."[1] In 1936, the music magazine *The Gramophone* reported that children had "developed the habit of dividing attention between the humdrum preparation of their school assignments and the compelling excitement of the

1. As quoted in Van Bell, "Don't Touch That Dial!" Slate.February 15, 2010. https://slate.com/technology/2010/02/a-history-of-media-technology-scares-from-the-printing-press-to-facebook.html, accessed February 12, 2024.

loudspeaker"[2] and lamented how radio programs were interrupting the equilibrium of their impulsive minds.

One of the problems inherent in any paradigm-shifting technology is that every technology evolves faster than humanity's ability to recognize its unintended consequences or our knowledge of how to use it responsibly. In the middle of the nineteenth century, for the first time in human history, the fastest way to travel was no longer by horse. The coasts of the United States were connected by over 3,000 miles of railroad tracks, and passenger trains were rapidly becoming very popular. However, since this was a new technology, people had to figure out how to act in a crowded public space. So, people would purchase etiquette guides on how to be polite on a train. The guides would give their readers advice like:

- No whispering, loud talking, immoderate laughing, or singing.
- Passengers should not embarrassingly gaze at one another.

Conductors cracked down on passengers who "indulged personal preferences at the expense of other passengers."[3]

---

2. Ibid.

3. Stephen Carter, *Civility: Manners, Morals, and the Etiquette of Democracy* (New York: HarperPerennial, 1999), 3–4. Based on some of my personal experiences with air travel and some internet videos I have seen, it probably wouldn't hurt to revise and revive this practice of etiquette guides for public travel!

While the advent of the internet age will invariably continue to bring about many excellent outcomes for human beings, it will take us a while to figure out how to mitigate its unintended consequences. Despite its upside, the internet is the single greatest distributor of ignorance and stupidity in the history of the world. If a person wants to find someone to affirm their racism, bigotry, or hate, it is just a couple of keystrokes away. By our nature, we humans rarely appreciate our own ignorance. Still, the internet makes it much easier to consume news that aligns with our beliefs, corresponds with our ideological alignment, and has been fine-tuned to make us feel self-righteous and angry. The big-tech search algorithms are not concerned with beauty, transcendence, awe, etc. They note which data attracts heat with your demographic, and they send that data to your feed. As a result, the internet is an ecosystem that runs on exploiting attention and monetizing the self.

DRINKING FROM A FIREHOSE

Every year, billions of dollars are spent to keep you and me in the internet rabbit hole, constantly clicking to the next thing. Never have human beings been the target of such a well-put-together effort to grab your eyeballs. The cultural critic Jia Tolentino reflects that the internet "has already become the central organ of contemporary life. It has already rewired the brains of its users, returning us to a state of primitive hyperawareness and distraction while overloading us with much more sensory input than was ever possible in primitive times."[4]

For most of human history, people lived in small villages. Usually, in these small communities, there was a person who functioned as the "village elder"—someone who was older and wiser and helped you sort through what matters and what doesn't. You could ask them, "What should I do with myself, and what should I not worry about?" The internet does not do this for us. Political opinion, X (formerly Twitter) rants,

4. Jia Tolentino, *Trick Mirror: Reflections on Self-Delusion* (New York: Random House, 2019), 11.

speculation about Taylor Swift and Travis Kelce, cat videos, and hard news about the Middle East are all intertwined and presented in the same size font. Our unfortunate paleolithic minds cannot handle the firehose of information our ancestors could never imagine. Nor is our central nervous system capable of handling the onslaught of dopamine rushes we get with every ding and click.

It may be obvious, but the internet is not going away. So, the question is, if we want to be spiritual people, how do we minimize the damage this new technology is doing to our souls? What are some boundaries that can keep us and others from destroying ourselves? Like the etiquette guides railroad passengers used in the nineteenth century, how do we interact with our fellow passengers as we ride this new technology wave?

"We need to rethink our strategy of hoping the Internet will just go away."

ESCAPE FROM THE HERE AND NOW

If you are familiar with the Enneagram, I'm an Enneagram 5.[5] This means that my personality has a strong propensity to become, in the words of Ian Morgan Cron and Suzanne Stable, "roadkill on the information

5. If you are unfamiliar with this language, the Enneagram is a model of human personality that describes nine interconnected personality types. Each type has certain fundamental driving motivations, fears, desires, and patterns of thinking and behaving. For those interested in learning more, the Ian Morgan Cron and Susan Stabile book in the next footnote is a good introduction.

highway."[6] I have had more than one partner ask me in frustration to put my phone down and engage with the humans in front of me. As such, I write the following words not from the vantage point of a success story but as a fellow struggler on this journey.

In the spirit of "The Five Whys" from chapter 4, a question that I have had to learn to ask myself when caught in a rabbit hole of the internet is this: "What am I looking for, really? What is it that I *really* want?" In other words, am I looking to fulfill something I can't find right here and right now that I think will make me happier, satisfy my boredom, soothe my anxiety, lift my depression, or fulfill my craving for affirmation?

It is easy to experience an internet dopamine rush ten, twenty, thirty, or more times a day. The problem with dopamine rushes is that they last only a few moments, leaving us unsatisfied and wanting more. This contrasts with some of our brain's other "feel good" chemicals: serotonin, endorphins, and oxytocin, which instead create feelings like contentment, connection with others, and well-being. Dopamine is what often drives our brains to addiction—short-term pleasure with the illusion that if we do it again, *this time*, it will be enough, and we will be content and satisfied. Anyone who has binge-eaten junk food has experienced this dopamine death spiral vividly. Many of us know what it is like to look at an empty bag of chips and feel bloated, disgusted, and unsatisfied.

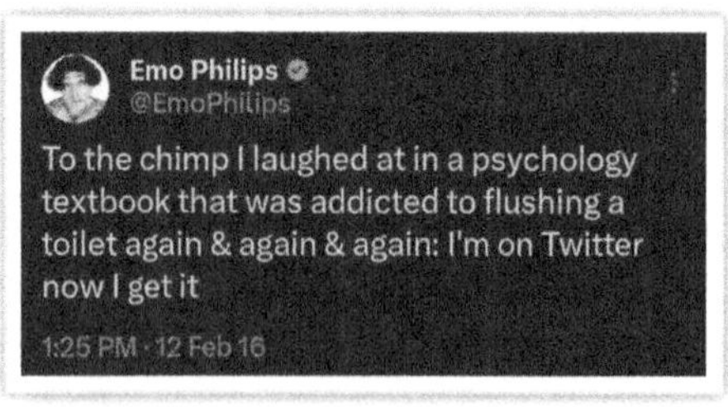

The pleasure death spiral was famously observed by researchers James Olds and Peter Milner in the late 1950s when researchers were mostly indifferent to ethical standards for animal research. Their experiment involved placing electrodes in the brains of rats associated with pleasure and reward. The rats were able to self-stimulate these brain regions by pressing a lever. When the rats pressed the lever,

6. Ian Morgan Cron & Susan Stabile, *The Road Back to You: An Enneagram Journey to Self-Discovery* (Downers Grove, IL: IVP Books, 2016), 174.

an electrical current would stimulate the pleasure centers of their brains. What they observed was that some rats would repeatedly press the lever to the point of exhaustion, foregoing food and water and, in extreme cases, continuing to self-stimulate until they died.[7]

I'm not sure any human beings have ever died from being unable to put their phones down. However, it is not surprising that anxiety and depression are rapidly on the rise in the internet era. The internet is a toxic place for the quest to find answers to questions like: Am I important? Am I loved? Am I good enough? Who notices me? These used to be questions that humans would find answers to with our face-to-face relationships rather than on social media.

So, when I realize that I am trying to escape the here and now, chasing a dopamine rush and behaving like a rat pushing the buttons on my phone, I try to step back and ask myself a simple question: "What am I looking for, really? What is it that I *really* want?"

INTERNET *SHABBAT*

For thousands of years, Jewish spirituality has used a spiritual practice that has benefited people's souls. Sabbath ("Shabbat" in Hebrew) is a period of time observed from Friday evening at sunset until Saturday evening at nightfall. *Shabbat* was considered by the Jewish people a sacred time and reserved for rest from work, reflection, community, spiritual enrichment, and renewal. The spiritual teacher Rob Bell describes it as "one day a week to remind themselves that

7. James Olds & Peter Milner (1954). "Positive Reinforcement Produced by Electrical Stimulation of Septal Area and Other Regions of Rat Brain." Journal of Comparative and Physiological Psychology, 47(6), 419–427.

they are human beings, not human doings."[8] We get the English word "sabbatical" from this ancient idea.

In our modern world, Sabbath and sabbatical can be reimagined as necessary components of using the internet healthily. Intentionally pulling away from the gravitational pull of the internet for a few hours, a few days, or even a few weeks can be an essential spiritual practice. It is setting down the fire hose to simply "be."

I've noticed in recent years that people have begun to practice internet *Shabbat* in all kinds of small ways: stacking everyone's phones in the middle of the table in a restaurant, "silencing" our phones to focus on the people we love, turning off our notifications so as not to be constantly distracted, or not having our phones in our rooms while we sleep so that it is not the first thing we go to when we wake up. Some are practicing even longer internet *shabbats*—from days to weeks. The comedian Paula Pell quipped, "I just found an app on my iPhone that helps you find deeper human connection. It's called the off button."

THE BURDEN OF KNOWLEDGE

For the vast majority of human history, we humans had no clue what was happening in the next village, much less what was happening halfway around the world. But now, for the first time in human history, we are flooded with the awareness of human suffering in every corner of the earth. When we see others suffering, we naturally empathize and want to do something. But our paleolithic minds are not designed to handle the firehose of knowledge about human suffering that the internet brings us. The feelings of helplessness and futility can quickly lead to stress, anxiety, cynical futility, and fear that the world is an unsafe and unpredictable place.[9]

8. Rob Bell, *How to Be Here: A Guide to Creating a Life Worth Living* (New York: HarperCollins, 2016), 166.

9. There is a growing body of research that shows a tight correlation between the amount of cable news a person consumes and how dangerous they perceive the world to be. Cf. Bryan McLaughlin, Melissa R. Gotlieb & Devin J. Mills (2023) "Caught in a Dangerous World: Problematic News

I find it interesting that in the Alcoholics Anonymous (AA) literature, our need to control outcomes is named as the root cause of addiction. Moreover, the activator of our need to control these outcomes is anxiety and fear.[10] While being aware of what is happening in the world is part of being a good global citizen, being constantly bombarded with problems, pain, and suffering that we cannot solve takes an enormous toll on our psyches. How do we respond to the depths of human suffering we cannot control?

People who are "working the steps" in AA have an interesting ritual they utilize to deal with their collective dysfunctional need for control over their worlds. Bill W., the founder of AA, adopted the prayer by American Christian theologian Reinhold Niebuhr ("The Serenity Prayer") that is traditionally cited at the end of every AA meeting:

Consumption and Its Relationship to Mental and Physical Ill-Being." Health Communication, 38:12, 2687–2697, DOI: 10.1080/10410236.2022.2106086.

While cable news is not technically part of the internet, it is worth noting that the shift in the 1980s and 1900s from news being a service of television networks and a loss leader to becoming for-profit was driven by a combination of regulatory changes, technological advancements, market competition, and economic incentives. What now drives most of the news consumed in the US is dollars that come from viewers in the form of ad revenue. As a result, the incentives naturally create a system in which networks produce programming that keeps viewers "tuned in." In particular: news that does not challenge our beliefs, corresponds with our ideological alignment, and has been fine-tuned to make us feel self-righteous and angry. Truth is a much smaller financial incentive for most of our news sources; consequently, nuance is virtually non-existent in the news ecosystem.

Chapter 7 of Jon Stewart's book, *America (The Book)* on "The Media" holds up 20 years later as a humorous and thoughtful critique of the cable news industrial complex. Cf. Jon Stewart, *America (The Book): A Citizen's Guide to Democracy Inaction*. (New York: Warner Books, 2004), 133ff.

10. Bill W., *Twelve Steps and Twelve Traditions*. (New York: Alcoholics Anonymous World Services, 1953), 76. This dysfunctional need for control is why the first step of the 12 steps in AA is typically stated as: "We admitted we were powerless over alcohol and that our lives had become unmanageable."

God grant me the serenity
To accept the things I cannot change;
Courage to change the things I can;
And wisdom to know the difference.
Living one day at a time;
Enjoying one moment at a time;
Accepting hardships as the pathway to peace;
Taking, as He did, this sinful world
As it is, not as I would have it;
Trusting that He will make things right
If I surrender to His Will;
So that I may be reasonably happy in this life
And supremely happy with Him
Forever and ever in the next.
Amen.[11]

We all have some ability to act independently and to make our own free choices in how we deal with our worlds: how we treat our loved ones, how we react when someone cuts us off in traffic, which government officials we vote for, whether we help our neighbor who can't pay their utility bill, etc. But there are also parts of our worlds, situations, or events that we ultimately cannot alter, no matter how much we may want to or try to: how my partner or my children choose to act, how the people around me drive their cars, who is elected to political office, my government's policy on climate change, geopolitical unrest in the Middle East, etc. As Reinhold Niebuhr noted, sometimes it takes a lot of wisdom to discern if a particular situation is within my control to some degree or if I need to "accept it." The advice columnist Cheryl Strayed said it more directly and poetically, "You don't have a right to the cards you believe you should

11. Robert McAfee Brown, ed., *The Essential Reinhold Niebuhr: Selected Essays and Addresses* (New Haven: Yale University Press, 1986), 3–4. I recognize the use of "God" and implied ideas of eternal rewards and divine power and/or providence are problematic for some readers. In keeping with the AA tradition, I would encourage readers to insert "The Divine as you understand it/him/her" into Reinhold Niebuhr's prayer.

have been dealt. You have an obligation to play the hell out of the ones you're holding."[12]

The second Noble Truth in Buddhism (*Samudaya* in Sanskrit) recognizes that there is a unique kind of suffering that happens when we are unable to accept the world as it is. Accepting the world as it is does not mean we have to like it. It just means that we are not expending hand-wringing energy wishing life was different or frustrated when the world does not behave the way we think it should in areas over which we have no control.

Obviously, "acceptance of the world as it is" is much easier said than done. How do we learn to remove ourselves from being overwhelmed with the suffering of the world and the anxiety of future possibilities and live, in the words of Reinhold Niebuhr, "one day at a time, enjoying one moment at a time"? A practice that has been around for thousands of years has helped millions of people do this. As we begin the "Reconstruction" stage, we will examine this practice more deeply.

---

12. Cheryl Strayed, *Tiny Beautiful Things* (New York: Vintage Books, 2012), 205.

Deconstruct
Clarify
Remove
Quest
Re-Construct
Cultivate

QUEST

Your Pursuit of Truth and Spirituality Requires a Mindset of Humility and Courage.

Our Brains Evolved to Help Us Survive,
Not to Show Us the Truth. Having A "Beginner's Mind"
Allows Us to Be Open to New Possibilities.

10

Quincy and the Holy Man's Question

The Quest for Thin Places

"It really is easier to experience a spiritual connection when your life is in the process of coming apart."

–Anne Lamott–
(American author)

"There are all kinds of addicts, I guess. We all have pain. And we all look for ways to make the pain go away."

–Sherman Alexie–
(Native American author – from, "The Absolutely True Diary of a Part-Time Indian")

A few years ago, I had a dog named Quincy. She was a miniature Australian Shepherd who weighed about 25 pounds but barked way above her weight. Like many small dogs, she was on constant patrol duty—very aware of any creature that ventured near or through our property.

Her world was tiny; it consisted of the border of our backyard surrounded by a fence. She had a powerful nose and excellent hearing, so she could hear sounds and smell scents undetectable to us. She was often convinced that something was on the other side of the fence. She would lay around on the lawn furniture for most of the day and do mostly

Quincy "Wiggle Butt" Hicks

nothing. But now and then, her ears would stand at attention, her head would quiver like a bobble-head doll, and her muscles would get as stiff as a soldier's.

Then, the DNA resulting from generations of breeding proud Australian Shepherds would kick in, and she would become frantic. She would sniff and bark and look for an opening in the fence. God only knows what she was barking at—a squirrel, a rabbit, or maybe a handsome young boy dog? Whatever it was, something would have her in its grip, and it would not let her go. And she was frantic to see it.

THIN PLACES

During my many years as a pastor, I oversaw many funerals. I would tell this story about Quincy, and then I would remind people:

> In moments like these, we become more aware that we are also living in a small universe. Outside the door of my house and yours is a backyard called the Universe. At the border of the universe is a fence. Our Universe is very small, like Quincy's. Only we often don't realize how small it is. This fence is a barrier that traps you and me in our backyards and cuts us off from a larger presence in the world—it cuts us off from seeing and experiencing The Divine. Some people are convinced that there is nothing behind the fence, that our backyard is all there is—what you see is what you get. But, like Quincy, I keep smelling stuff. I keep sensing stuff. The whispers and rumors of people sometimes get loud.

Most of the time, we don't pay attention to our fences. But now and then, we experience what Celtic Spirituality calls "Thin Places"—those moments in which our worlds and something bigger than us come together at their narrowest. It might be at the birth of a child, the sight of the sun setting over the ocean, some great music or art, or hiking in the mountains. We often experience these thin places during the most painful moments of our lives.

Sometimes, the fence seems so thin that it is almost transparent. We have moments of clarity when we recognize the futility of our soul's searching, such as, the things we thought were important in middle school (being accepted by a particular group or looking a certain way). In hindsight, the energy we put into all this was quite silly, and we can't believe we got caught up in all that. Now that we are older, we realize the futility of being on the capitalist hamster wheel—the endless pursuit of a bigger house or paycheck. In these thin moments, we recognize that, in many ways, we can observe our current lives like our middle school selves—the stuff we thought was important ultimately doesn't matter. We can see that having more money or more stuff will not satisfy our souls. Being in the perfect relationship won't satisfy our deepest inner longings.

One of the most extraordinary mysteries of life is that the times that we think spirituality would be the most distant from us are when it shows up in our backyard. One spirituality writer said this: "We can ignore even pleasure. But pain insists upon being attended to. [The Divine] whispers to us in our pleasures, speaks in our conscience, but shouts in our pains: it is [The Divine's] megaphone to rouse a deaf world."[1]

I would never argue that pain is a good thing in and of itself or to suggest that pain should be pursued. I am not advocating masochism. When I have a headache, I reach for some ibuprofen. The renowned psychiatrist and author M. Scott Peck liked to distinguish between "neurotic" pain and "existential" pain. There is a kind of pain that points us to better outcomes—the physical pain we feel that keeps us safe, or the emotional pain of guilt that drives us to act better. It is the kind of pain that enhances our existence.

---

1. Jana Harmon, "CS Lewis on The Problem of Pain" September 1, 2012. C.S.Lewis Institute. https://www.cslewisinstitute.org/resources/c-s-lewis-on-the-problem-of-pain, accessed August 18, 2023.

Dr. M. Scott Peck

But Dr. Peck says there is also a neurotic kind of pain in which our minds are racked by too much guilt that limits our existence. Anxiety or depression are examples of neurotic sufferings in which we are too focused on regret in our past or have too much concern for something that may happen in the future.

Dr. Peck suggests that we ask ourselves, "Is this pain enhancing my existence or limiting it?"[2] In other words, some pain leads to thin places or nudges us to better outcomes for ourselves, and different kinds of pain can be a psychological death spiral.

The first and most important teaching of The Buddha reminds us that life always involves pain[3]—both neurotic and existential pain. Pain will come to all of us, but how we respond to it varies. How we respond to pain usually has more to do with the stories we tell about ourselves and the world.

After Dr. Peck had been practicing psychotherapy for many years, he observed a curious difference in the way religious people and atheists responded to pain. He observed that most times that religious people came to him for therapy, their pain would lead them to more questions and doubts and usually to agnosticism or atheism. (We might label this as "deconstructing.") Whereas when atheists or agnostics would come to him for therapy, their pain would typically lead them to become either profoundly religious or deeply spiritual.

2. M. Scott Peck, *Further Along the Road Less Traveled* (New York: Touchstone, 1993), 22.

3. Dhammacakkappavattana Sutta, "Setting the Wheel of Dhamma in Motion." Trans. Thanissaro Bhikkhu. 1993. Access to Insight, http://www.accesstoinsight.org/tipitaka/sn/sn56/sn56.011.than.html, accessed August 18, 2023.

My hypothesis is that most religious people in the U.S. are theists who believe in an omnipotent god. When pain and suffering arrive in their lives, they don't have a framework with which to understand how a loving god would allow it. So, instead of giving up on either their god's goodness or a misguided perception of divine power, they give up on God's existence and choose atheism or agnosticism.[4]

However, people who are not hampered by preconceived ideas of divine control seem open to the thin places that pain brings. As a result, atheists and agnostics in pain seem inevitably to stumble upon The Divine.

THE HOLY MAN'S QUESTION

Regarding physical pain, healthy pain can point us to physical problems to which we should pay attention. Unhealthy pain is chronic pain that doesn't help us identify a problem, but similar to what Dr. Peck calls "neurotic pain," it does not enhance our existence. The medical profession has spent a lot of time and energy seeking solutions to unhealthy chronic pain. The opioid epidemic in the U.S. is a byproduct of the pursuit of resolving unwanted or unnecessary pain.

In previous eras of human history, if a king didn't like the message he was given, he may have the messenger killed. This is tantamount to suppressing your symptoms or your feelings because they are unwanted. Killing the messenger and denying the message or raging against it are not helpful ways of approaching healing. What we don't want to do is to ignore or rupture the essential connections that can complete relevant feedback loops and restore self-regulation and balance.

4. For readers who are theists and wish to remain so, the discussion of divine love and power and the problem of evil is outside the scope of this book. However, if you want to hang on to your theistic beliefs and struggle with the problem of pain and suffering, I highly recommend Thomas Jay Oord's book: *God Can't: How to Believe in God and Love after Tragedy, Abuse, and Other Evils* (Nampa, ID: SacraSage Press, 2019). For a more academic treatment of the issue, I suggest his book, *Pluriform Love: An Open and Relational Theology of Well Being* (Nampa, ID: SacraSage Press, 2022).

When fear of pain is intense, it can feel like we are going to drown in it. The human mind, as it has evolved over millions of years, pushes us to cut off the raw emotions in our bodies. This is one of our body's survival mechanisms. But our unwillingness to experience certain emotions can lead to depression, anxiety, loneliness, restlessness, boredom, and often addictive behavior. As Bessel A. Van der Kolk famously instructed us, our bodies really do keep the score of past pain:

> Traumatized people chronically feel unsafe inside their bodies: The past is alive in the form of gnawing interior discomfort. Their bodies are constantly bombarded by visceral warning signs, and, in an attempt to control these processes, they often become expert at ignoring their gut feelings and in numbing awareness of what is played out inside. They learn to hide from their selves.[5]

A few years ago, I happened upon this story from a Tara Brach book that changed the way I see my own fears:

> In a distant land, word spread far and wide of a holy man with magic so powerful it could relieve severe suffering. But to reach his wilderness refuge and receive his healing, a seeker had to trek through dense forests and over precarious mountain passes. Those who persevered arrived at the holy man's simple hut exhausted and dirty. After guiding them to a refreshing stream and then offering tea, he'd sit with them in silence, gazing out at the

5. Bessel A. Van der Kolk, *The Body Keeps the Score: Brain, Mind, and Body in The Healing of Trauma* (New York, New York: Viking, 2014), 97.

> pines and sky. When he finally spoke, it was to swear them to secrecy about what was next to pass between them. Once they took the vow, the holy man asked a single question: "What are you unwilling to feel?"[6]

For many of us, our spiritual quest is an act of courage. It is the courage to lean into what is often painful and to feel what is difficult to feel in order to heal.

I once heard an interview with the actor Jamie Foxx in which he spoke of an experience during his college days that changed how he saw his life. Foxx wanted to do stand-up comedy at an open-mic night but was terrified of failure and ridicule. As he thought about the root of his fear—the idea of a room full of people thinking he wasn't funny—he decided it wasn't something worth fearing. There was very little natural consequence on the other side of his fear and anxiety. So, this became his life mantra. Now, he reminds his children of this advice with a simple question and answer: "What's on the other side of fear?" Most often, the answer is, "Nothing."

When we lean into the fear of what we are unwilling to feel, we usually discover nothing on the other side except those thin places in which heaven and earth seem close.

---

6. Tara Brach, *Radical Compassion* (New York: Viking, 2019), 90.

11

More Slippery than a Greased Pig

More than a Little Humility is in Order

"The first principle is that you must not fool yourself and you are the easiest person to fool."

—Richard P. Feynman—
(American theoretical physicist)

"Whoever undertakes to set himself up as a judge of Truth and Knowledge is shipwrecked by the laughter of the gods."

—Albert Einstein—
(American theoretical physicist)

According to the New Testament, toward the end of Jesus's life, he was arrested by the Roman authorities and brought before the Roman leader, Pilate. John's Gospel records a philosophical discussion in which Pilate tried to bait Jesus about the nature of truth. Jesus told Pilate, "For this I was born, and for this I came into the world, to testify to the truth. Everyone who belongs to the truth listens to my voice."[1] Pilate, perhaps a bit sarcastically and rhetorically, asked, "What is truth?"[2]

---

1. John 18:37

2. John 18:38

If I am honest, I can appreciate Pilate's cynicism. Truth, or at least our perception of truth, can be slippery. The evolutionary psychologist Robert Wright reminded us that the human brain evolved not to discern what is true and accurate but to find the best way for humans to survive and pass on their genes to the next generation. He wrote:

> The human brain is, in large part, a machine for winning arguments, a machine for convincing others that its owner is in the right—and thus a machine for convincing its owner of the same thing. The brain is like a good lawyer: given any set of interests to defend, it sets about convincing the world of their moral and logical worth, regardless of whether they in fact have any of either. Like a lawyer, the human brain wants victory, not truth; and, like a lawyer, it is sometimes more admirable for skill than for virtue.[3]

The lens through which we see the world and frame the stories we tell ourselves to make sense of our world may not be as accurate as we think.

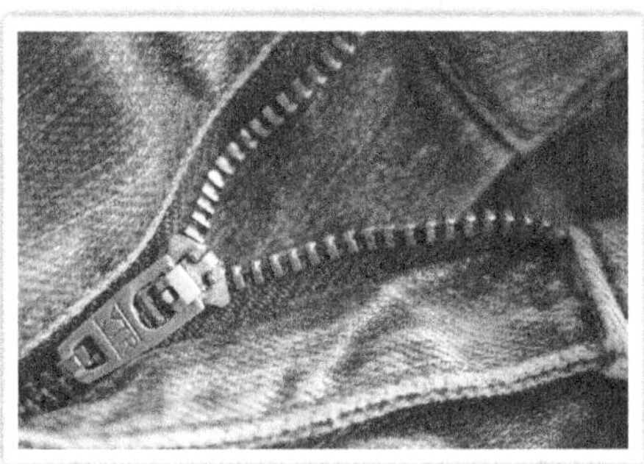

In a recent psychological experiment, people were asked to evaluate how well they understood the workings of an ordinary zipper. Most people confidently asserted that they understood zippers very well—after all, they used them all the time. However, when asked to describe in as much detail as possible all the steps involved in how a zipper works, most people had no idea. Authors Steven Sloman and Phillip Fernbach called this phenomenon "The Knowledge Illusion."[4] We modern humans think we know a lot, but it turns out we know embarrassingly little about the

3. Robert Wright, *The Moral Animal: Why We Are the Way We Are: The New Science of Evolutionary Psychology* (New York: Vintage Books, 1994), 280.

4. Steven A. Sloman and Phillip Fernbach, *The Knowledge Illusion: Why We Never Think Alone* (New York: Riverhead Book, 2017), 20.

world we live in. We assume that the knowledge in someone else's mind is somehow our own.

While a hunter/gatherer in the Stone Age may have known a lot about their world—how to make clothes, start a fire, kill small animals, etc.—as history has progressed, we know less and less about our worlds and how things work. For example, I am writing this chapter on a computer using software for which I have only the most cursory understanding of how my fingers moving on a keyboard will translate into letters on a page.

We know much less than we think. The real problem, though,. is that we trick ourselves into being confident we know much more than we do. Since opening my Facebook account in 2006, I have been constantly amazed at the confidence people display on subjects about which they know next to nothing. For example, people confidently propose policies regarding climate change and vaccinations with little to no knowledge in biology or meteorology. The anthropologist and historian Yuval Noah Harari reflects, "[People] lock themselves inside an echo chamber of like-minded friends and self-confirming news feeds, where their beliefs are constantly reinforced and seldom challenged."[5].

Samuel Perry
@profsamperry

The human capacity to delude ourselves, as individuals and in groups, never ceases to astound this social scientist. We can literally convince ourselves of anything contrary to evidence.

4:36 AM · Nov 23, 2022 · Twitter Web App

BLIND SPOTS

Since our brains are more interested in victory than truth, they come with a collection of blind spots. The most prominent blind spot is the comforting delusion that we do not have any blind spots. In recent years, dozens of researchers have documented and named countless ways our minds can ignore reality to win a victory. Here is a small sample of some of those ways:

5. Yuval Noah Harari, *21 Lessons for the 21st Century* (New York: Spiegel & Grau, 2018), 223. See also Eli Pariser, *The Filter Bubble* (London: Penguin Books, 2012).

- **The Totalitarian Ego**[6] is when our core beliefs are questioned, the oldest parts of our brain are activated. These parts of our brain are much less interested in rational discussion and instead respond with fight, flight, or freeze behaviors. As a result, we tend to shut down rather than open up. Adam Grant observed, "It's as if there's a miniature dictator living inside our heads, controlling the flow of facts to our minds, much like Kim Jong-un controls the press in North Korea."[7]
- **Confirmation Bias**[8] is our inclination to seek, interpret, emphasize, and recall information in a way that confirms what we already believe.
- **Anchoring Bias**[9] is our tendency to "anchor" and hold on tight to our assumptions based on the first piece of information we hear on a subject.
- **The "I'm Not Biased" Bias**[10] is the illusion that we are more objective than others. Intelligent people are more likely to fall into this trap. The brighter you are, the more difficult it can be to see your limitations and to see the world as it is. Some researchers have noticed that the faster a person recognizes patterns, the more likely they are to manufacture stereotypes in their minds.[11]

---

6. Anthony G. Greewald, "The Totalitarian Ego: Fabrication and Revision of Personal History," American Psychologist, no. 35: 1980: 603–618.

7. Adam Grant, *Think Again: The Power of Knowing What You Don't Know.* (New York: Viking, 2021), 59.

8. Raymond S. Nickerson, "Confirmation Bias: A Ubiquitous Phenomenon in Many Guises," Review of General Psychology 2 (1988): 175–220.

9. G.L. Iverson, B. L. Brooks, and J. A. Holdnack. "Misdiagnosis of Cognitive Impairment in Forensic Neuropsychology." In *Neuropsychology in the Courtroom: Expert Analysis of Reports and Testimony*, edited by R. L. Heilbronner, 243-265. (New York: Guilford Press, 2008).

10. Emily Pronin, Daniel Y. Lin, and Lee Ross, "The Bias Blind Spot: Perceptions of Bias in Self verses Others," Personality and Social Psychology Bulletin 29 (2002): 369–381.

11. David J. Lick, Adam L. Alter, and Jonathan B. Freeman, "Superior Pattern Detectors Efficiently Learn, Activate, Apply, and Update Social Stereotypes," Journal of Experimental Psychology: General 147 (2018): 209–227.

- **The GI Joe Effect** is the capstone of all cognitive biases. It is the belief that knowing about cognitive biases or being aware of them automatically enables us to overcome them.[12] The phrase "GI Joe Effect" comes from the 1980s children's television series, *GI Joe,* which ended with the tagline: "Now you know. And knowing is half the battle."

Social psychologist Lee Ross calls these phenomena *naïve realism*—the human mind's tendency to assume our perceptions and beliefs are accurate and unbiased. We think that other reasonable people perceive things the way we do, and when they don't, they are "unreasonable."[13]

CHANGING OUR MINDS

In a classic paper, sociologist Murray Davis argued that when ideas survive, it is not because they are true; it is because they are interesting. What makes an idea interesting is that it challenges our weakly held opinions. We get a dopamine rush when we discover or learn new things—but only when those new ideas do not threaten *our core beliefs*.[14] When ideas threaten our core beliefs, we do mental gymnastics to defend our beliefs. The legendary comedian Lenny Bruce observed this in action many years ago:

> I would be with a bunch of Kennedy fans watching the debate and their comment would be, "He's really slaughtering Nixon." Then we would all go to another apartment, and the Nixon fans

---

12. Ariella S. Kristal and Laurie R. Santos, "G.I. Joe Phenomena: Understanding the Limits of Metacognitive Awareness on Debiasing" Working Paper 21084: Harvard Business School, https://www.hbs.edu/ris/Publication%20Files/21-084_436ebba8-c832-4922-bb6e-49d000a77df3.pdf, accessed February 24, 2023.

13. Joyce Ehrlinger, Thomas Gilovich, and Less Ross, "Peering into the Bias Blind Spot: People's Assessments of Bias in Themselves and Others," Personality and Social Psychology Bulletin 31:2005: 680–692.

14. Murray S. Davis, "That's Interesting!: Toward a Phenomenology of Sociology and a Sociology of Phenomenology," Philosophy of Social Science, no. 1: 1971: 309—344.

> would say, "How do you like the shellacking he gave Kennedy?" And then I realized that each group loved their candidate so that a guy would have to be this blatant—he would have to look into the camera and say: "I am a thief, a crook, do you hear me, I am the worst choice you could ever make for the Presidency!" And even then his following would say, "Now there's an honest man for you. It takes a big guy to admit that. There's the kind of guy we need for president.[15]

Lenny Bruce in 1961

In our modern world, the quantity of information is pervasive. The amount of information at our fingertips overshadows what we had in front of us just a few decades ago. Adam Grant observes:

> In 2011, you consumed about five times as much information as you would have just a quarter century earlier. As of 1950, it took about fifty years for knowledge in medicine to double. By 1980, medical knowledge was doubling every seven years, and by 2010, it was doubling in half that time.[16]

Logically, one would assume that if people had more accurate information, we would be better able to discern what is true, make more

15. As quoted in Carol Tavris and Elliot Aronson, *Mistakes Were Made (But Not by Me): Why We Justify Foolish Beliefs, Bad Decisions, and Hurtful Acts* (Boston: Mariner Books, 2020), 26.

16. Adam Grant, *Think Again,* 17.

informed and better decisions, and be much better off as a species. Using this line of reasoning, scientists and politicians throw facts and figures at people, hoping to sway public opinion. But, as Robert Wright reminded us, the human brain wants victory, not truth. So, bombarding people with "facts" tends to backfire and make them more entrenched in their beliefs.

For example, the journal *Pediatrics* studied public health messages aimed at boosting childhood vaccination rates. Facts, images, and stories of disease-ridden children not only didn't sway anti-vaxxers, but the anti-vaxxers became *more* wary and *less* inclined to vaccinate their children.[17]

THE DUNNING-KRUGER EFFECT

Two psychologists from Cornell University, David Dunning and Justin Kruger, conducted an experiment in 1999 measuring the ability to analyze one's thoughts or performance.[18] After taking an exam, they found that participants with the worst scores overestimated their test performance and abilities. Despite low test scores that placed them in the 12th percentile, participants estimated they outperformed 62 percent of their peers. People are lousy at assessing their knowledge and ignorance.

"Let me interrupt your expertise with my confidence."

Dunning and Kruger also studied the peculiar case of McArthur

17. Kathryn M. Edwards and Jesse M. Hackell, "Countering Vaccine Hesitancy." Pediatrics 138, no. 3 (2006), https://doi.org/10.1542/peds.2016-2146, accessed October 12, 2023.

18. Justin Kruger and David Dunning, "Unskilled and Unaware of It: How Difficulties in Recognizing One's Own Incompetence Lead to Inflated Self-Assessments." Journal of Personality and Social Psychology. 77, no 6 (1999): 1121–1134.

Wheeler, a bank robber who was immediately caught after robbing two banks in broad daylight.

Wheeler had opted for not wearing a mask during his heists, because he believed putting lemon juice on his face would make him invisible to cameras. Wheeler's thought process went like this: since lemon juice is used as invisible ink, lemon juice should make a person's face invisible to security cameras. After being apprehended, Wheeler was legitimately incredulous that his plan with the lemon juice didn't work. Since their paper was published, additional research on the Dunning-Kruger Effect has proven it consistent across various situations: a person's driving skills, aviation, business, literacy, chess, and debating skills. We see the phenomenon play out in virtually every human domain.[19] We are blind to our ignorance and abilities, particularly in areas where we have a small amount of knowledge. David Dunning himself quipped, "The problem with [The Dunning-Kruger Effect] is we see it in other people, and we don't see it in ourselves. The first rule of the Dunning-Kruger club is you don't know you're a member of the Dunning-Kruger club."[20] People often diagram the Dunning-Kruger Effect something like this:

McArthur Wheeler robbing the bank. Note that his face is indeed very visible to cameras despite the generous application of lemon juice.

19. I often think about an offhanded comment made by comedian and actor Bryan Callen that may be the only exceptions to the Dunning-Kruger Effect, "There are three things you can't really fake: one is fighting, the second is sex, and the third is comedy." [Tim Ferris, *Tools of Titans: The Tactics, Routines, and Habits of Billionaires, Icons, and World-Class Performers.* (Boston: Houghton, Mifflin, Harcourt, 2017), 484.]

20. Brian Resnick, "Intellectual Humility: The Importance of Knowing You Might Be Wrong." Vox. January 4, 2019. https://www.vox.com/science-and-health/2019/1/4/17989224/intellectual-humility-explained-psychology-replication, Accessed December 14, 2023.

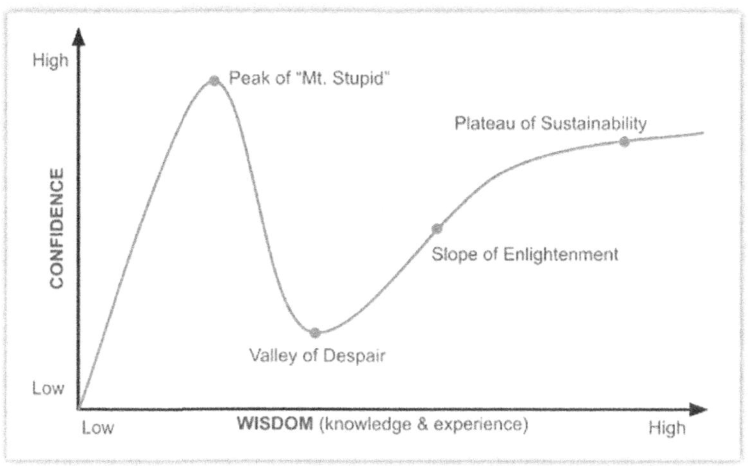

Satirical diagram inspired by the XY scatter plot representation of data from the original Dunning and Kruger study and illustrating a subject's self-report during skill acquisition.

Whether it is the annoying mansplainer on a date correcting you concerning your area of expertise, Monday morning quarterbacks ranting about how dumb their team's coach is, your uncle playing a foreign policy expert on Facebook, most financial investors in a bull market, the patient arguing with their physician because they had Googled their symptoms, or people who have never had children giving parenting advice, the Dunning-Kruger Effect is ubiquitous. While people who know *nothing* about a topic rarely opine about it, when we make the small step from novice to amateur, we suddenly discover inordinate amounts of confidence. As the saying goes, "Knowing just enough to be dangerous." Author Adam Grant calls it being "stranded on the summit of Mount Stupid."[21]

BEGINNER'S MIND

During the Enlightenment, spirituality elevated the individual's mind as the center of reality. It turns out that the human mind has, at best, a precarious relationship with truth. Our ability to discern truth is more

21. Adam Grant, *Think Again,* 43.

slippery than a greased pig. Even more than that, we are often most confident that we know the truth when we understand it the least.

If there is a takeaway from this discussion about our mental processes, it is this: we need to have a deep humility about what we perceive to be true. Another way to say it is that we need to be a little more open-minded to the possibility that the lens through which we see the world and the framing stories we tell ourselves to make sense of our world may not be as accurate as we think.

There's a beautiful scene in the TV show Ted Lasso where Ted makes a massive bet on a game of darts to help a friend. His opponent assumes Ted knows nothing about the game, as Ted makes a few less-than-excellent throws with his right hand. But then Ted reveals he's not right-handed and hits a bullseye with his left. While Ted is hustling his opponent, in typical Ted Lasso fashion, he gives his opponent a life lesson:

> **Ted**: Guys have been underestimating me my entire life. And I never used to understand why. It used to really bother me. But then one day, I was driving my little boy to school, and I saw this quote by Walt Whitman, and it was painted on the wall there. It said, "Be curious, not judgmental." I like that.
>
> [Ted throws a dart and hits his first triple 20]
>
> 
>
> **Ted**: So, I get back in my car and I'm driving to work, and all of a sudden it hits me. All them fellas that used to belittle me, not a single one of them were curious. You know, they thought they had everything all figured out. So, they judged everything, and they judged everyone. And I realized that their underestimating me— who I was had nothing to do with it. 'Cause if they were curious, they would've asked questions. You know? Like, "Have you played a lot of darts, Ted?"

[Ted throws another dart and hits his second triple 20]

Ted: To which I would've answered, "Yes, sir. Every Sunday afternoon at a sports bar with my father, from age 10 until I was 16 when he passed away."

[Ted throws his third dart and hits the bullseye; crowd cheers wildly]

Ted: Good game, Rupert.[22]

Being curious, not judgmental, is a way of approaching the world that is essential to our spiritual journeys. Zen Buddhists have a similar concept called the "beginner mind" (*shoshin*). The idea is this: to approach life with a sense of curiosity and lack of preconceptions or judgment—as if we are beginners or novices. This is true even in situations where we have expertise or experience. This practice enables us to experience the world as if it were new and full of possibilities. Zen master Shunryu Suzuki begins his classic book on the beginner's mind with this statement, "In the beginner's mind, there are many possibilities; in the expert's, there are few."[23] By cultivating a mind free from preconceptions and judgment, we can experience greater clarity, insight, and a deeper connection with the world. It's a way to approach life with wonder and humility.

If you are disheartened by the human mind's inability to perceive what is really real, you have only seen the tip of the iceberg. Our distorted perception of reality is probably worse than you think.

---

22. "The Diamond Dogs." Ted Lasso, season 1, episode 8, directed by Declan Lowney, written by Joe Kelly, Apple TV+, September 4, 2020.

To view this scene in its entirety and context, please visit: https://www.youtube.com/watch?v=3S16b-x5mRA&ab_channel=TheBestMovieClipsOnThePlanet

23. Shunryu Suzuki, *Zen Mind, Beginner's Mind* (Boulder: Shambhala, 2011), 1.

12

The Red Pill

The Courage to Experience New Possibilities

"Most people end up being conformists; they adapt to prison life. A few become reformers; they fight for better lighting, better ventilation. Hardly anyone becomes a rebel, a revolutionary who breaks down the prison walls. You can only be a revolutionary when you see the prison walls in the first place."

—Anthony de Mello—
(Indian Jesuit priest and psychotherapist)

"We are not human beings having a spiritual experience. We are spiritual beings having a human experience."

—Teilhard de Chardin—
(French Jesuit priest, scientist, theologian, and philosopher)

While it did not initially have much box office success, the 1999 film *The Matrix* quickly gained a cult following, and its social impact remains today. For many people, including myself, the film felt like no film that had ever existed before.

The Matrix is about a guy named Neo who, through a long series of events, discovers that he has been living in a dream world—an elaborate hallucination. While his mind is hallucinating, his actual physical body (along with most of humanity) resides inside a coffin-sized pod, where it was placed by robot overlords. He and other humans are pacified by dream lives created by "the machines."

Neo is given a choice: keep living the delusion or wake up to reality. This choice is famously captured in the "red pill" scene. Neo makes contact with rebels who meet him in his dream state. Their leader, Morpheus, explains the situation to Neo:

MORPHEUS: The Matrix…is the world that has been pulled over your eyes to blind you from the truth.

NEO: What truth?

MORPHEUS: That you are a slave, Neo. That you, like everyone else, was born into bondage… kept inside a prison that you cannot smell, taste, or touch. A prison for your mind. Unfortunately, no one can be told what the Matrix is. You have to see it for yourself.

NEO: How?

MORPHEUS: Hold out your hands.

In Neo's right hand, Morpheus drops a red pill.

MORPHEUS: This is your last chance. After this, there is no going back.

In his left hand is a blue pill.

MORPHEUS: You take the blue pill and the story ends. You wake up in your bed and you believe whatever you want to believe. You

> take the red pill, and you stay in Wonderland and I show you how deep the rabbit-hole goes.[1]

It is a stark choice: a life of delusion and bondage or a life of insight and freedom. It is very dramatic—even for Hollywood. But the film captured for many a growing sense that nothing is real, and everything is manipulated on some level (a feeling that has only intensified in the years since the movie was released).

Others saw the red pill/blue pill choice as one they must actually make. Many who have experienced holotropic states of consciousness, including religious experiences, plant medicines, and psychotropic drugs, understand clearly that the world we humans experience is a kind of illusion. While perhaps our lives are not full-blown hallucinations, they are more like a trick mirror that one might see at a carnival—a warped picture of reality that results in a warped approach to life.

From a more scientific framework, Evolutionary psychology is, in the words of Robert Wright, "the study of how the human brain was designed—by natural selection—to mislead us, even enslave us."[2] Neuroscientists and cognitive psychologists have likewise begun to explore one of humanity's biggest mysteries—how accurately can the human mind perceive what is real?

CONSCIOUSNESS

While the sciences have made vast improvements in our understanding of our world, one of the biggest remaining areas of mystery in scientific research today is human consciousness. In a 2005 issue of the journal *Science*, editors ranked the top 125 open questions in science. "What is

1. Wachowski, L., & Wachowski, L. 1999. *The Matrix.* Warner Bros.

2. Robert Wright, *Why Buddhism is True,* 3.

the universe made of?" was the first-place winner.[3] But "What is the biological basis of consciousness?" was a close second.

If you hit your thumb with a hammer, consciousness is the experience of pain. If you see a blue sky, consciousness is the experience of the blue. Neuroscientists have been wrestling with this relationship between our perceptions and their relationship to reality.

Dr. Donald Hoffman

At the University of California at Irvine, Professor Donald Hoffman has spent his life wrestling with the big questions of consciousness: How did consciousness evolve in the human mind? What is the evolutionary purpose of consciousness? How should we understand our perceptions and their relationship to reality?

Most of us assume we know the answer—our perceptions show us reality. Maybe not all of it, but when I see the moon, there really is a moon. I don't see everything about the moon, but I see what I need to see. When I see an apple, I'm seeing the truth. If I pick it up, I see the correct shape, color, and weight.

However, Dr. Hoffman's research has led him to what he calls the "Interface Theory of Perception." If we take evolution and natural selection seriously, we could ask, "Would evolution by natural selection shape sensory systems to tell truths about the physical world around us?" Through theorems and computer simulations, the results seem to point

3. Since we don't know about 96 percent of the matter ("dark matter") in the universe, this is a very vast question!

in one direction: the probability that our senses have shaped us to see the truth about the world around us is zero.

According to Dr. Hoffman, our senses have shaped us to guide adaptive behavior so that we can live long enough to make babies. In other words, natural selection didn't shape us to see the truth, but it shaped us with sensory systems that are like a user interface to the truth.

To explain how this works, Dr. Hoffman uses the metaphor of a computer:

> Suppose you are writing an email, and the icon for its file is blue, rectangular, and in the center of your desktop. Does this mean that the file itself is blue, rectangular, and in the center of your computer? Of course not. The color of the icon is not the color of the file. Files have no color. The shape and position of the icon are not the true shape and position of the file...
>
> The purpose of a desktop interface is not to show you the "truth" of the computer—where "truth," in this metaphor refers to circuits, voltages, and layers of software. Rather, the purpose of an interface is to hide the "truth" and to show simple graphics that help you perform useful tasks such as crafting emails and editing photos.[4]

Evolution gave us a simple user interface that lets us interact with reality in the ways that we need to interact with it to stay alive and reproduce without having any idea what that reality is. You don't have a

4. Donald D. Hoffman, *The Case Against Reality: How Evolution Hid the Truth from Our Eyes* (New York: Penguin Books, 2019), xii.

need to know, so you don't know. According to the Interface Theory of Perception, reality is a trick mirror.

Very few of us know exactly how the desktop interface on our computers works. When you drag an icon to the trash can to delete a file, a lot is going on inside the CPU and memory to delete the file. In the same way, we're blissfully ignorant about the nature of reality. Evolution gives us "icons" that allow us to control reality, but they are not the reality itself.

To take it a step further, things that we usually think of as fundamental realities, like space and time, turn out to be merely the format of our desktops.[5] The colors, shapes, and objects we see have nothing to do with true colors and shapes in an objective reality. They're just a nice format that evolution gave us, and that format will vary from species to species. They're not pointers to objective reality in any sense.

Skeptics may reply, "If that speeding train is just an icon on your interface, just jump in front of it, and it will show you how real it is!"

Dr. Hoffman clarifies that he wouldn't jump in front of a speeding train for the same reason he wouldn't carelessly drag a blue file on his computer to the trashcan icon. "Not because I take the icon literally—the file is not blue. But I do take it seriously: if I drag the icon to the trashcan, I could lose my work."[6]

THE INTERSECTION OF SPIRITUALITY

While these discussions at first glance seem to be for the realm of neuroscience and physics, at its core, spirituality is concerned with ultimate reality—the lens through which we see our worlds and the stories we tell that provide meaning to what happens. The mystics have been telling us for centuries that the world as we first perceive it is not an accurate reflection of what is real. "You will know the truth, and the truth will set you

5. Physicists' abandonment of spacetime and the pursuit of a more satisfying story to understand the universe is laid out in Ron Cowen, "Simulations Back up Theory That Universe is a Hologram." Nature. 2013. https://doi.org/10.1038/nature.2013.14328, accessed December 12, 2023.

6. Donald D. Hoffman, xiii.

free,"[7] Jesus was known to say to his followers. Modern Buddhists who follow the Dharma (The Buddhist path) often use the shorthand, "I took the red pill," to describe their new way of seeing the world. Spirituality is about learning to see the world through a new, more accurate lens, not through the trick mirror we have inherited.

Author Tara Brach tells a story about a tiger named Mohini who was rescued from an animal sanctuary and placed in a zoo. The story has become a helpful metaphor for me for transformational spirituality:

> Mohini had been confined to a 10-by-10-foot cage with a concrete floor for 5 or 10 years. They finally released her into this big pasture: With excitement and anticipation, they released Mohini into her new and expansive environment, but it was too late. The tiger immediately sought refuge in a corner of the compound, where she lived for the remainder of her life. She paced and paced in that corner until an area of 10-by-10 feet was worn bare of grass.[8]

Freedom is possible, but our own mind's limitations trap us.

7. John 8:32

8. Tim Ferris, 612.

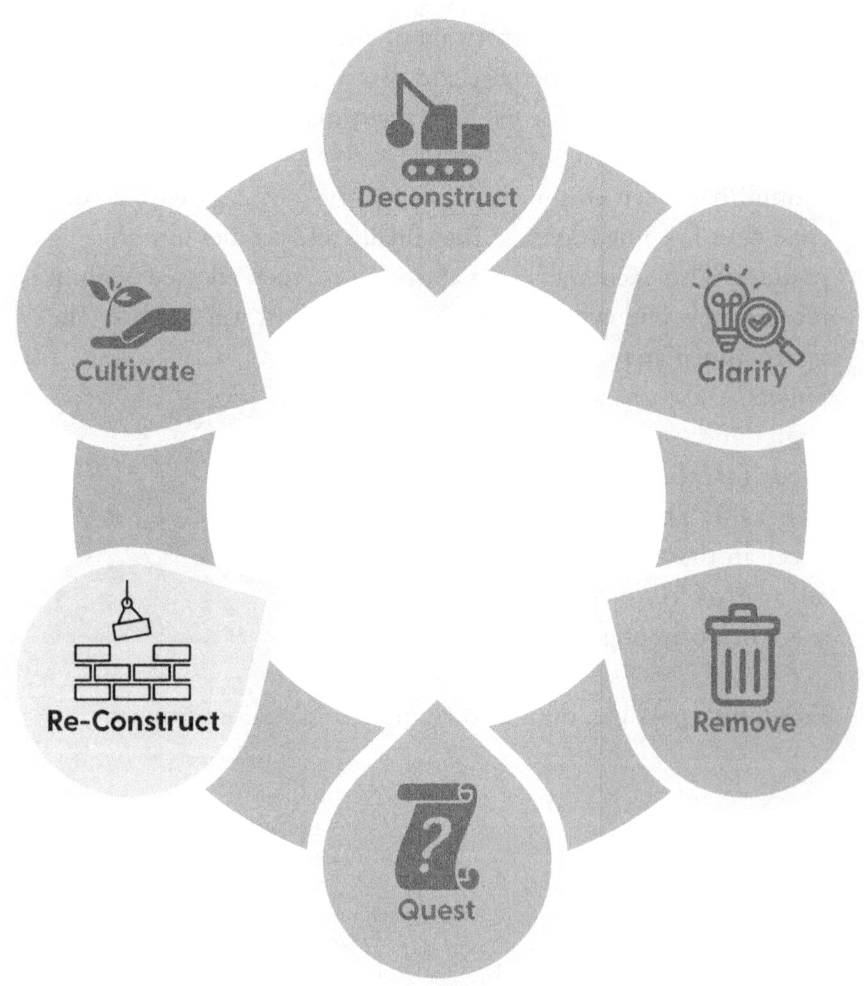
Deconstruct
Clarify
Remove
Quest
Re-Construct
Cultivate

RE-CONSTRUCT

Re-Building Your Spirituality with New Tools.

We can rebuild by cutting through our illusions and delusions and understanding how our brain's default mode network works. In their quests for spirituality, our ancestors used different technologies than we do, and we are just beginning to rediscover them.

13

The Most Common Verb in English

Silencing the Default Mode Network

"Our obsessive desire to make and have and do and say and go and get—six of the seven most common verbs in English—may ultimately steal away our ability to be, the most common verb in English."

—John Green—
(Author, from *The Anthropocene Reviewed*)

"'To be is to do' —Socrates
'To do is to be' —Sarte
'Do be do be do' —Sinatra"

—Kurt Vonnegut—
(American writer and humorist)

When I first started meditating, about 15 years ago, it was a painful and discouraging project. I was stressed out, worried, and taking anti-depressants. I needed to find a way to calm my mind down from the anxiety of the future and the memories of the past and focus on the here and now. So, I downloaded a meditation app on my phone and tried to do self-directed meditation for about 10 minutes daily. Here is what happened: my mind would not shut up! Thought after thought would race through my head, demanding my attention. I later learned that

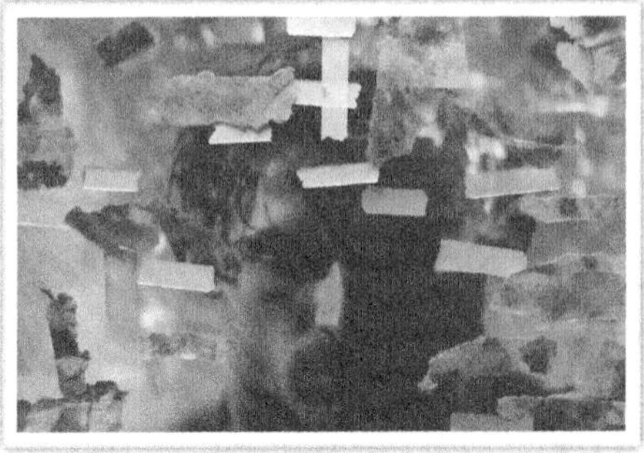

meditation teachers affectionately call this "monkey mind." After a few days, I began bringing a notepad to my meditation time to write down things I needed to do that day, hoping that I could try and get my mind to quit obsessing about them. Making a to-do list helped a little bit, but I got discouraged with the whole meditation process and quit after a couple of months.

I have spoken to many others who have had similar experiences with "monkey mind" as they started to meditate. I resonated deeply with Yuval Noah Harari's first experience with meditation when he wrote:

> Despite my best efforts, I couldn't observe the reality of my breath coming in and out of my nostrils for more than ten seconds before my mind wandered away. I had lived under the impression that I was the master of my life, the CEO of my own personal brand. But a few hours of meditation were enough to show me that I had barely any control over myself. I was not the CEO; I was barely the gatekeeper.[1]

Even when not meditating, research shows that our minds wander, lost in thought, for 30 to 50 percent of our waking hours. My meditation practice slowly turned a corner when a mentor taught me to "observe" my thoughts, emotions, and bodily sensations without engaging or trying to control them.

While different religions and groups of people have meditated for thousands of years and developed hundreds of meditation techniques, meditation is not a religious practice per se. In the same way that many

1. Yuval Noah Harari. *21 Lessons for the 21st Century,* 317.

religions have books, reading a book is not inherently a religious practice. Meditation empowers us to observe our minds at work and, over time, observe the tricks that our minds can play on us. So, while meditation has a strong scientific foundation among neurological researchers because meditation can "lift the veil" off the way we see the world, it often leads to what people self-describe as "spiritual experiences."

When I learned to "observe" my thoughts, my emotions, and my bodily sensations without engaging with them or trying to control them, unbeknownst to me, I was beginning to become aware of what scientists call the "Default Mode Network" of our minds. The Default Mode Network (DMN) is like an auto-pilot mode for the brain. Just as an airplane's auto-pilot system takes over when the pilot isn't actively controlling the aircraft, the DMN becomes more active when our conscious attention isn't focused on external tasks.

When we're not consciously engaged in a specific task, the DMN becomes more active, and our thoughts drift, daydream, or engage in introspective thinking: "Can you believe what she said to me?" "When was the last time I changed the oil in the car?" "Do I like cabbage?" "If I won the lottery, I would buy a new car first." When we are on auto-pilot, the DMN takes charge. It recalls memories, imagines the future, and processes emotions. The DMN also plays a role in cognitive processes like self-awareness, identity, creativity, and problem-solving. But the DMN can have a dark side. Our ruminations about the past are often negative emotions of regret or pain. Our brains' attempts to work through the uncertainty of the future usually lead to some level of anxiety.[2]

2. The "auto-pilot" analogy of the DMN is a broad oversimplification of a very complex process that, frankly, neuroscientists don't fully understand. As noted earlier in this book, many parts of the human mind remain a mystery.

Another way to think of the DMN is in terms of time zones. Our minds can process three kinds of time: the past, the present, and the future. Whenever we feel pain or stress, we learn to "travel" between these time zones, drawing on our past experiences and projecting our hopes or anxieties into the future. Usually, we are not very present in the here and now.

By observing our thoughts and feelings through meditation, without judgment or engagement, we stand back and observe the DMN as the "third-party observer." We begin to loosen the grip of the DMN's self-centering, ego-driven narrative, and distracting patterns. We can eventually learn to quiet the DMN's incessant chatter through practice. Instead of focusing on what has happened or what might happen, we can focus on the here and now.

Robert Wright wrote of the DMN, "When the default mode network subsides—when the mind stops wandering—it can be a good feeling. There can be a sense of liberation from your chattering mind, a sense of peace, even deep peace."[3] In that space, we quickly gain a deeper sense of clarity and well-being. We shift from incessantly trying to grasp the past and/or control the future to allowing everything to be as it is.

That is a lot of neurobiology. What does this look like in real life?

THE CURIOUS CASE OF JILL BOLTE TAYLOR

In December 1996, at the age of 37, Jill Bolte Taylor experienced a severe hemorrhage in the left hemisphere of her brain caused by a rare form of stroke known as an arteriovenous malformation (AVM). What made her experience doubly unique is that Jill Bolte Taylor is a neuroscientist. As such, she was uniquely positioned to observe and analyze her neurological condition as it unfolded.

In her book, *My Stroke of Insight,* Dr. Taylor recounts that during the stroke, she lost the functions in her brain that govern analytical thinking, language, and the perception of time—past and future. This also meant

3. Robert Wright, *Why Buddhism is True,* p. 47.

that her entire Default Mode Network (DMN) went offline. Suddenly, there was no more brain chatter or monkey mind. There was no more inner voice that could navigate her five senses by looking to the past to determine the best future course of action. She lost the linear and rational capabilities of our brain that we develop as infants that help us get through our days—remembering to eat and where to go when nature calls, etc. Essentially, she was an infant in a woman's body.

But far from being terrifying, her experience was euphoric and profoundly moving. Since her DMN was not working, she felt an intense connection with the present moment and the world around her. She entered an expanded state of consciousness, feeling a sense of unity and interconnectedness with the universe. For Jill Bolte Taylor, it was a transformative and transcendent spiritual experience.

It may be that this way of being is how infants see the world before they learn that they are separate from their mothers. I vividly recall my children as babies discovering the wonder and delight of themselves: "Look at my hand! It is so weird!"

Dr. Taylor felt no anxiety, fear, or anguish, and like "a great whale gliding through a sea of silent euphoria," she got ready to die. But she didn't die. Instead, she was reborn with fresh eyes and childlike wonder. She would later write:

> To the right mind, no time exists other than the present moment, and each moment is vibrant with sensation. Life or death occurs

> in the present moment. The experience of joy happens in the present moment. Our perception and experience of connection with something that is greater than ourselves occurs in the present moment. To our right mind, the moment of now is timeless and abundant.[4]

What is remarkable about her story is the clear contrast of her experience: what it is like to move from a "normal" state of being to allowing the right hemisphere of the brain to run free. For those interested in spirituality, awe, wonder, and beauty, the possibility of expanding this state of being, even in small doses, can be beneficial.

BE. HERE. NOW.

My original motivation to start meditating and to quiet down my Default Mode Network (DMN) was to slow down my mind, focus more, and reduce stress. Most people are likewise introduced to meditation through some mindfulness exercises. It wasn't until later that I began to view meditation as more of a spiritual practice: listening to my life, becoming aware of my anxieties, fears, and stress, and allowing what I have been "pushing down" to rise to the surface.[5]

Then something else happened: the more I became fully present in my meditation practice, the more it became apparent how much of my life was spent in the time zones of the past and future and not here and now. The more I would slow down to meditate, the more I became aware of how fast I was moving in the rest of my life. I slowly started paying more attention to my life as I went about my daily tasks.

---

4. Jill Bolte Taylor, *My Stroke of Insight: A Brain Scientist's Personal Journey* (New York: Viking, 2008), 29.

A great summary of her story can be seen on her TED Talk: https://www.ted.com/talks/jill_bolte_taylor_my_stroke_of_insight?language=en.

5. How to meditate is, frankly, way too big of a question for this small book. If you are interested in starting a meditation practice and are not sure where to start, I have tried to put together some very brief suggestions in "Appendix A" of this book.

Engaging with the here and now and focusing on one thing is what Buddhist teachers call "right concentration." It is learning to see meditation beyond simply sitting quietly and instead allowing it to become part of our mundane lives while washing the dishes, driving to work, eating, or almost any other activity we are engaged in.

I once had a partner named Christina who had many years of practice with "right concentration." One of her routines was to remove her shoes before she would enter the house.[6] I noticed once how slow she was at removing her shoes and made some satirical comments that were pathetic attempts at humor. She patiently explained to me:

> When I get home, I don't want to be already thinking of what I need to do when I get inside or be in a hurry to get through this moment to get to the next moment. I want to be present here and now. By intentionally and deliberately removing my shoes and putting them where they belong, I am staying engaged in *this* moment. Moreover, when I put them away neatly and in an orderly fashion, I am not living in the future by "borrowing" the time it will take to straighten things up later.

Slowly, I began paying more attention to my life and noticing the many things I had skimmed over. I observed landmarks and buildings during my morning commute that I had never noticed before. I quit quickly gobbling down my food with all the dignified restraint of a wolverine devouring a fatburger and instead focused on the delight of amazing

6. In most Buddhist traditions, removing shoes before entering a home reflects a recognition of the sacredness inherent in all aspects of life and the importance of maintaining a sense of mindfulness and respect in everyday actions.

food, relishing each bite. I realized that the most important things in my life were my partner and my adult children and the limited time I could spend with them. I became much more present with them and would repeat the mantra in my mind, "Savor this...Savor this...Savor this" to remind myself that the meals we share and the time we spend together are fleeting.

Eventually, I began to become more and more aware of a spiritual presence flowing through me. I first noticed the presence during quiet meditations. Eventually, it would appear in the mundane aspects of life, especially when I was relaxed and fully present at that moment.[7] It's hard to explain to those who have not experienced it other than to say that I can feel a presence arise in different parts of my body from time to time. Sometimes, it is subtle; other times, it is overwhelming, but the experience usually brings a heightened awareness and a deep sense of connection to others and the universe. For lack of a better word, it has always been beautiful.[8] The Vietnamese Buddhist monk and author Thích Nhất Hạnh explains it beautifully: "People usually consider walking on water or in thin air a miracle. But I think the real miracle is not to walk either on water or in thin air, but to walk on earth. Every day we are engaged in a miracle which we don't even recognize: a blue sky, white clouds, green leaves, the black, curious eyes of a child—our own two eyes. All is a miracle."[9]

These experiences of beauty, awe, and wonder in my ordinary life remind me of the "Plastic Bag Scene" in the movie *American Beauty*. The

---

7. I think of this energy as a Divine Presence or, in the words of the Christian theologian Alfred North Whitehead, an "initial aim" or "the creative advance into novelty" that underlies all existence and influences the ongoing process of reality's becoming. Those in the Eastern tradition, whose language is much more robust for spiritual experiences, often refer to this as *Kundalini*. Hinduism and Tibetan Buddhism vary in their understanding and role of *Kundalini* in spiritual practice. However, the awakening of *Kundalini* is broadly seen as a transformative process that leads to spiritual awakening, heightened awareness, and a deepening of insight into the nature of reality.

8. I recognize that the experience of *Kundalini* is a deeply personal and subjective experience, and its manifestations can vary widely from person to person. *Kundalini* can sometimes be difficult for people, particularly if it occurs spontaneously or without adequate preparation or support.

9. Thích Nhất Hạnh, *The Miracle of Mindfulness* (Boston: Beacon Press, 1999), 12.

character of Ricky Fitts (played by Wes Bently) is new to his high school and is an outcast who spends most of his time videotaping "beautiful" things. Through Ricky's lens, we notice what most people overlook. Beauty and wonder can be found not only in grand gestures or extraordinary experiences but also in the ordinary moments of life in which we are fully present in the moment. At the climax of the movie, Ricky shows Jane (Thora Birch) some of the videos he shot and explains what it means to him:

Ricky Fitts played by Wes Bently

> Do you want to see the most beautiful thing I have ever filmed? It was one of those days when it was a minute away from snowing. And there's this electricity in the air, you can almost hear it, right? And this bag was just...dancing with me...like a little kid begging me to play with it. For fifteen minutes. That's the day I realized that there was this entire life behind things, and this incredibly benevolent force that wanted me to know there was no reason to be afraid. Ever. Video is a poor excuse, I know. But it helps me remember...I need to remember...Sometimes there's so much beauty in the world...I feel like I can't take it and my heart is just going to cave in.[10]

---

10. Sam Mendes, director. 1999. *American Beauty*. DreamWorks Pictures.

As I mentioned in Chapter 3, I am aware that this film has generally not aged well and that Kevin Spacey is distracting at best and problematic at worst. I hope you can nevertheless feel the weight of what the writer, Alan Ball, was trying to convey. To view this clip in its entirety, see: https://www.youtube.com/watch?v=tcW-CER03NU&ab_channel=BingeSociety

There is so much beauty and wonder in the world if we can just notice. If we can slow down enough to be. Here. Now.

LET IT BE

This finally gets us to the question at the end of chapter nine: How can we begin to remove ourselves from the stress and anxiety of living in a world with so much that we can't control and instead live one day at a time, enjoying one moment at a time?

When we begin to practice meditation, we slowly start to identify less and less with our thoughts and feelings. We learn to observe our thoughts and feelings without judgment or engagement as the "third-party observer." Instead of centering on what has happened or might happen, we focus on the one time zone in which we have influence: here and now. Our mindset shifts from compulsively trying to control future outcomes—or "doing"—to simply "being." We let go of the things we cannot control and instead remain fully present.

In Tara Brach's book *Radical Acceptance*, she used a helpful metaphor to explain this mindset:

> In the 1950s, a few highly trained pilots in the U.S. Air Force were set a life or-death task—to fly at altitudes higher than ever before attempted. Going beyond the earth's denser atmosphere, they found, much to their horror, that the ordinary laws of aerodynamics no longer existed. As Tom Wolfe describes it in The Right Stuff: "A plane could skid into a flat spin, like a cereal bowl on a waxed Formica counter, and then start tumbling—not spinning and diving but tumbling end over end."
>
> The first pilots to face this challenge responded by frantically trying to stabilize their planes, applying correction after correction. The more furiously they manipulated the controls, the wilder the ride became. Screaming helplessly to ground control, "What do I do next?" they would plunge to their deaths.

This tragic drama occurred several times until one of the pilots, Chuck Yeager, inadvertently struck upon a solution. When his plane began tumbling, Yeager was thrown violently around the cockpit and knocked out.

Chuck Yeager

Unconscious, he plummeted toward earth. Seven miles later, the plane reentered the planet's denser atmosphere, where standard navigation strategies could be implemented. Yeager came to, steadied the craft and landed safely. He had discovered the only lifesaving response that was possible in this desperate situation: Don't do anything. You take your hands off the controls. This solution, as Wolfe puts it, was "the only choice you had." It countered all training and even basic survival instincts, but it worked.[11]

Every day, we are aware of situations we can't control that can be disorienting and annoying. It might be an interpersonal situation like a conflict with a friend, office politics, or some geopolitical tension halfway around the world. Our helplessness leads us to the impulse to flail against it, to try and manage it in some way, strategizing, turning it over in our minds, verbally processing it, etc.

Metaphorically taking our hands off the controls lets us see the desires and fears driving us. I once heard a spiritual teacher muse that 90 percent of our thoughts are fear-based and only 10 percent desire-based. That is more anecdotal observation than a scientific statement, but the point was well taken. Often, our thoughts or feelings that something is amiss keep us trapped in the time zones of the past and future. We can either

11. Tara Brach, *Radical Acceptance: Embracing Your Life with the Heart of a Buddha* (New York: Bantam Books, 2003), 52–55.

continue our futile attempts at control or meet our vulnerability with the wisdom of acceptance. We can let it be.

A beautiful picture of this is Cheryl Strayed's memoir, *Wild.* The book describes her feelings of being lost—her trauma over the death of her mother, the dissolution of her marriage, and her descent into self-destructive behaviors. Strayed found herself hiking the Pacific Crest Trail, starting in California's Mojave Desert. The closing words of the book find her reflecting on the Bridge of the Gods in Washington State and "letting go":

> It was all unknown to me then, as I sat on that white bench on the day I finished my hike. Everything except the fact that I didn't have to know. That it was enough to trust that what I'd done was true. To understand its meaning without yet being able to say precisely what it was, like all those lines from The Dream of a Common Language that had run through my nights and days. To believe that I didn't need to reach with my bare hands anymore. To know that seeing the fish beneath the surface of the water was enough. That it was everything. It was my life—like all lives, mysterious and irrevocable and sacred. So very close, so very present, so very belonging to me.
>
> How wild it was, to let it be.[12]

---

12. Cheryl Strayed, *Wild: From Lost to Found on the Pacific Crest Trail* (New York: Alfred A. Knopf, 2012), 312.

14

There Once Was a Chinese Farmer

Seeing Beyond the Stories

"Meditation is like an oven that forces the truth out."

—Adyashanti —
(Buddhist teacher, from *True Meditation*)

"Do you know what you are?
You are a manuscript of a divine letter.
You are a mirror reflecting a noble face.
This universe is not outside of you.
Look inside yourself;
everything that you want,
you are already that."

—Rumi—
(Thirteenth-Century Persian poet)

The human mind is a story-making machine. Our mind always tries to turn the most obscure patterns of what we are experiencing into meaning. This is why people see various things in the abstract ink blots of a Rorschach test: our mind can easily make meaning out of *literally* nothing. An old joke illustrates this: A man sees a psychiatrist for a Rorschach inkblot test. The psychiatrist shows him a series of abstract ink blots and asks him what he sees. The man eagerly responds with each inkblot,

"That looks like a couple making love. And that one looks like two naked women. Oh, and that one resembles a steamy bedroom scene."

After several rounds of this, the psychiatrist, feeling exasperated, says, "Your problem seems clear: you are obsessed with sex." The man replies, "*I'm* obsessed with sex? *You're* the one who keeps showing me the dirty pictures!"

The human mind is indeed a story-making machine. We can create stories from literally anything. This is why so many are drawn to conspiracy theories: weaving seemingly unrelated events together into a neat and tidy story gives a dopamine rush and a feeling of satisfaction—even superiority. It doesn't matter if the story is true: it *feels* true and is enjoyable.

It may not be an exaggeration to say that stories shape human beings more than any other force in our world. Stories transmit cultural beliefs, values, and norms from generation to generation. Stories can help simplify abstract ideas and complex processes. Understanding other people's stories gives us empathy and compassion for their unique experiences. On a cultural level, stories can sway opinions, inspire action, and shape public discourse on social and political issues.

STORIES AND MEANING

The stories we tell ourselves help us make sense of our past, present, and future and establish a sense of selfhood and purpose. Stories also help us place ourselves in the world and give meaning to what we experience. When events happen to us, we automatically put them in the context of our own story or the larger stories we believe about ourselves and our place in the world.

Our minds do not care if the story is *true* or not; we glean meaning and our emotional response to the events based on what we *believe* to be true. In one experiment, researchers observed subjects' brain activity while they tasted a variety of wine samples, each labeled with a different price. However, the bottles labeled $10 and $90 were the same wine. Many people reported liking the $90 wine better than the $10 bottle. Researchers also noted that, while drinking the $90 sample, those subject's brain activity reflected their greater enjoyment of the $90 bottle, as the mOFC region of the brain lit up in the scams. The researchers concluded that this brain region seems to be where stories mix with our sensory data to create what they call "the hedonic experience of flavor."[1]

In other words, wine tastes better if we have a good story to attach to it. This is just one small example of how our brains filter and interpret our experiences based on the stories we tell ourselves. The reality of our experience and our interpretation of that experience are two—sometimes very different—things. The stakes are low if our perception of a wine's deliciousness is regulated by the stories we tell. But when it comes to other aspects of our lives, the stories we tell ourselves can cause us all kinds of suffering.

HOW STORIES CAUSE SUFFERING

At its most basic and obvious level, the stories we tell about ourselves and our world can cause us suffering by being the filter through which we experience our world. If we tell ourselves that everyone is out to get us, we will interpret and respond to everything that happens to us through this lens. We will be suspicious, guarded, and untrusting of everyone. A lot of the suffering associated with mental illness—schizophrenia, bipolar disorder, obsessive-compulsive disorder, post-traumatic stress disorder

---

1. Plassmann, Hilke, John O'Doherty, Baba Shiv, and Antonio Rangel. "Marketing Actions Can Modulate Neural Representations of Experienced Pleasantness," Proceedings of the National Academy of Sciences of the United States of America 105, no. 3 (2008): 1050–54.

(PTSD), and even anxiety and depression—arises from a warped story of the world.[2]

Self-Fulfilling Prophecies

Moreover, the stories we tell ourselves can often become a self-fulfilling prophecy—for ourselves or others. Someone who believes that they are inadequate and their partner will eventually leave them may become overly clingy, jealous, or insecure in the relationship, which can create tension and ultimately push the partner away, confirming their belief in the story's truth.

Or, a teacher or an employer may have low expectations for a student or employee based on a story they believe about their race, gender, or some other aspect of their identity. As a result, they may unconsciously provide less support, opportunities, and positive feedback to them. In doing so, they inadvertently hinder their performance and confirm their story of low expectations.[3]

Our Interpretation of What Happened

At a deeper level, the stories we tell about ourselves and our world can cause us suffering by how we interpret those events. Imagine a car on a freeway cuts you off, forcing you to slam on your brakes. People often respond by honking, yelling, showing them the "one-fingered salute," or exhibiting road rage.

But there are two layers of experience in this scenario: what happened, and the story we tell ourselves about what happened. We may think, "This

2. If you or someone you love is suffering from a serious mental illness, the recommendations of this chapter are not meant to be a way to "fix" these issues. Please seek the help of a mental health professional who can help with your healing, or at the very least, help manage your symptoms.

3. I find it fascinating that in the Protestant Christian tradition, the Calvinistic doctrine of total depravity often becomes a self-fulfilling prophecy among its adherents. It doesn't take much time on X (Twitter) to notice that some of its most vile and cruel participants come from the Reformed Christian tradition. There is a troublesome correlation between Calvinism and cruelty.

guy is an insensitive jerk!"—but how do we know that? Our assumption is a story we have made up in our minds. What if they were having a medical emergency? Or what if they were having some mechanical failure with their car? Would those alternative stories change the feelings we experience in that scenario?

What we *know* when someone cuts us off, is that it will delay our arrival at our destination by about three seconds. That is all we know for certain. The anger that arises within us comes from the story we tell ourselves about the incident, *not the incident itself.* We become so wrapped up in the story we have created that we no longer pay attention to our lived reality. We are living in a story in our heads. We are no longer present here and now.

About a year ago, I took a certification course on trauma coaching. One of the insights I took away from that training is that the greater trauma we experience is often not the incident itself but the *stories* we tell ourselves about the incident. Some horrific things have happened to human beings that I would not wish on anyone. But a significant part of why trauma is difficult to overcome is the meaning we give to the traumatic event through the stories we tell ourselves about it.

Our minds so desperately want to make sense of what happens that it plays a mental trick on us. I have often heard people say, "Everything happens for a reason. These events may not make sense now, but someday, it will all make sense." That is, the meaning is out there; we need time to understand it fully. What that saying *really* suggests is that our brain needs a little more time to create a satisfying narrative. Like the Rorschach Inkblot Test, our minds can make a story (and meaning) out of anything if we give it enough time.

Cultural Narratives

On a broader cultural level, anthropologists say that our collective values and culture are shaped through stories. Stories sometimes give meaning to actions that cause suffering and while baffling those who do not believe the story. For example, people who live outside of the United States find our gun culture and violence incomprehensible. But our attitudes toward guns make perfect sense when you pay attention to the stories we tell about guns and violence. In 2022, the comedian Bill Maher gave a monologue about the stories Hollywood tells and how it justifies violence. Obviously, the problem of gun violence is not one-dimensional. Still, the monologue pulled back the curtain on how human behavior is understood by the stories we tell. Maher said:

Bill Maher

> They call them "action" movies, but they should be called "revenge" movies. Because that's the plot of every one of them. And there's a sick similarity in the revenge fantasies Hollywood turns out, and those of school shooters. "I want revenge. I want them to know that death is coming, and there's nothing they can do to stop it."
>
> Here's a list of just of the action movies that have vengeance in the title: Blind Vengeance. Bitter Vengeance. Cry Vengeance. Sweet Vengeance. Dark Vengeance. Fast Vengeance. Blue Vengeance. Forced Vengeance. Heated Vengeance. Naked Vengeance. Acts of Vengeance. Deadly Vengeance. Out for Vengeance. Bound

> to Vengeance. Fistful of Vengeance. Streets of Vengeance. Angel of Vengeance. Ministry of Vengeance. With a Vengeance. Code Name Vengeance. Fort Vengeance. Kickboxer Vengeance. Ninja Vengeance. And Taste of Vengeance. (My Least Favorite Chinese Restaurant!).
>
> Vengeance has been in more movies than pets in sunglasses!
>
> There's even a movie called "I am Vengeance: Retaliation," even though retaliation means vengeance. It's like calling your movie "I am Pregnant: Expecting."
>
> Getting revenge on them that wronged you is what happens—it's all that happens—in movies that are made for, and loved by, young men. It's the male version of getting your groove back or Meryl Streep getting a big kitchen!
>
> Like every school shooter, our movie heroes are grievance collectors, and when it comes to "action" movies, there's one story: "He was a nice guy, but they pushed him too far and now it's on." "They took my daughter!" "They killed my father!" "They killed my fiancé!" "They killed my family!" "They killed my family again!" "They killed my puppy!"[4]

The collective stories we tell help us to make sense of the world around us. Our stories don't have to be good, accurate, or helpful; they just need to make sense of the chaos we experience.

Metanarratives

At the most insidious level, the stories we tell about ourselves and our world cause suffering because of how groups of people use stories as mechanisms of power and control. The 20th-century French philosopher Michael Foucault argued that the culturally-shaping stories we tell ("metanarratives") become instruments of power and control. These stories

4. "New Rule: Hollywood's Culture of Violence. Real Time with Bill Maher Transcript." June 15, 2022. Scraps from The Loft. https://scrapsfromtheloft.com/tv-series/new-rule-hollywoods-culture-of-violence-real-time-with-bill-maher-transcript/, accessed January 13, 2024.

Michael Foucault

shape knowledge, frame how we talk to each other, and create social institutions that spread the majority's dominance and marginalization of the minority.[5]

People put their faith in stories—whether they are religious stories or political stories. The metanarratives we believe are bigger than ourselves, but they give us a role to play in it. These metanarratives are usually distortions of the truth that have tidy heroes, villains, and enemies. In these stories, we often find good excuses to use violence or go to war.

If we doubt or question the metanarrative, our social group often ostracizes or persecutes—because if the story is false, the entire world we've created with our stories is merely an illusion. Social constructs like laws, norms, and economic institutions become endangered. Since our identity is wrapped up in the metanarrative, an attack on the metanarrative feels like an attack on *us*. It is impossible to doubt the metanarrative, not because so much evidence supports it but because its collapse is unthinkable. In the words of the historian and anthropologist Yuval Noah Harari, "In history, the roof is sometimes more important than the foundation."[6]

The stories we tell are seductive because they give us a sense of certainty. Whether they are *true* stories is beside the point. But great freedom comes with releasing ourselves from the stories that cloud our perception—and being okay with not always understanding the situation or circumstances that we find ourselves in.

5. Cf. Michael Foucault, *The Archaeology of Knowledge*. Translated by A. M. Sheridan Smith, (London: Routledge, 2002).

6. Yuval Noah Harari, *21 Lessons for the 21st Century*, 287.

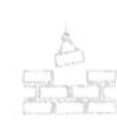

THE CHINESE FARMER

Let me tell you a story from the Taoist tradition about stories: Once upon a time, a farmer lived in a small Chinese village with his son. He owned just one horse, which he used for plowing his fields. One day, the horse ran away. All the villagers came to console him over his loss, saying how unfortunate his circumstances were. However, the farmer replied, "It could be good; it could be bad. Who is to say?"

A few days later, the horse returned, bringing with it a magnificent wild stallion. This time, the villagers congratulated the farmer on his good fortune, exclaiming how lucky he was. But again, the farmer simply said, "It could be good; it could be bad. Who is to say?"

The farmer's son rode the wild stallion, attempting to tame it. In the process, he was thrown off the horse and broke his leg. The villagers once again came to express their sympathy for the misfortune that had befallen the farmer's family. Yet, the farmer simply replied, "It could be good; it could be bad. Who is to say?"

A war broke out not long after, and all able bodied young men were conscripted into the army. The farmer's son, with his broken leg, was deemed unfit for military service, sparing him from the horrors of war. The villagers, realizing the wisdom of the farmer's words, remarked how everything had turned out for the best. And once again, the farmer replied, "It could be good; it could be bad. Who is to say?"

I've heard this story told in several different contexts with several different spins on its meaning. Some interpret this story to mean that we need to reframe the *stories* that happen to us to minimize suffering. We should spin our stories to recognize that good can sometimes come from bad circumstances. Or we should reframe our *place* in a story from "passive victim" to something more empowering. Or the story is about re-framing our *identity* in some way. Often, in the Christian Scriptures, a person who goes through a radical transformation is given a new name, indicating that their essence—including the stories they tell about themselves—has changed. For example, in the New Testament, Simon became Peter, and Saul became Paul.

That may be a reasonable way to think about the stories we tell ourselves. But I would advocate for something even more transformative—the elimination of stories altogether. Not just a shift of identity, but an elimination of identity.

THE BRAIN HACK TO LESSEN SUFFERING

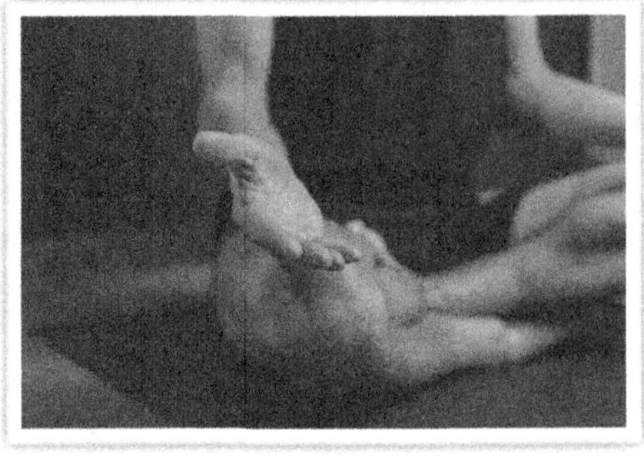

The creation of stories and identities in our minds draws on a complex neural process involving various brain regions. However, it is the Default Mode Network (DMN) region of the brain that does much of the self-processing, autobiographical memory, and narrative construction about ourselves and our worlds. But an interesting thing happens to the stories we tell when we slow down our brain's DMN through meditation.

The more we shut down the DMN through meditation to "be" instead of "do," the more we begin to let go of the stories and identities that can cause suffering in ourselves and the world. In meditation, we realize that the idea of "self'" is something our minds manufacture, update, and rewrite. Like the political spin doctors who explain the latest political happenings, our DMN is the storyteller who explains who I am, where I came from, where I am going, and what this all means. And like the political spin doctors on your favorite news network, our mind's DMN often gets things wrong—but rarely, if ever, admits it.

In my own journey, letting go of the myth-making stories I told myself and posted on my social media feeds was the first step away from a lot of suffering.[7] For many years, I believed these stories and identities, and when they were attacked, I thought it was me who was being attacked. It was no wonder that I got angry and defensive! I could let go of some of my stories and identities through meditation. I am not at my core a pastor, a father, a husband, an American, or even a Christian. I realized there was something deeper than those stories that was essentially "me." More importantly, I became increasingly detached from those stories I told about myself, which enabled me to become more genuinely me.

Through meditation, we begin to observe the flow of our bodies and minds. Thoughts, emotions, and desires appear and disappear randomly in our consciousness like the wind blowing in. Just as we are not the wind, we are also not our thoughts, emotions, and desires. So, who or what are we?

The Buddhist teacher Adyashanti teaches a practice he calls "Meditative Self-Inquiry" to begin to find one's true nature. Meditative Self-Inquiry is finding a question to meditate on repeatedly. He wrote:

> The most intimate question we can ask, and the one that has the most spiritual power, is this: What or who am I? Before I wonder why I am here, maybe I should find out who this "I" is who is asking the question. Before I ask "What is God," maybe I should ask who I am, this "I" who is seeking God. Who am I, who is actually living this life? Who is right here, right now? Who is on the spiritual path? Who is it that is meditating? Who am I really? It is this question which begins the journey of self-inquiry, finding out, for your own self, who and what you truly are.[8]

7. Like so many others, I confess to having been caught up in creating a perfect online persona with the belief that it was reflective of the truth of my "self." No, my life is not really a nonstop collection of sunsets, fun trips, perfect dinners, and smiling children. The truth is, most of my life is pretty mundane. Cf. Ray Williams, "How Facebook Can Amplify Low Self Esteem/Narcissism/Anxiety." Psychology Today. May 20, 2014.

8. Adyashanti, *True Meditation: Discover the Freedom of Pure Awareness.* (Boulder: Sounds True, 2006), 48.

As people meditate on this question, "Who am I?" they slowly begin to let go of the stories they tell and the identities they have created. Like the Chinese farmer, events do not have intrinsic meaning for them, but instead, they can say: "Is it good? Is it bad? Who is to say?" In doing so, they still experience the pain of an event but are freed from the suffering that they attach to the event through the meaning they ascribe to it.

15

Fecal Matter in The Pool

There is No "Them"

"Survival is the second law of life. The first is that we are all one."

—Joseph Campbell—
(American writer and professor)

"I have always found it quaint and rather touching that there is a movement [Libertarians] in the US that thinks Americans are not yet selfish enough."

—Christopher Hitchens—
(British and American author and journalist)

There is a profound maxim in cultural anthropology: "Trying to explain a person's culture to them is like trying to explain water to a fish." This powerful metaphor suggests that, from the moment we are born, we are so deeply immersed in a specific set of values, norms, customs, and ways of thinking and behaving that they become like 'water' to us—an all-encompassing environment we swim in without actively noticing or questioning it.[1] We may not realize how ridiculous or absurd a way of thinking or behaving is because we can't conceive of how life would be different without our "water."

---

1. The technical phrase for this is "an unconscious logico-meaningful universe."

When European settlers first came to the Americas for religious freedom and economic opportunity, pilgrims had to carve out their existence with limited resources. This quickly created a spirit of self-reliance and rugged individualism in European Americans that became the water we swam in.

Our subsequent struggle during the American Revolution heightened our collective beliefs in individual liberty and our distrust of centralized authority. Not long after that, our westward expansion of the 19th century, with its promise of land ownership and the frontier spirit, solidified individualism as *the* core American value.

Alexis de Tocqueville

In 1831, the French historian Alexis de Tocqueville spent ten months in the United States observing Americans up close. In his now notorious book on American life, *Democracy in America,*[2] Tocqueville was astonished by Americans' strong emphasis on individual rights, freedoms, and the pursuit of self-interest. For Tocqueville, at no time in human history had a culture been so individually focused. The upside to these unique values was virtues like independence and initiative. But Tocqueville was wary of the negative consequences of excessive individualism: the potential for isolation of individuals, disconnection from their communities, a lack of a sense of belonging, social fragmentation, an erosion of civic engagement, and a lack of concern for the common good. Tocqueville observed almost

2. Alexis de Tocqueville, *Democracy in America*, translated by Henry Reeve. (New York: J. & H. G. Langley, 1840. Reprint, Chicago: University of Chicago Press, 2000).

200 years ago how a lack of concern for the rights and well-being of others, particularly minority groups, could easily lead to exploitation and marginalization.

It is impossible to understand American culture without understanding that rugged individualism permeates all our institutions and even our religious and spiritual pursuits. It is the water of which we are unaware but nonetheless shapes our values, norms, customs, and ways of thinking and behaving.

THE DARK SIDE OF INDIVIDUALISM

Nearly 200 years after Tocqueville, we Americans have become even more individualistic. In 2000, Robert Putnam wrote *Bowling Alone,*[3] arguing that traditional American forms of social interaction, such as participation in clubs, religious organizations, and community groups, have decreased significantly since the 1960s. There are many reasons for this increase, including suburbanization, television, electronic entertainment, and changes in work patterns that have made people busier and less inclined to engage with others. According to Putnam, this decline has weakened civil society and reduced our trust and cooperation.

For those living through this experiment in rugged individualism, it has been a slow-moving train wreck of isolation, loneliness, and a growing public health

3. Robert D. Putnam, *Bowling Alone: The Collapse and Revival of American Community.* (New York: Simon & Schuster, 2000).

concern.[4] We are such social creatures that being isolated and lonely is dehumanizing. The years of the COVID-19 pandemic put a magnifying glass on how isolation can be destructive to our psyches. Similarly, prisoners who are sent into solitary confinement tend to experience mental health problems.[5] It is considered by many to be a violation of the 8th Amendment of the Constitution against "cruel and unusual punishment."

While we live in the most technologically connected age in history, rates of loneliness have doubled since the 1980s. Like eating cotton candy, social technology gives us the illusion of connectedness but leaves us malnourished and craving something more substantive. Many of us are dying of loneliness.

One hot summer afternoon, when my oldest daughter was in middle school, she and a friend decided to cool off in her friend's community pool. When they arrived at the pool, a sign on the gate read, "Fecal Matter in the Pool." The girls looked at each other and, unable to decipher the meaning of this vague pronouncement, decided that the water looked acceptable to them. After about ten minutes of swimming, the pool guy arrived to clean up the mess. With a confused look on his face, he said to the girls, "You know there is poop in the pool, right?" The girls were, understandably, both disgusted and mortified. They spent the next few hours trying to scrub off residue from the pool.

4. A meta-analysis of studies on loneliness by Brigham Young University discovered that medical outcomes for lonely people were worse than other negative health risk factors, including obesity, alcoholism, and air pollution. Cf. Julianne Holt-Lunstad, Timothy B. Smith, and J. Bradley Layton, "Social Relationships and Mortality Risk: A Meta-analytic Review," PLOS Medicine (July 27, 2010), https://doi.org/10.1371/journal.pmed.1000316, accessed January 14, 2024.

5. Cf. Angad Singh Bhalla, director. *Herman's House*. PBS, July 9, 2013.

In my current work life, I manage a social services nonprofit that runs programs to empower foster kids and alleviate poverty. During a recent staff meeting, I told the "Fecal Matter in the Pool" story to all the employees of our company. I then told them:

> The human need that we deal with every day is not something that is "out there" that we can just ignore. We humans are all swimming in the same pool. What happens in your part of the pool affects me and vice versa. When there is "fecal matter in the pool," it is not another city's or another person's problem. We can't just swim to our side of the pool and wish them well from a distance. Just because we don't see the fecal matter doesn't mean we are not affected by it. The idea that we are isolated individuals without an impact on each other is an illusion.

There is a seductive lure to the illusion of rugged individualism. In 1967, American psychologists Edward E. Jones and Victor Harris identified the "Fundamental Attribution Error."[6] When judging others, we tend to attribute their actions to their character (they are "lazy," "greedy," or "dishonest") while ignoring or minimizing their external circumstances. Yet when it comes to our actions, we know our bad behavior is because of our circumstances, not our character. For example, when we see a parent yelling at a child in a grocery store, we are tempted to think, "What an impatient, terrible parent." When we yell at our kids in the grocery store, we think, "These kids are such brats!"

Of course, The Fundamental Attribution Error works the other way around, too: We tend to attribute the good actions of others to their circumstances and our good actions to our character. This is why rugged individualism is so seductive: it allows us to feel superior to others as we reflect on our good actions (our "good character"). It lets us off the hook for helping others in dire circumstances because of their "bad character."

6. Jones, Edward E., and Victor Harris. "The Attribution of Attitudes." Journal of Experimental Social Psychology. 3, no. 1 (1967): 1–24.

Steve Jobs

But the truth is that we are all in the pool together. Our lives and circumstances are so interconnected and interdependent on other people and the environments in which we live that the notion of being a self-made, self-reliant, self-sufficient, self-sustaining, autonomous master of one's destiny is ridiculous. A few days before Apple co-founder and CEO Steve Jobs died of pancreatic cancer, he made a quick note to himself:

From: Steve Jobs, sjobs@apple.com
To: Steve Jobs, sjobs@apple.com
Date: Thursday, September 2, 2010 at 11:08PM

I grow little of the food I eat, and of the little I do grow I did not breed or perfect the seeds.

I do not make any of my own clothing.

I speak a language I did not invent or refine.

I did not discover the mathematics I use.

I am protected by freedoms and laws I did not conceive of or legislate, and do not enforce or adjudicate.

I am moved by music I did not create myself.

When I needed medical attention, I was helpless to help myself survive.

I did not invent the transistor, the microprocessor, object-oriented programming, or most of the technology I work with.

I love and admire my species, living and dead, and am totally dependent on them for my life and well-being.

Sent from my iPad[7]

We are all swimming in the same pool and depend on others for our lives and well-being. The actor and comedian Patton Oswalt has been known to phrase this truth slightly differently: There is no "Them."

There is no isolated "me" apart from "you." No "other" that is somehow separate from "us." The idea of "them" is a carefully crafted illusion created by our minds and reinforced through rugged individualism, tribalism, and diabolical leaders who know that unity is easily made by demonizing a group of people as "them."

Let me push you a little bit further. There is also no isolated individual "me" apart from the rest of the universe.

7. Steve Jobs Archive. "Put Something Back." https://putsomethingback.stevejobsarchive.com/, accessed December 18, 2023.

16

One

Even The Phrase "Each Other" Doesn't Make Sense

"In a relational world, no entity, be it cell or society, can exist apart from its receiving and giving to others."

—Marjorie Hewitt Suchocki—
(Christian theologian in *God-Christ-Church*)

"All differences in this world are of degree, and not of kind, because oneness is the secret of everything."

—Swami Vivekananda—
(19th Century Indian Hindu monk and author)

Humans must intentionally try to find the differences between ourselves and others. How we all love our kids, laugh or cry, and love the people closest to us is so universal that we must find nearly arbitrary categories to differentiate ourselves. We quickly point out our superficial differences: we wear different clothes, speak other languages, and eat different foods. But the fact remains that everyone wears clothes, speaks languages, and eats food. We must go out of our way to find our differences, but our similarities are ubiquitous. In the 21st century, I can read a book like *The Iliad,* written over 2,000 years ago, halfway around the world, in a different language. Yet the universality of the human

experience in the story can still resonate with me: anger and wrath, pride and honor, grief and loss, loyalty and friendship, and love and family.

Despite the myriad differences among the world's religions, a common thread of unity and oneness of humanity weaves through many of them. This shared belief is usually championed by spiritual mystics:

- In Hinduism, the concept of *Brahman* emphasizes the ultimate reality or divine essence that pervades the entire universe, including individual souls (*Atman*).
- In Buddhism, the "dependent origination" principle teaches that nothing, including human beings, exists in isolation. Instead, everything arises in dependence on other causes and conditions. This concept of interdependence is further reinforced by the notion of 'emptiness' (*Shunyata*), which asserts that everything lacks an intrinsic, independent existence and is interconnected with the whole. These teachings underscore the profound interconnectedness of all beings, fostering a sense of unity and oneness that we all share.
- In ancient Chinese philosophy, the Tao is seen as the unity that encompasses and transcends all duality and opposites.
- In Christianity, the concept of unity and oneness is embedded in the poetry of John the Evangelist in the New Testament as he recounts the vision of the universe being absorbed into divine love.[1] In Alfred North Whitehead's theology, there is a fundamental unity

1. Revelation, Ch. 21—22

underlying all of existence, with every supposedly separate entity intimately tied to and influenced by all other entities. Each entity inherits from the past and contributes to the unfolding future reality into a unified experience.[2]

- In Islam, the concept of *Tawhid* (unity of God) teaches that all creation and existence emanate from and is sustained by The Divine. The Qur'an emphasizes the unity of all existence with the divine source by stating, "To Allah, we belong, and to Him is our return."[3]
- In many indigenous traditions worldwide, the interconnectedness of all life and the unity of humans with nature, the earth, and the cosmos is central to their worldview.

So, where does our sense of separateness come from? How and why do we have this sense of "individual self"?

THE HUMAN MIND AND OUR SENSE OF SELF

The influential evolutionary psychologist Robert Wright argued that our sense of self evolved in us as a species because it helped us do what evolution always wants us to do: survive and procreate. The psychologically constructed feeling of being a coherent personal agent served essential functions for our highly social, intelligent species.[4]

2. Cf. Alfred North Whitehead, *Process and Reality: An Essay in Cosmology* (New York: The Free Press, 1978).

3. Qur'an 2:156

4. Robert Wright, *Why Buddhism is True*, 196ff.

From a neurological vantage point, there are several ways in which our minds have an intuition of selfhood. The most superficial sense of selfhood is *embodiment*: the feeling of being contained within a body. Another sense of self is our *social self*, which creates our identity from the social contexts in which we live. For example, a person might sometimes identify as a father, sometimes a husband, sometimes an employee, sometimes a member of a nation, etc. Finally, there is also the *narrative self* in which we feel like we are the boss or the CEO of ourselves, making decisions and exerting our agency.[5]

Despite our mental perceptions of these different aspects of ourselves, neuroscientist Thomas Metzinger argues that they are illusions. Instead, Dr. Metzinger proposes a theory called the *self-model theory of subjectivity*.[6] In his theory, we really have no self as such. Instead, we have a persistent self-model in our brains with which we identify. There is no *you* causing your thoughts to appear, but we nonetheless persistently identify with those thoughts.

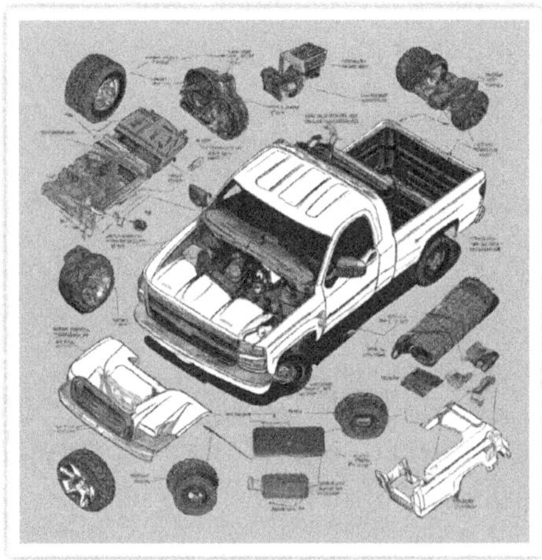

This idea of "non-self" (*anatta*, as the Buddhists call it) is difficult, if not impossible, to grasp. The 20th-century Thai monk Ajahn Chah would remind his students that it was only through meditation that we could begin to grasp this concept. Trying to grasp this

5. There are parts of our brain that are associated with our sense of self, such as the prefrontal cortex and posterior cingulate cortex. When these parts of our brains are not functioning correctly, conditions such as schizophrenia, depersonalization disorder, and certain forms of dementia can warp the sense of self and make it difficult to relate to others and function in human society.

6. Thomas Metzinger, *Being No One: The Self-Model Theory of Subjectivity*. (Cambridge, MA: The MIT Press, 2004).

perception through "intellectualizing" alone would cause your "head to explode."[7]

Let me try an analogy at the potential risk of your head exploding. I own a Toyota Tacoma pickup truck. If you saw my truck in a parking lot, you would see an independent object, separate and distinct from everything around it. But the truth is, my truck depends on all the parts and processes that allow it to exist. If you were to take it apart and spread its thousands of parts across the parking lot, you couldn't point to any one singular part that was essentially "my truck." This is no single part of my truck—the engine, the wheels, the seats—that *is* the truck. My truck is the sum of all its parts. All the parts depend on causes or conditions that allow my truck to be a truck.

Likewise, we humans depend on everything that makes us who we are. "You" are the sum of all your parts. There is no part of you—your memories, experiences, emotions, all the different parts of your mind, all the different parts of your body—that is essentially *you*. Moreover, you are part of other entities that depend on you: families, communities, societies, etc.

Alfred North Whitehead

In the early 20th Century, Alfred North Whitehead taught and wrote about applied mathematics and explored foundational

7. Robert Wright, *Why Buddhism is True,* 58.

I am happy to report that my head is firmly intact despite trying to wrap my mind around the concept of *anatta*. At the advice of my attorney, however, I am obliged to inform you that any head explosion on your part from reading these pages is not my responsibility. Read and reflect at your own risk.

concepts in physics like space, time, relativity, and quantum theory. Through these disciplines, Whitehead put a scientific spin on what mystics have told us for centuries: fully self-contained, independent entities do not exist. Instead, everything is intimately tied to and impacted by other entities through a constantly evolving network of relations and interconnections. What we perceive as distinction and separateness of our selves is an illusion. There is no unchanging you or essence of you. There is only the momentary "you" that is continually changing and being changed by your environment. While many things are the same, "you" are not the same "you" as when you were five years old. Nor will it be the same "you" 10 years from now.[8]

Like a river continually flowing downstream to the ocean, there is no permanent aspect to the river. The water from upstream is always new. The banks constantly evolve as the sediment and rocks wash away and erode the soil. Similarly, the cells of your body are continually regenerating and splitting. Your older memories are fading, and new memories are being created. Your thoughts, ideas, preferences, and opinions are changing over time.

So, if this is true, what is the benefit of knowing there is no essential "you"? What are the spiritual benefits of recognizing this unity and "oneness" of the universe?

BRAIN HACKS THROUGH MEDITATION

As noted earlier, spiritual mystics from the world's religious traditions have tried to articulate this idea of connection, interdependence, and unity of all things from their experiences for centuries. Today, meditation is the most common way people begin to have this epiphany of oneness.

8. Alfred North Whitehead, *Process and Reality: An Essay in Cosmology* (New York: The Free Press, 1978) is Whitehead's magnum opus in which he outlines his "philosophy of organism" emphasizing the interdependence of all entities. Building on Whitehead's metaphysic with a Christian theology spin, David Ray Griffin's *Reenchantment Without Supernaturalism: A Process Philosophy of Religion* (Ithaca, NY: Cornell University Press, 2001) lays out a naturalistic process of universal interrelatedness.

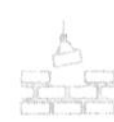

Like Ajahn Chah would tell his students, these ideas of unity and oneness of everything and the diminishment of self are less something we understand rationally and more something we experience. If we can slow down the Default Mode Network (DMN) in our minds, those aspects of our minds that create a perception of "selfhood" begin to diminish. This is not a fast process. It often takes meditators years to start to experience it. But the side effects of one's slow diminishment of self can be profound.

In a very general sense, I'm sure everyone would agree that our world would be a much better place if there were fewer self-absorbed people! The root cause of most of the suffering in our world comes from cherishing and centering the "self" above all else. One Buddhist monk put it starkly:

> According to the teachings of the Buddha, the idea of self is an imaginary, false belief which has no corresponding reality, and it produces harmful thoughts of 'me' and 'mine,' selfish desire, craving, attachment, hatred, ill-will, conceit, pride, egoism, and other defilements, impurities, and problems. It is the source of all the troubles in the world from personal conflicts to wars between nations. In short, to this false view can be traced all the evil in the world.[9]

This is why the first step in war, genocide, or nationalistic atrocities is the dehumanization of the "other." When we call people names like "cockroaches" or "vermin," we allow our minds to draw a greater distinction between "us" and "them" so we can justify the violence we inflict.

But when we experience the reduction of that line between ourselves and others, we realize that we are all swimming in the same pool. When we realize there is no "them," it makes us more generous, empathetic, and compassionate toward other people. Other people's suffering becomes *our*

---

9. Walpola Rahula, *What the Buddha Taught* (New York: Grove Press, 1959), 51.

suffering. Harming other people is the same as harming ourselves.[10] One person committed to serious meditation over a long period was asked whether, if everyone in the world meditated intensively, there would be any wars. He answered the question with a question, "Why would someone want to harm themself? In that sense, I don't think there would be, because it's like, why would you cut off your right hand?"[11]

Additionally, when people experience a sense of the transience and impermanence of all things, they often find themselves with a significantly reduced fear of death. Death is frightening to a linear personal identity, but research is showing that meditators who can transcend the individualistic fear of non-existence and instead experience a sense of connection with all things showed significantly lower levels of death anxiety compared to non-practitioners.[12]

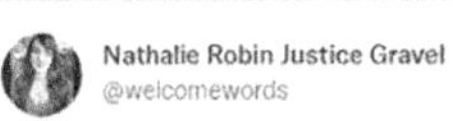

If a monkey hoarded more bananas than it could eat, while most of the other monkeys starved, scientists would study that monkey to figure out what the heck was wrong with it. When humans do it, we put them on the cover of Forbes.

3:02 PM · Feb 2, 2021 · Twitter for iPad

Experiencing the perception that there is no "them," of the oneness of the universe, of the unity of all things, of the transience and impermanence of all things can be a profoundly spiritual experience. Psychological researchers like Daniel X. Freedman and Ido Hartogosohn use terms like "portentousness" and "meaning-enhancement" to describe experiences like this that become an all-consuming, overarching conviction. It is

10. The general idea of the "golden rule" finds itself in virtually every religious tradition. In the teachings of Jesus, I find it intriguing that Matthew 7:12 seems to have the same underlying idea that what I do to others, I am in some way doing to myself. In the original language—Πάντα οὖν ὅσα ἐὰν θέλητε ἵνα ποιῶσιν ὑμῖν οἱ ἄνθρωποι, οὕτως καὶ ὑμεῖς ποιεῖτε αὐτοῖς·. can be literally translated, "Always, therefore, whatever you want people to do to you, do even so to them." Like other spiritual teachers, Jesus' teaching seems to blur of the lines between "me" and "them" when it comes to our ethical treatment of "others."

11. Robert Wright, *Why Buddhism is True,* 206.

12. Suzanne C. Danhauer, Nancy O. Totten, David Fenster, John P. Stukey, Brian J. Lawlor, Keith G. Meador, and Alycia A. Ciccolo. "Meditators and Non-Meditators: A Descriptive Study of Age, Gender, Health Practice Characteristics." Consciousness and Cognition. 33 (October 2015): 135–141.

much less an intellectual epiphany and more a profound, "more real than real," intense experience with deep meaning for the person experiencing it. The experience usually carries a weight of truth more significant than anything the person has felt or believed before. The 13th Century Persian poet Rumi captured some of this weight when he wrote:

> Out beyond ideas of wrongdoing and rightdoing,
> There is a field. I'll meet you there.
> When the soul lies down in that grass,
> The world is too full to talk about.
> Ideas, language, even the phrase *each other*
> Doesn't make any sense.[13]

13. Rumi, *The Essential Rumi,* Trans. Coleman Barks and John Moyne, (New York: HarperCollins, 1995), 36.

17

Back to The Future

Once You've Plunged into The Ocean...

"You go deep enough or far out enough in consciousness and you will bump into the sacred. It's not something we generate; it's something out there waiting to be discovered."

—Michael Pollen—
(Author, from *How to Change Your Mind*)

"How is it that hardly any major religion has looked at science and concluded, 'This is better than we thought! The Universe is much bigger than our prophets said, grander, more subtle, more elegant?' Instead, they say, 'No, no, no! My god is a little god, and I want him to stay that way.'"

—Carl Sagan—
(American astronomer, from *Pale Blue Dot: A Vision of the Human Future in Space*)

A couple of years into my meditation journey, I listened to a podcast episode with the author Michael Pollen. The podcast led me to Pollen's massive 450-page book, *How to Change Your Mind: What the New Science of Psychedelics Teaches Us About Consciousness, Dying, Addiction, Depression, and Transcendence.* Growing up evangelical, I didn't start drinking alcohol until I was in my 30's. Even though I grew up in Oregon, I have never tried cannabis in any form. I had no experience with or desire for experimentation with drugs of any kind, much less psychedelics. In short, I was an improbable candidate to be the kind of person who would take an interest in psychedelics. But my personality, being what it is,[1] I took a deep dive into the history and science of some of the substances that have shaped human history in ways that we moderns in the Western world do not appreciate.

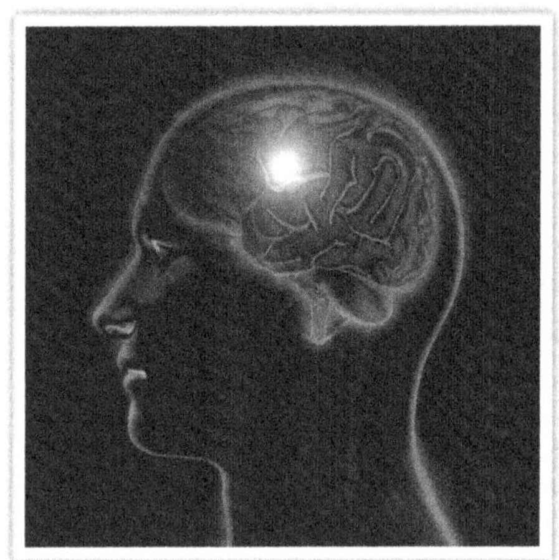

I discovered that, not until the advent of the industrial civilizations of the West did a culture exist that did not hold mystical and altered states of consciousness in high esteem. For the vast majority of human history, people have induced altered states of consciousness for religious reasons, to diagnose and heal sickness, and for creative expression.

For thousands of years, humans have used what Stanislav Grof calls "technologies of the sacred"[2]—techniques and substances that alter the human mind for spiritual purposes. There is evidence of shamanic practices as far back as 30,000 years ago during the Paleolithic era. In the last few thousand years, rituals of most native cultures have used mystical states for healing. In other ancient places, there is considerable evidence of using "technologies of the sacred": Egypt, Greece, China, Persia, the Caribbean, Africa, Tibet, and Mesoamerica. The technologies and symbols vary, but what is similar is humanity's ability to find different

1. If you are familiar with The Enneagram I self-identify as an Enneagram 5. The Enneagram is a model of human personality that describes nine interconnected personality types, each with its own motivations, fears, and patterns of thinking and behaving. It is used as a tool for self-understanding, personal growth, and improving relationships by helping individuals recognize their core drives and blind spots.

2. Stanislav Grof, *The Cosmic Game: Explorations of the Frontiers of Human Consciousness.* (New York: State University of New York Press, 1998), 254

technologies to create altered states of consciousness to enable their desire for the spiritual—for awe, wonder, transcendence, and healing.[3]

In recent years, some technologies-of-the-sacred compounds that have been used for thousands of years—psilocybin, ergot, ayahuasca, and peyote—are experiencing a revival and are getting a lot of attention from the scientific community for their healing potential. Additionally, substances that have been developed in a modern lab, like MDMA and LSD, are getting a close examination.

SPIRITUALITY AND PSYCHEDELICS

What interested me most about Michael Pollen's book on psychedelics and what continues to capture my imagination today is the new amalgamation of what most people don't usually put together: spirituality and science. Despite most of these compounds being used as technologies of the sacred for centuries, many researchers were surprised and unsure how to handle this spiritual side effect.

Prof. Dr. Roland Griffiths

In 2006, Dr. Roland Griffiths at Johns Hopkins University began digging deeper into this connection between spirituality and psychedelics. Based on his research, Dr. Griffiths published an article with the clunky title, *Psilocybin Can Occasion Mystical-Type Experiences Having Substantial and Sustained Personal Meaning and*

3. I won't bore you with all the detail surrounding the history of technologies of the sacred in the Christian tradition as well as the modern re-discovery of psychedelics as a spiritual technology. However, if this has piqued your interest, I spell all this out In Appendix B of this book for your reading pleasure.

Spiritual Significance.[4] The study was designed as a double-blind, placebo-controlled study with 30 volunteers who had never used psychedelics. Volunteers were overseen by two therapists and were given a high dose of psilocybin (the active agent in magic mushrooms). They then lay on a couch wearing eyeshades and listened to music.

Not surprisingly, the drug could quickly and reliably create a profoundly spiritual experience for the participants. What was surprising, however, was that most participants ranked their psilocybin experience as one of the most meaningful experiences in their lives. Many compared their experience to the birth of their first child or the death of a parent. Most of them rated their experience as among the top five "most spiritually significant experiences" of their lives. One-third of them described it as their life's *most important* spiritual experience.

Over time, the effects of the experience had only dropped slightly. In a follow-up, fourteen months later, volunteers reported significant improvements in their "personal well-being, life satisfaction and positive behavior change."[5]

By the time he died in 2023, Dr. Roland Griffiths had written over fifty peer-reviewed publications on his psilocybin research. In his TED talk, Dr. Griffith asserted that psilocybin-induced states generated in his laboratory have produced "virtually identical" experiences to those reported by prophets, visionaries, and mystics throughout human history.[6]

Dr. Griffith's colleague, Dr. William Richards, wrote a book in 2015 in which he described the typical psilocybin journey as being beyond limits like time and space. It includes a perception of the oneness and holiness of all things and the epiphany of new insights. Often, the experience is a sense of merging the self with a larger whole. For most people, mere words cannot encompass the deep belief that they have glanced at

---

4. Roland R. Griffiths, William A. Richards, Una McCann, and Robert Jesse, "Psilocybin Can Occasion Mystical-Type Experiences Having Substantial and Sustained Personal Meaning and Spiritual Significance." Psychopharmacology. 187, no. 3 (2006): 268–283.

5. Ibid.

6. Dr. Griffith's TED Talk, *The Science of Psilocybin and Its Use to Relieve Suffering* is fascinating and can be viewed here: https://www.youtube.com/watch?v=81-v8ePXPd4&ab_channel=TEDMED

the ultimate nature of reality. This perception seems "blatantly obvious" as they experience it. For most people, it is not a fearful experience but rather elicits powerful feelings of joy, tranquility, exaltation, and awe.[7]

A surprising result from studies like these is that these overwhelming spiritual experiences happen to people regardless of their religious background or self-identification. One staunch atheist in a psilocybin study described her experience like this:

> "I'm an atheist, I don't believe there is a God," she affirms. "But then I began to feel this love. Just overwhelming, all-encompassing love." There is a long silence. "And the way I describe it is being bathed in God's love," she goes on, her voice cracking, "because I find no other way to describe it. I felt that I belonged, that I was part of everything and had the right to be here. How else do I describe it? Maybe what your mother's love felt like when you were a baby. This feeling of love was suffusing the entire experience."[8]

One researcher distilled his decades of observing the strange paradox of the "spiritual atheists" by noting with a hint of resignation, "Once you've plunged into the ocean, does it really matter whether or not you believe in water?"[9]

7. William A. Richards, *Sacred Knowledge: Psychedelics and Religious Experiences.* (New York: Columbia University Press, 2015).

8. Brian C. Muraresku, *The Immortality Key,* 3.

9. Ibid, p. 8. The symbolism of Christian baptism in these conversations with "spiritual atheists" is not lost on me. In my mind, it demonstrates how far modern Christianity has veered from its roots of being a spiritual movement to an institution that polices beliefs.

BACK TO THE FUTURE

The re-discovery of these technologies of the sacred may be a major path for the future of spirituality. Despite (or maybe because of) religious institutions' attempts at monopolizing spirituality, firsthand mystical experiences are once again being handed back to the masses in the industrialized world and away from religious professionals. Many are tired of those attempting to be tour guides to The Divine, hawking a three-tiered universe. It doesn't matter how great the pictures look in the cookbook; it's no substitute for the actual meal. It doesn't matter how slick the brochure is; it's no substitute for seeing the sunset over the ocean. As the ancient Hebrew poet urged us thousands of years ago, "Open your mouth and taste, open your eyes and see—how good [The Divine] is."[10]

Before the cultural backlash of the 1960s and the Nixon Administration's war on psychedelics, the 20th-century English philosopher and writer Aldous Huxley had a life-altering experience with Peyote. In an opinion piece penned for the *Saturday Evening Post* in 1958, Huxley accurately predicted the mass exodus of people from churches in Europe and America and the growth of the "nones." Huxley also pushed for a link between ancient technologies of the sacred and the future of spirituality. He concludes his article with these words:

> My own belief is that, though they may start by being something of an embarrassment, these new mind changers will tend in the long run to deepen the spiritual life of the communities in which they are available. That famous "revival of religion," about which so many people have been talking for so long, will not come about as the result of evangelistic mass meetings or the television appearances of photogenic clergymen. It will come about as the result of biochemical discoveries that will make it possible for large numbers of men and women to achieve a radical

---

10. Psalm 34:8, *The Message*.

> self-transcendence and a deeper understanding of the nature of things. And this revival of religion will be at the same time a revolution. From being an activity mainly concerned with symbols, religion will be transformed into an activity concerned mainly with experience and in-tuition—an everyday mysticism underlying and giving significance to everyday rationality, everyday tasks and duties, everyday human relationships.[11]

Despite enormous efforts to keep "technologies of the sacred" as relics of the past, they will likely play a prominent role in the future of spirituality.

ONCE AGAIN, THE DEFAULT MODE NETWORK

In 2009, across the pond at the University of Bristol, a researcher named Robin Carhart-Harris began working on a question that many were wondering: from a neuro-biological perspective, what exactly is happening in people's brains when they are on psychedelic drugs? The theory at the time was that brains on psychedelics would show an increase in activity in the emotional centers of the brain.

---

11. Aldous Huxley, *Moksha: Aldous Huxley's Classic Writings on Psychedelics and the Visionary Experience*. Michael Horowitz and Cynthia Palmer, eds. (Rochester, VT: Park Street Press, 1977), 146–56.

Dr. Robin Carhart-Harris

Dr. Carhart-Harris' study was simple: volunteers were injected with psilocybin, placed inside an fMRI scanner, and had their brains imaged to see where the activity was. When the data began to be compiled, Carhart-Harris was surprised. Instead of increased blood flow and activity, they saw *decreased* brain activity. The decrease was especially pronounced in one brain network: The Default Mode Network.

At the time, the Default Mode Network (DMN) concept was a new concept. It was discovered by accident in 2001 by brain researchers. Researchers in fMRI experiments often try to find a "baseline" of brain activity to work from as their volunteers prepare for whatever tests they are about to administer. They noticed that several areas in the brain showed increased activity when people were not explicitly asked to do anything. They were observing the mind in its "default" state: where we go to roam, daydream, obsess, reflect, and worry when we are not asking our brains to do anything in particular.

Upon further research, they found that the DMN lights up when we focus on high-level thinking processes that probably only belong to adult human beings. Processes like self-reflection, moral reasoning, and our ability to imagine what it is like to be someone else are all part of the DMN's function. But most importantly, the DMN creates our sense of self.

THE DMN AND SPIRITUALITY

As you may recall from previous chapters of this book, the positive spiritual outcomes people hope for in meditation mostly come from the ability to quiet the DMN's incessant chatter slowly. By slowing down the DMN, we can focus not on what has happened or what might happen but on the here and now. The more we shut down the DMN to "be" instead of "do," the more we begin to let go of the stories and identities that can cause suffering in ourselves and the world. The aspects of our minds that create a perception of self diminish when the DMN diminishes. When we experience the reduction of that line between ourselves and others, we realize that we are all swimming in the same pool and that there is no "them." It makes us more generous, empathetic, and compassionate towards others because other people's suffering becomes our suffering.

This is a very crude and over-simplified illustration, but I sometimes think the goal in my cognitive processes is to slowly move the "sliders" to dial in the mental space that is most helpful to me:

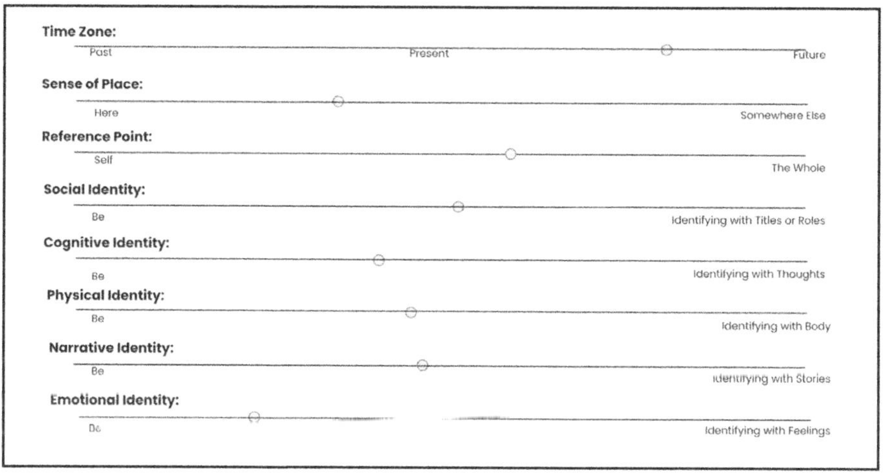

As I read book after book and my internet search history threw up all kinds of red flags from the DEA (Drug Enforcement Administration), I began to wonder: could it be that psychedelics are a quick fix to bypass years and years of meditation? Are psychedelics a Get-God-Quick scheme?

DISCLAIMER:

As you read this chapter, please keep in mind that despite the potentially beneficial effects of altering consciousness with psychedelics, I do not condone any illegal activity. In most of the world, it is unlawful to possess psychedelics such as mescaline, DMT, LSD, and psilocybin.

18

My Pilgrimages to Mexico

Adventures with the Niños Santos

"You only live once; but if you do it right, once is enough."

—Mae West—

(American actress, comedian, screenwriter, and playwright)

"Last summer...I went to Montana with one of my best friends for three days and we went hiking and then we did [LSD]. She's like a born and bred downtown New York girl and staunch atheist. And she had this moment, it was overpoweringly beautiful and also, we were on acid, and she was like, 'How is it that we're alive at the same time as each other and as all this beauty?' She was like, 'I feel so scared and I feel so grateful.' We're both starting to cry and I said, 'Girl, this is why people believe in God.'"

—Jai Tolentino—

(American author, as recounted to Rachel Martin on NPR's *All Things Considered*)

Once upon a time, a former evangelical pastor in his fifth decade of life who had never used an illegal drug in life and had only begun drinking alcohol in his thirties decided he wanted to take a psilocybin trip to experience it for himself. I didn't know much about buying illegal drugs, but I knew that Amazon didn't offer Prime service for them and Googling "drug dealers near me" probably wasn't going to work very well, either.

I also knew that ingesting psychedelics does not automatically generate mystical or spiritual experiences. The outcome of the experience has a lot to do with what researchers call "set and setting." This is why people using the same drug can have very different experiences. Simply put, "set" is the state of being of the person taking the psychedelic: their mental and physical health and their previous experiences with psychedelics (good or bad). Important to "set" is one's expectations and intention: What do you think will happen? What are your fears? What are you hoping to get out of this?

"Setting" is the environment in which you take the psychedelic: inside or outside? Alone or with a guide or with a group? With friends or strangers? etc.[1]

I knew I wanted a "set" and "setting" to maximize my chances for a good experience. After searching online, I figured out that there were a few psilocybin retreat centers in the US that offered good preparation, guidance, and supervision. But as you might imagine, they were very secretive about where they were—and expensive.[2]

Not surprisingly, there is an abundance of all kinds of drugs and retreat centers in The Netherlands. They advertise their mushrooms with pride and boast about how much you can take under their supervision. However, I didn't want to pay their European prices or have a mushroom trip while recovering from jetlag from a nine-hour time zone difference.

In Mexico, psilocybin has been used by indigenous people in religious ceremonies for at least 2,000 years. As a result, consuming psilocybin for spiritual purposes is not illegal there. Since spirituality was my intention, I found a retreat center in Playa del Carmen, Mexico, that looked safe.

1. In Appendix "C" of this book, I outline in more detail these concepts and some other possible considerations one should think about before going on a psychedelic trip.

2. While the legal status of psilocybin in the US is rapidly changing, two years ago when I was looking for a good retreat center, it wasn't legal anywhere. In case you were wondering, the retreat centers I found were in Colorado and California.

After an interview with Juan, the director, I booked the nonstop flight from Phoenix to Cancun.

PLAYA DEL CARMEN

We would be experiencing this five-day retreat together, a group of nine people who were perfect strangers to each other.[3] Most of us were scattered from around the US but a couple were from London and Dubai.

We would have two psilocybin sessions over the five days, giving us lots of time for planning, talking, journaling, and learning. After my first session, I wrote in my journal, *"I'm not sure what I was expecting, but it was different than I expected."*

At 1.5 grams of psilocybin, what was most powerful for me was the removal of my identification with the stories I told about myself and the stories people told about me. I wrote, *"I am adequate. I am enough. My healing has mostly to do with overcoming my constant feelings of inadequacy and shame."*

The "Nine Perfect Strangers" during our last meal together

At one point during the experience, I recall looking at my legs and thinking, "I really like my legs." I know that sounds odd, but I was experiencing an emotion I hadn't felt since being a preschooler or maybe even a toddler. The feeling of my legs being this fantastic extension of me that got me to places and allowed me to play and run. Gone were all the messages about how they should look or how they should function. They just were. And they were beautiful.

---

3. At the time, Hulu had a popular limited-series drama called "Nine Perfect Strangers" about people who go on a 10-day health and wellness retreat only to be tricked into taking psilocybin. We all thought this was a funny coincidence and began to call each other "The Nine Perfect Strangers."

Meditation was easy and the deepest I had ever experienced up to that point. My Default Mode Network (DMN) was mostly silent, and I left the session with a deep sense of gratitude and joy. There was also a strong connection with the other people in the group. Part of it was from the mushrooms, of course, but part of it was the vulnerability that many people put forward as they wrestled with past trauma and past hurts. For many of us, the experience was intense yet beautiful.

Receiving a blessing from the Mayan shaman

For our second session, we traveled deep into the jungle in Quintero Roo. We met up with a Mayan shaman who gave us psilocybin and took us through a sweat lodge ceremony that included letting go of some of our past trauma. After the sweat lodge, the religious ceremony included a dose of Ayahuasca in the form of Tepezcohuite smoke.

I took 2.25 grams of psilocybin during this experience. Some of my experiences during this session included some profound breakthroughs that are too personal to write about. Some experiences were so "woo woo" that I hesitate to talk about them because they are outside most of our ordinary human experiences. Frankly, I don't want you to think that I am crazy.

There is a saying among the indigenous healers, "The mushrooms won't necessarily give you what you want, but they will give you what you need." I found this to be profoundly true.

What became as clear to me as if I had been slapped in the face was the scope and direction of my life. I wrote in my journal:

> *"The overall feeling is that it all belongs. Every emotion, every experience, everything that has brought me to this point is soaked in grace and love from the Divine. The experience of the Divine is an experience of this world*

– including each other. There is no need to look 'outward' or to some 'other' place – it is right here, right now. I can't believe that I didn't see it before."

The genesis of this book came while I was in that Mexican jungle. For the first time in a long time, the path forward for my life was obvious.

Being a typical guy, I'm often emotionally constipated. I haven't had a good history of dealing directly with my emotions. The mushrooms didn't seem to care about that. I lay on the jungle floor for about two hours in the yoga "child's pose" and sobbed. A few months before this experience, my partner Christina had died of gallbladder cancer. I thought I had grieved in a pretty healthy way, but all that loss, pain, and grief came to the surface and poured out of me.

PUERTO VALLARTA

Eighteen months later, I made a second pilgrimage to Mexico for another psilocybin session. This time, I traveled to Puerto Vallarta. I met up with an American woman named Morgan, who had trained with the indigenous Mexicans in the ways of what they call the *Nino Santos* ("Children Saints") or the *Buena Medicina* ("The Good Medicine"). I wanted this experience to be more internal and was hoping to experience a complete dissolution of self, so this time, I would almost double the dose. I would also be alone in an Airbnb I had rented next to the Pacific Ocean, except for Morgan monitoring to ensure I didn't do anything dangerous or go anywhere. I had a blindfold over my eyes and headphones playing a setlist of music Morgan had prepared.

Citing the traditional ritual, Morgan handed me a cup of tea laced with 5 grams of The Good Medicine and said, "I give this to you with love." I recited the ancient ritual back by saying, "I receive this with love."

On the flight home, I wrote in my journal, *"I am having a hard time discussing the experience with people who have not been there. I want to say, 'How much do you want to know?' Or 'Are you sure you want to hear about it?'"*

Let me be clear that this was undoubtedly the most powerful experience of my life. I can confirm that consciousness survives the disappearance of the self. Our sense of self is not as indispensable as it likes to think. Far from being a terrifying experience, it felt familiar and peaceful. I understood why people in the psilocybin studies who had death anxiety no longer felt that anxiety. "I" am already part of all that is. Losing "myself" is not losing anything.

I was conscious but conscious apart from "me" or all the stories, identities, and baggage I associated with my identity. What I read in a Michel Pollan book made complete sense to me:

> The usual antonym for the word "spiritual" is "material." That at least is what I believed when I began this inquiry—that the whole issue with spirituality turned on a question of metaphysics. Now I'm inclined to think a much better and certainly more useful antonym for "spiritual" might be "egotistical." Self and Spirit define the opposite ends of a spectrum, but that spectrum needn't reach clear to the heavens to have meaning for us. It can stay right here on earth. When the ego dissolves, so does a bounded conception not only of our self but of our self-interest. What emerges in its place is invariably a broader, more openhearted and altruistic—that is, more spiritual—idea of what matters in life. One in which a new sense of connection, or love, however defined, seems to figure prominently.[4]

Language was difficult during this stage of my trip because my brain was "thinking" in symbols and images, not in words or syntax. At one point, I removed my blindfold and, after a moment of trying to grasp the words, asked Morgan, "How long has it been?"

"About two hours," she replied, "Does it seem longer?"

I laughed and laughed because it seemed like such an absurd question, given what I was experiencing. "What is time but a social construct?" I asked Morgan. She laughed knowingly.

---

4. Michael Pollan, *How to Change Your Mind: What the New Science of Psychedelics Teaches Us About Consciousness, Dying, Addiction, Depression, and Transcendence.* (New York: Penguin Press, 2018), 316–317.

I heard people speak of mushrooms in a way that anthropomorphized them: "The mushrooms spoke to me and told me…" they would say. I thought it was a quaint metaphor. But then the *Nino Santos* spoke to me. It wasn't a metaphor. They had incredible wisdom and insight—about the people closest to me, my divorce, Christina, power, fear, and control and how it controls people. I wrote in my journal the next day:

> *Isn't it a little odd that a rabbi from the Ancient Near East would make it his life's work to free humanity from human systems and structures of oppression to set them free. And the response of his followers was to say, "Let's start a new institution based on new systems and structures."*

When the psilocybin started to wear off, Morgan hung around for about an hour, and we processed some of what I had experienced. When it was clear that I wasn't hallucinating any longer and that I was safe, Morgan headed home.

I slowly made my way to the restaurant below where I was staying. I hadn't eaten anything since breakfast, and for the first time, I was starting to think about food and feel my blood sugar dropping. I took my journal with me with the intention of writing down what I had experienced. However, I discovered quickly that when the DMN is not working very well, it is difficult to reflect on one's experiences or to think about what it might mean going forward.

So, instead, I basked in the moment. I ordered fresh seafood and watched the sunset over the Pacific Ocean. I was completely present in the moment, slowly and quietly absorbing the overwhelming beauty of it all: the sound of the ocean, the sight of the sunset, the smell and taste of the magnificent food. At one point, I had to remind myself, "Don't cry so much that you draw attention to yourself!"

NOW WHAT?

Neurologically speaking, a lot was happening in my brain during these experiences.[5] Psilocybin, the active compound in magic mushrooms, allows for increased brain neuroplasticity. In other words, it often helps people begin new thought patterns, let go of deeply embedded thought processes, and make new neurological connections. It's not hard to imagine how this can be incredibly freeing and healing for those who use it. The effects of these experiences have been long-term. They changed how I see the world and still impact me today.

My psychological experiences with mushrooms were not like the dreams I have while I am sleeping. Instead, they were like what psychological researchers Daniel X. Freedman and Ido Hartogosohn call "portentousness." They were much less an intellectual epiphany and much more a profound "more real than real" experience with a profoundly deep weight of truth attached to it.

Spiritual practices like a magic mushroom ceremony are not for the faint of heart. Nor are they, like I initially thought, a "get-god-quick" scheme. Beyond the travel time and expense, the time and preparation to create the appropriate "set and setting" for a positive experience was daunting. It probably took me five decades of spiritual practice to prepare for the psilocybin experience. Traveling home from Puerto Vallarta, it took me a solid week to emotionally recover from the intensity of the experience. I've concluded that for me, high-dose magic mushroom ceremonies are so intense that an annual pilgrimage was about the most I can handle.

The premise of this book is that spirituality is not something we "arrive" at. There is no moment in which we "graduate" from growing spirituality. Spirituality is a continual mindset of shedding unhealthy and

---

5. If you are like me and the neuroscience of psychedelics fascinates you, I would recommend to you chapter 5 of Michael Pollan's book, *How to Change Your Mind: What the New Science of Psychedelics Teaches Us About Consciousness, Dying, Addiction, Depression, and Transcendence.*

un-useful ideas and habits, clarifying what we really want, removing the barriers holding us back, and developing new, intentional habits. For me, an annual pilgrimage to Mexico might be on the menu, but I recognize other everyday practices as critical for my journey. However, everyday practices are more challenging to maintain than annual ones.

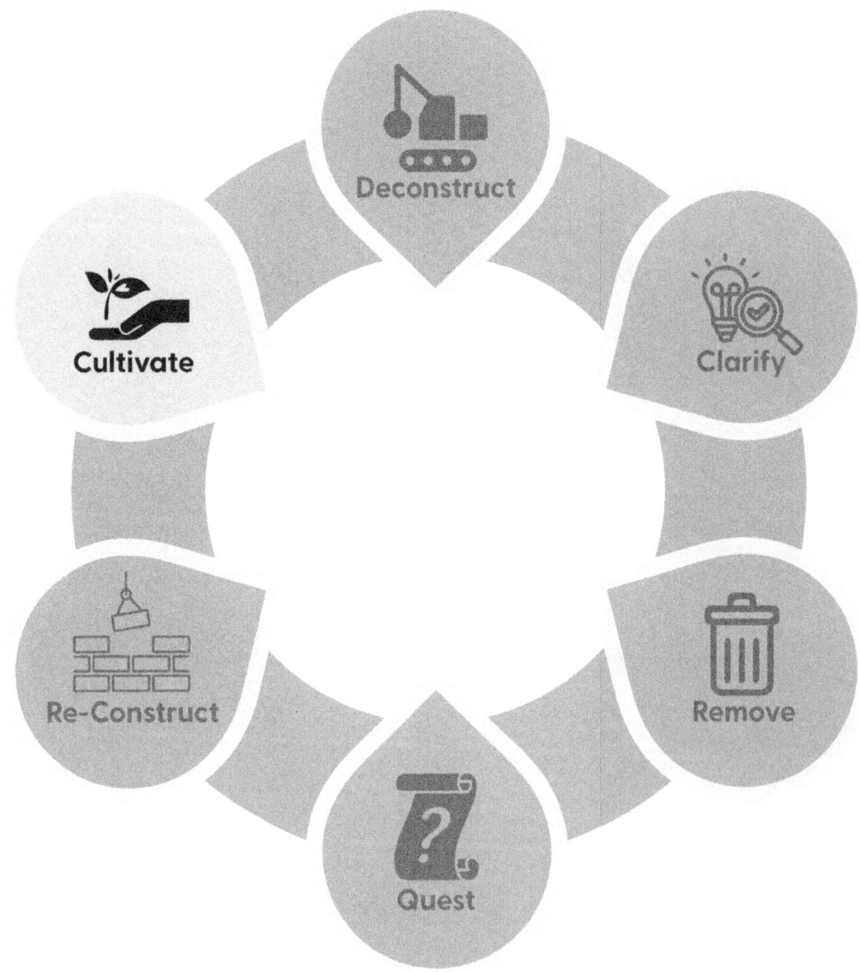
Deconstruct
Clarify
Remove
Quest
Re-Construct
Cultivate

CULTIVATE

Sustaining Habits for a Life of Spirituality.

Deconstruction is not a one-time event but a lifetime of shedding unhealthy and un-useful ideas and habits. Unlike our get-it-quick society, spiritual growth is a slow and deliberate process. Even though they can be difficult, others can be crucial to this process.

19

The Law of The Farm

There is No Such Thing as Microwave Spirituality

Disciple: "Is there anything that I can do
to make myself enlightened?"
Zen Master: "As little as you can do to
make the sun rise in the morning."
Disciple: "Then of what use are the spiritual
exercises you prescribe?"
Zen Master: "To make sure you are not
asleep when the sun begins to rise."

—Anthony de Mello—
(Indian Jesuit priest and psychotherapist)

"The only thing that endures over time is the 'Law of the Farm.'
You must prepare the ground, plant the seed, cultivate,
and water if you expect to reap the harvest."

—Stephen Covey—
(Author and management consultant, from *The Seven Habits of Highly Effective People.*)

I often think about how different the world we live in today is from what most of human history has experienced. Since the agricultural revolution, humanity has lived chiefly on farms, grown most of their food, and lived in agricultural cycles: planting, growing, and harvesting.

But in recent history, most human beings' perception of the way the world works radically shifted. We developed machines and technology that quickly and efficiently did precisely what we asked them to do. The results of factory work were immediately recognizable. We could measure productivity and faster was better. We now live in an information-based world that worships speed. We get impatient when problems aren't solved quickly, like a 30-minute sitcom.

Not all of this "progress" is bad. I am an Amazon Prime member and love my benefits. But some things just can't be accomplished quickly. I learned the hard way in college that the idea that you can cram and learn a semester's worth of material in one night is a myth. That's not how the human mind works. Some things are organic: they are not machines that can do things quickly. Some things must develop naturally over time. You can't raise a child quickly. You can't rush a tree to grow quickly. You can't lose 20 pounds in a week to prepare for swimsuit season. You can't cram for your retirement by only saving the last year you work.

Humans who live on farms seem to understand this organic way of thinking more intuitively than those who live in an information or industrial world. On the farm, the rhythm of life is slow and cannot be forced or rushed. It's going to take what it's going to take. You can't cram seeds in a few weeks before harvest and expect a result. There is no quick fix, no hack, no secret formula.

Likewise, your soul is not a machine; it is organic. I'm sorry to say that spiritual change and spiritual growth are as slow and gradual as a plant growing. Trying to force organic things to grow quickly usually creates more problems than it solves. You can quickly produce physical growth in your child through anabolic steroids, but it will be very, very unhealthy growth. Likewise, developmental psychologists worry about children who show drastic, non-age-appropriate behavior; it usually means that they are growing up too quickly.

As a spiritual leader, I have seen people get impatient and try to find some magic prayer, manifestation, or spiritual experience that will quickly change their lives and fix all their problems. Sometimes, they may have some emotional experience that they think has changed everything. But usually, a year or two later, they are back where they started looking for another quick fix or emotional spiritual experience. The truth is, they opted for *guaranteed* failure: rapid growth through steroids. By trying to take the short route, we sometimes take longer than we would have had we taken the long route in the first place.[1]

The law of the farm reminds us: it's going to take what it is going to take. It is sometimes easier to recognize this in other areas of our lives: A get-rich-quick scheme usually gets us in financial trouble. A fad diet usually doesn't last, and we put the weight back on. But real growth takes time, whether it is a plant or our souls.

These may seem like obvious observations, but sometimes, we don't realize how industrial-age or information-age thinking has influenced our view of spirituality. Here are a couple of examples of how to think about spirituality as organic rather than mechanical.

ORGANISMS ARE CYCLICAL, NOT LINEAR

If you have gone through the painful process of deconstruction, I have unfortunate news for you: your deconstruction is not over. There is no "end" to growth for living things in an organic world; it is a constant process of pruning and renewal. This is why the cycle I described in the Introduction of this book is a cycle and not a linear line. Like the seasons of the year, there are constantly evolving seasons: for new life, for

1. I find it interesting that in the New Testament's telling of the life of Jesus, the "temptations" that Jesus faces in the wilderness in Luke 4 are, at their essence, temptations of impatience: instant relief from his hunger, instant glory, and instant safety. The story of Jesus' temptations in the wilderness is a cautionary tale about the temptations of spirituality.

thriving, for pruning, for loss, and for rebirth again. And again. And again.

It was the Protestants (the "protesters") in the Christian tradition who, during the Reformation, declared that they would self-describe themselves as *ecclesia reformata, semper reformanda* or "reformed and always reforming."[2] Meaning, the process of deconstructing, clarifying, reconstructing, and cultivating should always be an ongoing cycle and never-ending process of growth.[3]

These differences in mindsets between cyclical and linear, or static and dynamic may seem like subtle differences, but these different mindsets create enormously different outcomes for our spiritual journey. At Stanford University, Carol Dweck has extensively researched these mindsets and how they impact people's experiences with limitations, obstacles, failure, and change. Drawing on insights from the educational world, Dwek argues that people exist on a continuum of mindsets between a fixed mindset or a growth mindset.[4]

If a person has a fixed or linear mindset, their goal is to impress others and have them think, "Wow! He's got 'It.' He's made a lot of progress." Therefore, they must work on their image and post on social media to make them appear intelligent, beautiful, and "together."

---

2. Cf. Jaroslav Pelikan, *Reformation of Church and Dogma (1300-1700). Vol. 4 of The Christian Tradition: A History of the Development of Doctrine.* (Chicago: University of Chicago Press, 1984).

3. The irony is not lost on me that the most rigid and unwavering of today's American Christians are the Neo-Reformed types. While they hold the literal beliefs of the Protestant reformers, they have long departed from the spirit, methodology, and courage of the ones whose names they identify with.

4. Carol S. Dweck, Ph.D., *Mindset: The New Psychology of Success.* (New York: Random House, 2006) is a great introduction to Dr. Dweck's research. Her compelling TED talk on growth has almost 6 million views: https://www.youtube.com/watch?v=_X0mgOOSpLU&t=560s&ab_channel=TED

If a person has a fixed or linear mindset, they avoid challenges, give up easily when they face obstacles, ignore useful feedback, and are threatened by the success of others. People with that mindset will try to arrange their lives so that they always have success and never fail. They never want to make a mistake because if they do, people might think they don't have "it" or they haven't progressed very far.

Dr. Carol Dweck

Dweck says most people live with this fixed or linear mindset. It creates fear and constant pressure to prove ourselves. On the other hand, Dweck says that some have a growth mindset or a cyclical view of life. What matters in this mindset is not where you are but developing a growth process. What matters is not your raw ability but constant improvement. The goal is not to look more intelligent, more spiritual, or more competent than others. The goal is to grow beyond where you are today. Therefore, failure is indispensable and something to be learned from.You can persist in the face of setbacks, because setbacks are part of the growth cycle.

Dweck gives an example from her educational world: Researchers gave 10-year-olds increasingly difficult math problems to see how they would handle failure. Most of the kids would hit a point of failure, get discouraged and quit. However, some responded with a growth or cyclical mindset. One kid rubbed his hands together, smacked his lips, and said, "I love a challenge!" Another kid said, "I was hoping this would be informative." The kids wisely didn't think that having obstacles was failing; they assumed they were learning and growing.

Organisms like your soul are cyclical and not linear. This is why continual growth is a mindset that we need to nurture in our modern world.

TRUST THE PROCESS

In our scientific era, we are often under the illusion that understanding the mechanics of something means we can control it. The scientific mind does not like a mystery. But organisms are a mystery in that we can't predict their outcomes with scientific certainty. Farmers create a healthy environment and hope for the best. We can control the process of creating an environment, but ultimately, we cannot control the outcomes.

If you are a parent, you undoubtedly quickly realize that children are not machines. As a result, good parenting is more like being a good farmer than a good machine operator. Despite the best technologies and methodologies, sometimes good parents have kids that go off the rails. (And sometimes terrible parents have great kids!) Parents can't control the outcomes, but we can do our best to create the best environments that put the odds in our favor.

Organic growth is not something that we can grit our teeth, and it will happen. When we are depressed, it is not helpful to try and be un-depressed. It does help, however, to cultivate the soil of your life with things that make people less depressed: good diet, exercise, healthy relationships, maybe even a puppy, and if necessary, even some chemical interventions like anti-depressants.

In the competitive world of coaching, there has been a mindset change in recent years with the advent of the book *The Inner Game of Tennis* by W. Timothy Gallwey.[5] Central to his teachings, Gallwey made an important distinction between focusing on the process versus focusing on the outcome. He argued that becoming too fixated on the outcome–winning, scoring, etc.—is counterproductive. When the mind is

5. W. Timothy Gallwey, *The Inner Game of Tennis.* (New York: Random House, 1974).

preoccupied with a desired end result, it creates anxiety and tension that impedes performance. Instead, Gallwey suggests shifting one's attention to the process—the present actions and movements required to execute the skill successfully. Focusing on the process calms the mind and allows the body's natural abilities to express themselves freely.

Although spirituality is not a competitive sport, the lessons are nonetheless transferable. Judging yourself during the spiritual process based on whether you achieved some outcome creates self-criticism and fear of failure. I think of my Pentecostal friends who grew up concerned about whether they "got the gift of the Spirit" or the people in my tradition who wrung their hands, worried if they had achieved "entire sanctification."

As we work our way through different cycles of spirituality, the liminal space between where we were and what is next often feels fraught with anxiety. Where will I end up? What does this mean? But Gallwey reminds us that focusing on the process—the specific actions and techniques needed in the present moment—allows us to access our greatest skills and creates a sense of lightness, freedom, and joy.

Trust the process. Progress often happens when we least expect to see it. Progress is a side effect of the process and usually comes in spurts, not in a straight line. Any farmer who has followed the process of seeds from planting to harvest will tell you that often, it is the hidden, unseen, and unrecognized things that are the most significant. The good stuff usually lies below the surface—if we have the patience to allow it to grow.

20

Tribes and Tribalism

Can't Live with Them, Can't Live Without Them

"Being deeply loved by someone gives
you strength, while loving someone gives
you courage."

—Lao Tzu—
(Ancient Chinese philosopher)

"The only way out is through
And the only good way through is together."

—Robert Frost—
(American poet)

The 2009 romantic comedy "500 Days of Summer" encapsulated the rollercoaster of human relationships. It's a tale of unrequited love, where the protagonist, Tom, is head over heels for Summer, who is not as invested in the relationship. The film spans 500 days, oscillating between their blissful and turbulent moments.

As the film begins, Tom and Summer have just begun dating, and he is full of the joy of new relationship energy. He tells his friend: "I love her smile. I love her hair. I love her knees. I love this heart-shaped birthmark she has on her neck. I love the way she sometimes licks her lips before she

Joseph Gordon-Levitt and Zooey Deschanel as Tom and Summer.

talks. I love the sound of her laugh. I love the way she looks when she is sleeping."[1]

But later in the film, Tom and Summer are not doing well. He tells his friend: "I hate her crooked teeth. I hate her 1960s haircut. I hate her knobby knees. I hate her cockroach-shaped splotch on her neck. I hate the way she smacks her lips before she talks. I hate the way she sounds when she laughs."

It's not just romantic relationships; this film encapsulates humanity's love/hate relationship with other people. When it is good, it's great; but when it's bad, it's awful. For millennia, long before our modern world, humans lived as hunter/gatherers. As a species, we survived *and* thrived when we cooperated. This is why relationships, acceptance, belonging, and community are deeply ingrained in the human psyche. For most of human history, we literally could not live without each other. Going against the group often meant putting oneself at great risk or even death.

---

1. Marc Webb (Director). 2009. *(500) Days of Summer*. Performances by Joseph Gordon-Levitt and Zooey Deschanel. Fox Searchlight Pictures.

These two clips can viewed in their entirety at: https://www.youtube.com/watch?v=-d_Ieyza4oY&ab_channel=%D8%AA%D8%AD%D9%81%D9%81%D9%86%D9%8A%D9%87

RE-THINKING MASLOW

In 1943, Abraham Maslow published his now-famous paper arguing that humans have a hierarchy of needs. The "lower," physiological needs (food, sleep, safety, security), must be satisfied before the "higher" needs, like love, intimacy, and friendship, can be satisfied.[2] The idea sounds good on paper, but I've watched many people whose hearts were broken—by a romantic partner, by grief over the loss of another person, or by an interpersonal conflict—who couldn't eat or sleep. People often trade food and sleep for the more basic need of human connection.

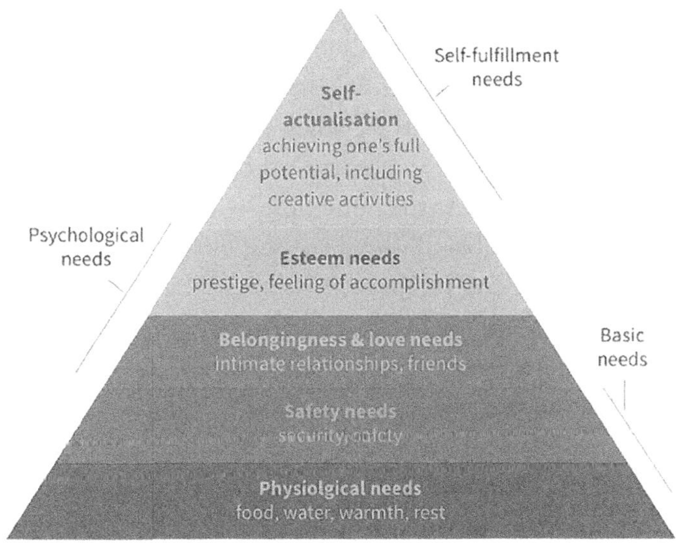

Illustration of Maslow's Hierarchy of Needs

In my current job, we wrestle with the challenge of 40,000 unhoused people in Maricopa County. One surprising aspect among the chronically unhoused that we have discovered is that they don't always want to be

2. Abraham Maslow, (1943). "A Theory of Human Motivation." Psychological Review. 50(4), 370–396.

housed. The reason is that their only sense of community and connection is among their friends on the streets. To move into a home means leaving their only support system and sense of belonging. When forced to choose, people often trade safety, security, and shelter for the more basic need of human connection.[3]

Maslow got the hierarchy of needs wrong. We have an irrational need for love and acceptance from other humans. Anyone who has witnessed a 13-year-old in love (or, for that matter, a 70-year-old in love) knows that people do irrational and foolish things for love. But, as Tom discovered with Summer in "500 Days of Summer," love can leave us in a vulnerable position. Whether in a romantic context or some other situation, when we trust someone else with our hearts, they can shatter it with a single action.

I don't know the specifics of your story, but I am guessing that the darkest moments of your life were when someone betrayed you. If you love someone, there comes a moment when they let you down—and when you let them down. At the same time, when you look back on your life, you may not remember all the successes, but you will always remember when you experienced acceptance, belonging, and intimacy.

This is true not only of interpersonal relationships but also of how we relate to groups of people. As anyone who has rebelled against their tribe's norms can tell you, we may not literally die, like our ancestor hunter-gatherers, but separation from the tribe feels like a kind of death. We may think of "peer pressure" as a middle school struggle, but with the possible exception of sociopaths, every human alive has a deeply ingrained aversion to going against the crowd.

Social scientists have documented this powerful tendency for individuals to conform to group norms and pressures, even when it means going against their beliefs or better judgment. A small sampling would include:

3. While outside the scope of this book, in the spirit of the "Five Whys" of chapter 4, if a person were to ask enough "whys," one of the root causes of the homeless issue (among many factors) is lack of community and human connection.

- **Solomon Asch's Conformity Experiments.** Asch had participants judge which line matched the length of a reference line. When surrounded by peers who intentionally gave the wrong answer, a high percentage of participants conformed to the obviously incorrect majority view.[4]
- **Irving Janis' Groupthink Studies**. Janis examined how groups can suppress disagreement and critical thinking. This strong pressure to conform to the group leads to catastrophic decision-making.[5]
- **Donelson Forsyth's Research on Group Norms**. Forsyth showed that people often miscalculate the consequences of group cohesion. They expect their unwillingness to conform will be punished more severely than it would be.[6]

SPIRITUALITY AND GROUPS OF PEOPLE

So, what does this have to do with spirituality? Our spiritual beliefs and experiences do not happen in a vacuum. We are tied together with the people closest to us. If you have gone through a religious deconstruction, you know that, almost always, the most difficult part is dealing with your tribe and their expectations.

Muslim gathering near Jama Masjid, Delhi, India

It is difficult to talk about spirituality without discussing religious institutions and communities. At their best, religious

4. S.E. Asch, "Effects of Group Pressure Upon the Modification and Distortion of Judgments." in H. Guetzkow (Ed.), *Groups, Leadership, and Men.* (New York: Carnegie Press, 1951), 177–190.

5. I.L. Janis, *Victims of Groupthink: A Psychological Study of Foreign-Policy Decisions and Fiascoes.* (Boston: Houghton Mifflin, 1972).

6. D. R. Forsyth, "Group Norms." in M. S. Clark (Ed.), *Review of Personality and Social Psychology, Vol. 12.* (Thousand Oaks, CA: SAGE Publications, 1990), 149–192.

communities are formed to give us a narrative that provides meaning to our lives and experiences and points us to something beyond ourselves. At their worst, religious communities are tools that an empire or institution uses to manipulate people into conformity and to keep the peace by oppressing marginalized people—or to convince the oppressed to accept the status quo with the promise of a better life in the afterworld. In short, finding other people to help you on your spiritual journey can be either incredibly helpful or extremely destructive, depending on the community.

Historically speaking, larger institutions, be they religious or secular, are relatively recent inventions. It wasn't until the agricultural revolution 10,000 years ago that humans congregated in groups larger than 50 people.[7] There is a reason why 80 percent of Christian religious communities in the US are less than 50 people: we have evolved to relate to no more than that number of people.

The advent of the Agricultural Revolution brought about the blessing and curse of larger institutions. For the first time in history, we could feed more people, but the unintended side effects included the advent of deep class divisions. This is part of why anthropologist Jared Diamond called the agricultural revolution "a catastrophe from which we have never recovered" and "the worst mistake in the history of the human race."[8] Food no

Bayaka people in the Dzanga Sangha Ndoki reserve - Central African Republic

7. The average hunter-gatherer band consisted of 25–30 individuals, though bands could range from as few as 10 to as many as 50 members. This number is consistent with ethnographic studies of modern hunter-gatherer societies and archaeological evidence from prehistoric hunter-gatherer sites and camps.

8. Jared Diamond, "The Worst Mistake in the History of the Human Race." Discover Magazine. April 30, 1999. https://www.discovermagazine.com/planet-earth/the-worst-mistake-in-the-history-of-the-human-race, accessed December 17, 2021.

longer functioned as a means of survival but as a pathway to wealth. He wrote:

> Hunter-gatherers have little or no stored food, and no concentrated food sources, like an orchard or a herd of cows: they live off the wild plants and animals they obtain each day. Therefore, there can be no kings, no class of social parasites who grow fat on food seized from others. Only in a farming population could a healthy, non-producing elite set itself above the disease-ridden masses.[9]

By 3,000 BCE, technology and communication had evolved enough to allow humans to invent the nation-state, and institutions eventually became empires. Of course, in the last 5,000 years, institutions and empires have grown. The way human beings gather now is entirely unrecognizable to our ancestors.

This is important because as groups increase in size, their social dynamics significantly change—how individuals relate to the group, what motivates the group, what holds the group together, how the group is led, and how the group views outsiders. Social psychologists like Donelson R. Forsyth, Professor Emeritus at the University of Richmond, have researched and written extensively on group dynamics and how they vary with a group's size.[10] As time has passed and institutions have grown increasingly larger, people have (understandably) become more suspicious and cynical of them. To oversimply Dr. Forsyth and other social psychologists, here is a broad generalization of how groups change as they get larger:

9. Ibid.

10. Cf. Donelson R. Forsyth, *Group Dynamics. 7th ed.* (Boston: Cengage Learning, 2019).

	COHORT	BAND OR TRIBE	INSTITUTION	EMPIRE
SIZE	8 to 12 People	25 to 50 People	500+ People	Nations
GLUE THAT HOLDS THE GROUP TOGETHER	Interpersonal Relationships	Boundary markers/virtue signaling	Conformity/ Submission	Force/ Violence
RESPONSIBILITY TO OTHERS	Personally accountable	"Someone should do something."	"Not my problem."	Answers to nobody.
VIEW OF OUTSIDERS	Outsiders are seen as individuals.	Outsiders are suspect.	Outsiders are threats.	Outsiders are obstacles to dominate.
ORGANIZATIONAL MOTIVATION	Relational Harmony	Conformity/ Control	Survival of the Institution	Prosperity/ Colonization
VIEW OF THE INDIVIDUAL	Individuality is celebrated	Individuality is minimized	Individual is anonymous	Individual is expendable
LEADERSHIP STYLE	Informal leadership by influence	Formal leadership by influence	Formal leadership by position	Formal leadership by force or coercion

Once you begin to understand what motivates a group and how they view individuals, it is not hard to predict how those who do not conform might be treated as a group grows larger. If you have ever worked for a large corporation or attended a large church, you may know that, contrary to what is said, large institutions are not motivated by truth, the common good, or justice, but rather by conformity, control, and survival of the institution. Space in this book does not allow me to give the hundreds of examples I have witnessed.[11]

We may not be able to avoid institutions (and maybe even empires) altogether, but it is helpful to have realistic expectations when dealing with them. Sometimes, people complain that corporations are greedy and will do anything to increase their bottom line. While I am sympathetic to the problem, I wonder, *What did you expect? Institutions exist to*

11. My favorite illustration of this is from the very quirky comedian Emo Phillips and his "Die, Heretic!" routine: https://www.youtube.com/watch?v=l3fAcxcxoZ8&ab_channel=MUskratty

self-perpetuate and survive. They don't care about anything else. Likewise, some are surprised when large religious institutions cover up abuse and scandals to avoid a public-relations scandal. But as groups like the Roman Catholic Church and the Southern Baptist Denomination have shown us in recent years, if forced to choose, a large institution will always choose survival over any values or ideals it claims to uphold, sacrificing individuals that get in the way.[12]

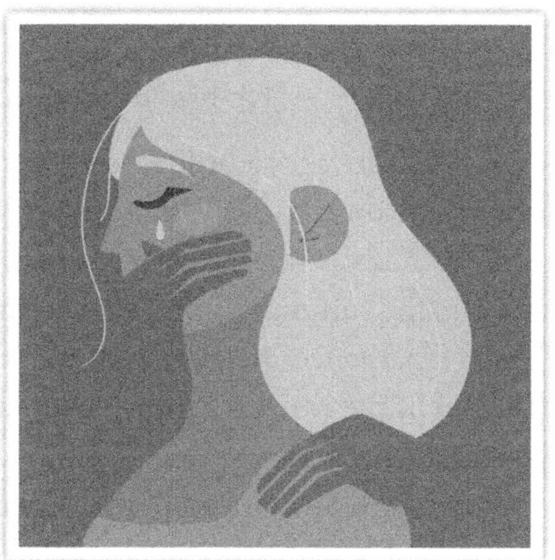

Many years ago, my father gave me advice that helped me survive 30 years of life inside religious institutions. He said, "Institutions are incapable of loving you. You will quickly become bitter if you think they will reciprocate your love." As a result, I always assumed that religious institutions served people, not vice versa.

My point in all this discussion is to remind you of this as you cultivate your spiritual life:

- It's impossible to avoid interacting with people. When it is good, it's great, but when it's bad, it's awful.
- It's often helpful to have groups of people help you on your spiritual journey through insight, teaching, friendship, support, etc.
- Set realistic expectations for any group or organization, religious or otherwise. In almost every measurable way, the larger the group, the worse it is for individuals who do not conform.[13]

---

12. There is a great example of how the institution sacrifices the individual in the Christian Scriptures. The Sanhedrin was discussing Jesus' fate, and John's Gospel records, "Then one of them, named Caiaphas, who was high priest that year, spoke up, 'You know nothing at all! You do not realize that it is better for you that one man die for the people than that the whole nation perish'" (John 11:49–50).

13. One of my editors pointed out to me the humorous irony that my first book's message was, "You need *more* people in your life," whereas this book argues, "You need *fewer* people in your life."

Because I spent 30 years getting a paycheck from Christian institutions, in the last part of this chapter, I want to address this unique moment in history and how these group dynamics play into Christian institutions. If this is not your world (or if you don't care), please feel free to go on to the next chapter. But if you are still embroiled in Christian institutions, since I was in them for decades and now can see them as an outsider, I believe I have a unique vantage point into their future.

THE FOURTH GREAT EMERGENCE

A few decades ago, a brilliant woman named Phyllis Tickle began to write and speak on a concept she called "The Great Emergence."[14] Her book's central thesis is that every 500 years, Christianity cleans out its attic and has a giant rummage sale. It goes through a major transitional period or "great emergence" that dramatically shifts Christianity in significant ways. The fall of the Roman Empire around 500 AD, the Great Schism between the Eastern Orthodox and Western Catholic churches in 1054, and the Protestant Reformation in 1517 were the first three "great emergences." She argues that Christianity is currently in the throes of another great transition driven by forces like globalism, the rise of the internet/social media, and postmodern philosophical shifts.

Phyllis Tickle

Phyllis was very influential on many young Christian leaders, including myself, who were looking for fresh expressions of institutional Christianity or "the next new thing." Many of us believed that we were on the tip of

14. Phyllis Tickle, *The Great Emergence: How Christianity Is Changing and Why* (Grand Rapids, MI: Baker Books, 2012).

the spear of a religious shift, not unlike the Reformation, in which all the rules and expectations would change. Like others, I started new churches and experimented with new liturgies, theologies, and attitudes.[15] While the "emergent" church movement quickly gained traction, it just as quickly faded into oblivion.

Hindsight being 20/20, I think the Christian church is indeed going through a fourth great emergence."However, the emergence is not necessarily theological, liturgical, or cultural, but structural. We assumed that the institutional structures we inherited were amoral and neutral. However, large religious institutions (like all large institutions) have always been centered around conformity and survival. Creating new institutions with new theologies, liturgies, and values was tantamount to rearranging the deck chairs on the Titanic. We were still on a behemoth institution that was sinking.

In my postdoctoral studies in church planting, I was shocked to discover that the Christian movement is growing fastest in environments with the least institutional control. For example, in 1949, when the Communist Party took control of China, they expelled all the Western missionaries and made Christianity illegal. Most Western religious leaders assumed that this would be the end of Christianity in China with its one million adherents. However, necessity was the mother of invention, and expressions of Christianity went underground, forcing them to meet in small cohorts of 8-20 people. These simple churches easily multiplied and did not carry the institutional baggage of conformity and submission.

As a result, while precise numbers are difficult to pin down given challenges with data collection in China, estimates suggest there are

15. An excellent summary of this short season in American Christianity that was so formative in my life is the *Emerged Podcast*: https://homebrewedchristianity.lpages.co/emerged-an-oral-history-of-the-emerging-church-movement/

now between 60-80 million Protestants and 10-12 million Catholics in China. In other words, if current growth rates continue, China could soon have the world's largest Christian population.

While this is a broad oversimplification of a convergence of many forces, as Phillip Jenkins pointed out in his book *The Next Christendom*, Christianity's center is shifting to the global East and South and moving away from large institutions to small grassroots networks.[16] There is a saying about Christian institutions, "When Christianity is working, what we care about is our neighbors. When Christianity is not working, what we care about is Christianity." Small cohorts of faith are not concerned with larger institutional concerns, like: What is our public image? What is our legal exposure? How will we fund the professional's retirement accounts? What are the financial policies and procedures for handling our investment accounts?

What I am trying to say to my friends who still identify as Christian (or even as "followers of Jesus") is this: if you want renewal or revival (or whatever your tradition calls it), don't look for it to come from or be part of a religious denomination or institution. Because of how we evolved, humans thrive in small cohorts and are chewed up and spit out in large institutions. The fourth emergence of Christianity will most likely be a continuation of the abandonment of institutions and a focus on smaller cohorts. De-centralization, diversity, accountability, and openness will be fertile soil to allow spirituality to thrive.

---

16. Philip Jenkins, *The Next Christendom: The Coming of Global Christianity*. (New York: Oxford University Press, 2002).

21

The Secret of The Secret

What are You Paying Attention to?

"Dwell on the beauty of life. Watch the stars and see yourself running with them."

–Marcus Aurelius–
(Ancient Stoic philosopher, from *Meditations*)

"This place could be beautiful, right? You could make this place beautiful."

–Maggie Smith–
(American poet)

In 2006, the author Rhonda Byrne released *The Secret*, which quickly became a cultural phenomenon and a worldwide bestseller. Celebrities like Oprah Winfrey praised it, and it gained an enthusiastic following, especially in the self-help and New Age communities.[1]

The book's central idea is the "law of attraction"—that positive thoughts can bring positive experiences into a person's life, while negative thoughts can lead to negative outcomes. The book argues that people can manifest their wants and desires by focusing their thoughts and feelings on positive visualizations of desired outcomes. It claims this law of

1. Rhonda Byrne, *The Secret* (New York: Atria Books, 2006).

attraction is a powerful universal force akin to the laws of physics. Of course, others have criticized the book as being pseudoscientific and overly simplistic. Nevertheless, *The Secret* popularized the law of attraction and manifestation techniques in mainstream culture.

It may be surprising to learn that I believe in the law of attraction—but not in the same way that Oprah and Rhonda Byrne do. My belief is much less "woo-woo" and instead rooted in neuroscience. As my friend Andy often says with his Louisiana drawl, "Sometimes ya'll just gotta take the spooky out of it."

THE RETICULAR ACTIVATION SYSTEM

The Reticular Activating System (RAS) is part of the human brainstem. It's job is to filter out unnecessary information so the most important stuff gets through. Even if you are unaware of it, you undoubtedly have experienced it at work.

For example, years ago, I was at my local Honda dealer negotiating the purchase of a brand-new Civic. Before I arrived, I had decided that I wanted a blue Civic. But once on the lot, the salesperson informed me they were out of the blue Civics and showed me a green one instead. It was a lovely shade of green, and I remember thinking, "This looks nice! Besides, I've never seen a green one. I'll probably be the only person in town with this unique color." But on the way home, I noticed two other green Civics. Over the next week or two, I saw green Civics everywhere!

Obviously, the green Civics didn't suddenly appear, and I didn't manifest them. They were there all along; I just didn't notice them. My RAS was at work, helping me notice what I now find worthy of attention: green Honda Civics. You've had experiences like this as well. Your RAS is why you can tune out a crowd of talking people as background noise yet immediately snap to attention when someone says your name. Your RAS takes what you think is essential and filters out the rest. It presents only important information to your conscious mind.

I recently saw this meme on a social media platform and thought it perfectly illustrated how the RAS works:

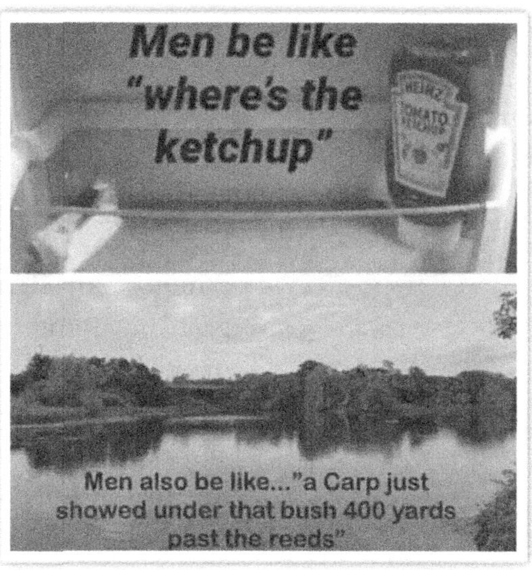

We often see and hear what we are looking for, not what is actually there.

TELL ME WHAT YOU WANT

A person's RAS is not static; instead, we can train it. If you intentionally focus on a goal, your RAS will look for the people, information, and opportunities that will help you achieve the goal. For example, If you want a pet turtle, and 15 times a day you say to yourself, "I will find myself the perfect pet turtle," you'll tune in to the right information, the right people, and the right opportunities that will help you find that turtle. That is an overly simple example, but salespeople do this with sales, researchers do this with research, and so on. They focus on a goal or what they want to notice and put their RAS to work at filtering out what doesn't fit that goal.

The dynamic at work with our RAS reminds me of Jesus' teaching on prayer in which he admonishes his followers, "Keep on asking, and you will receive what you ask for. Keep on seeking, and you will find. Keep on knocking, and the door will be opened to you."[2] In my humble opinion, Jesus' teaching is not necessarily about receiving supernatural intervention from The Divine but clarifying what we desire and activating our RAS.

Some religious traditions might call this kind of focus *prayer* or *meditation*, but frankly, I think those labels come with too much baggage to be helpful in this conversation. I want to call it "Priming the Pump of my RAS," but you can probably come up with a better name than that. There is nothing spooky or woo-woo about it. It's all neuroscience, but making it a spiritual practice will significantly help your spiritual journey.

To integrate this into your life, intentionally focus on an outcome that will be the filter through which you see the world. You might write this on a 3x5 card and repeat it to yourself about fifteen times daily, reminding your RAS that this is what you want to focus on.

Unsurprisingly, many people who read *The Secret* book wanted to manifest money, fame, or the perfect lover. However, as discussed in this book's "Clarify" section, what we initially think we want is often not what we really want. Do we really want money, or do we crave security and stability? Do we really want power or desire to feel like our lives are not out

2. Luke 11:9.

of control? What is the "why" underneath what we think we want? What presents as our desire is often a proxy for something deeper.

I suggest starting with this question, "What do I really want, and why do I want it?" If you ask yourself that question fifteen times a day and reflect on it, you will essentially be doing the "Five Whys" exercise of Chapter 4. As you dig deeper and deeper, you will see things you never noticed before. Your world will open up to people, information, and opportunities you never realized existed. You will see green Honda Civics that you did not know were there.

It may be that you need a better job and need to make money. There is nothing wrong with that. Reworking your 3x5 card of desires to say "I need a job that pays me a living wage and is meaningful" will open your eyes and ears to people, information, and opportunities you never realized were there.

Eventually, however, as you dig deeper into your desires, you will probably begin to realize that your soul desires outcomes like transcendence, intimacy, and meaning. If you dig even deeper than that, you may even find The Divine. That is why this is ultimately a spiritual exercise.

Let me give you a simple example of how this worked in my life. About ten years ago, I was living in Boise and came to Phoenix to visit my daughter, who was attending school here. I had lived in Arizona before and missed the climate, the people, and the lifestyle. Besides, my daughter would put roots down here, and there may be grandkids someday that I want to be here for. I thought, "I don't know how or when, but someday, I will move to Phoenix."

The coffee mug that got me to Phoenix

Coincidently, I bought a Starbucks "Been There" coffee mug while on that trip. It had all the icons of Phoenix on it: the Saguaro cactus, rattlesnakes, coyotes, baseball, etc. For the next five years, whenever the cup

was clean, I would drink my morning coffee from it and think, "I don't know how or when, but someday, I am going to leave Boise and move to Phoenix."

During the middle of the COVID-19 pandemic, I suddenly realized that my job was fully remote, and as a result, I could do my job just as easily from Phoenix as Boise. My RAS kicked in, and I noticed the people, information, and opportunities right before me. Several weeks later, I was in Phoenix (just in time to skip the Boise winter!) The process wasn't nearly as "woo-woo" as Ms. Byrne makes it out to be—but it worked. I attracted (more accurately, noticed) what I was focused on.

FINDING A "CREED"

Another part of the RAS is seeking information that validates our beliefs. If you think that people are basically selfish, greedy, and out for themselves, you will notice evidence everywhere that reinforces that belief. If you believe people are generally kind and generous, you will find proof of that, too. There is plenty of evidence for either of these beliefs, but your RAS finds evidence to reinforce what you have chosen to believe. This can be dangerous when the RAS traps us into biases or stereotypes and doesn't allow us to see another perspective.

Sometimes, our beliefs about the world or The Divine come not from our experiences but from what we *choose* to believe. In those instances, we can choose to believe ideas that become like a compass for how we *want* to see the world, other people, or The Divine.

Some counselors use repeated affirmations to rewire a person's brain to reinforce positive beliefs and thought patterns. Affirmations like "I am enough; I matter" repeated several times a day can trigger our RAS to notice circumstances that align with the affirmations, creating a self-fulfilling prophecy.

In many religious traditions, adherents recite statements of belief or "creeds" that become ways to activate their RAS. Their RAS then becomes the lens through which they see the world:

- In Christianity, the Apostles' Creed and the Nicene Creed are succinct expressions of the dogmas that believers publicly declare together.
- In Islam, *The Shahada* is the Islamic statement that declares belief in one God (Allah) and recognizes Muhammad as God's messenger.
- In Judaism, *The Shema* is a central prayer affirming the oneness of God found in the Torah.
- In Hinduism, *The Gayatri Mantra* is an essential Sanskrit mantra that expresses reverence for the divine.

You may not want to choose to see the world in one of those particular ways, but there may be other beliefs that you want to activate in your RAS to make it the lens through which you see the world. Eugene Peterson, who wrote and thought from a Christian framework, would tuck his young son into bed every night and recite a short set of beliefs that he believed was essential. Eugene hoped to activate his son's RAS to become like his lens of seeing the world. He would repeat, "God loves you. He's on your side. He's pursuing you. He's relentless."[3]

3. There is a beautiful eulogy given by Eugene Peterson's son, Leif, at his memorial service that tells this story: https://www.youtube.com/watch?v=gPl78KZmrYU&ab_channel=jaker599371, accessed June 13, 2024. I recognize the struggle of some readers who dislike referring to The Divine with gendered language. I get it. I see you.

Here are some other examples of creeds that I have recited in my own life to activate my RAS and shape the lens through which I see the world:

- "The world is full of awe, wonder, and beauty waiting for me to notice."
- "Despite their rough exterior, there is a well of goodness and kindness in most people."
- "People are doing the best they can given their circumstances."
- "Growth is more about unlearning old things than learning new things."
- "I will never regret being kind."
- "I can't win over the haters."
- "Love is greater than fear."

These are just examples, of course. My hope is that you will decide for yourself what kind of lens you want to see the world through and create a creed that activates your RAS to do just that.

I realize that some may feel too old and cynical to do this. Maybe you feel as if you have seen too much or experienced too much to *choose* to believe what you want to believe. You may need to recite your creed with another person. This is why many religious institutions say their creeds together, even when we don't believe it to be entirely true. Sometimes having someone next to me who believes enough for the both of us is enough.

It may be that, like Eugene Peterson tucking his son into bed, you need to start by passing on your creed to the next generation instead. Maggie Smith's poem *Good Bones* is a reminder of what it means to be a generational harbinger of hope despite my doubts:

Life is short, though I keep this from my children.
Life is short, and I've shortened mine
in a thousand delicious, ill-advised ways,

a thousand deliciously ill-advised ways
I'll keep from my children. The world is at least
fifty percent terrible, and that's a conservative
estimate, though I keep this from my children.
For every bird there is a stone thrown at a bird.
For every loved child, a child broken, bagged,
sunk in a lake. Life is short and the world
is at least half terrible, and for every kind
stranger, there is one who would break you,
though I keep this from my children. I am trying
to sell them the world. Any decent realtor,
walking you through a real shithole, chirps on
about good bones: This place could be beautiful,
right? You could make this place beautiful.[4]

The dirty little secret of The Secret is that there is no magic "woo-woo" force out there that we can summon and control.

It's you.

You could make this place beautiful.

4. Maggie Smith, *Good Bones*. (North Adams, MA: Tupelo Press, 2017).

22

The Elephant, The Rider, and The Path

I Don't Know Where I'm Going, But I Know Exactly How to Get There

"Start by doing what's necessary; then do what's possible; and suddenly, you are doing the impossible."

—St. Francis of Assisi—

(13th century Italian mystic, poet, and founder of the Franciscan Spiritual Order)

"Keep trying. Stay humble. Trust your instincts. Most importantly, act. When you come to a fork in the road, take it."

—Lawrence "Yogi" Berra—

(American professional baseball player and pithy observer)

A couple of days ago, I was partaking in my nightly ritual of watching ESPN, and sportscaster Scott Van Pelt recounted Tom Brady's heartfelt speech upon being inducted into the New England Patriots Hall of Fame earlier that day. When it comes to Tom Brady, I've always been more of a hater than a lover, but as he said in his speech, "Some may not have liked us, but they certainly ended up respecting us." True. I do have respect for Tom Brady. So, the end of his speech rang true to me:

> Life is hard. No matter who you are, there are bumps and hits and bruises along the way. And my advice is to prepare yourself

because football lessons teach us that success and achievement come from overcoming adversity and that team accomplishment far exceeds anyone's individual goals. To be successful at anything, the truth is you don't have to be special. You just have to be what most people aren't: consistent, determined, and willing to work for it. No shortcuts.[1]

Tom Brady in 2019

Life is hard. Spiritual growth is hard too. If it were easy, this book wouldn't exist.

The Deconstruction/Reconstruction Cycle has an emotional price many are unwilling to pay. It takes some self-awareness and self-reflection, which requires a good dose of emotional maturity. It also takes some ability to think critically about thoughts and ideas and to sort through all the crazy snake-oil salespeople in the spirituality industrial complex. But more than anything, the Deconstruction/Reconstruction cycle journey takes grit and perseverance.

As you read this book, I shared various practices that might aid you on your journey. As a reminder, here are some of them:

- **The Five Whys** (chapter 4). Find the root of your desires by repeating the question "Why?" five times. Sometimes, what we think we want is not what we really want.

1. Ian Logue, "TRANSCRIPT: Tom Brady's Hall of Fame Induction Speech." June 12, 2024. https://www.patsfans.com/patriots/blog/2024/06/12/transcript-tom-bradys-hall-of-fame-induction-speech/, accessed June 13, 2024.

- **Pay Attention** (chapter 5). Do the hard work of paying attention to the awe, beauty, and wonder surrounding you daily.
- **Marie Condo It** (chapter 7). Remove the "debris" you have accumulated over the years and thank it for its service to make room for The Divine to take root and blossom.
- **Treat Your Hurry Sickness** (chapter 8). Slow down the pace of your life to notice and experience the awe and beauty around you.
- **Take an Internet Sabbath** (chapter 9). Take breaks from the dopamine rush addiction of the internet to help your paleolithic mind and emotions not be overwhelmed.
- **Face Your Fears** (chapter 10). Come to terms with what you are unwilling to feel.
- **Develop a Beginner's Mind** (chapter 11). Cultivate the practice of being curious rather than judgmental. Our minds have many blind spots, and we vastly overestimate our abilities.
- **Be. Here. Now.** (chapters 13–18). Practice slowing down your Default Mode Network through meditation and/or other technologies of the sacred to:
  - Accept what you can't control.
  - Let go of the stories you tell yourself that cause suffering.
  - Experience your inter-connectedness to others and the rest of the universe.
- **Develop a Growth Mindset** (chapter 19). Learn to think of your spiritual journey as organic and cyclical, not linear; dynamic, not static. Become process-oriented, not outcome-driven.
- **Find Community** (chapter 20). Find a person or people who can help you on your spirituality journey by providing insight, teaching, friendship, support, etc.

- **Develop a Creed(s)** (chapter 21). Activate your Reticular Activation System (RAS) to intentionally shape the lens through which you see the world.

I have suggested these practices not because they are a checklist for becoming a spiritual person. There is no checklist. Instead, my hope is that you will begin to think of yourself as the type of person who embodies the qualities and practices necessary to be a spiritual person. I hope you will become the kind of person who is consistent, determined, and willing to work to find new ways to let awe, beauty, and transcendence into your life.

THE ELEPHANT, THE RIDER, AND THE PATH

If you have ever tried to break a bad habit or start a new practice, you know that maintaining the grit to persevere, while well-intentioned, is much easier said than done. We have a rational mind that deliberates, analyzes, and understands that we probably *should* focus more on our spirituality. We also have an emotional mind that would much rather doom-scroll on social media or eat ice cream. Humanity has wrestled with this dichotomy for millennia. The ancient Greek philosopher Plato likened our rational minds to a charioteer who must try and control the unruly horse of our emotional mind.

University of Virginia psychologist Jonathon Haidt uses the analogy of an elephant with a rider. Our emotional minds are like an elephant, and our rational minds are like a rider.[2] It appears as if the rider is the one calling the shots with the reigns and the whip. However, the elephant's size is so much greater that if the elephant decides it wants to do something different, there is not much the rider can do.

If you have ever overslept, overate, tried to quit smoking, tried to stick with a diet, skipped the gym, or procrastinated your homework, you

2. Jonathan Haidt, *The Happiness Hypothesis: Putting Ancient Wisdom and Philosophy to the Test of Modern Science.* (New York: Basic Books, 2007), 1–22.

know that sometimes, no matter how much the rider is trying to steer the elephant, the elephant does its own thing. The elephant prefers short-term payoffs (like impulse buys) to longer-term outcomes (like more money in our savings account next year). When it comes to change, the most difficult type of change is delayed gratification—the sacrifice of short-term gains for long-term benefits.

The elephant is not always the bad guy. Yes, he can be impulsive, but he also drives us to fiercely love our kids, be compassionate, be empathetic, and pursue the heart of spirituality—awe, wonder, and transcendence. The rider can be overly analytical and paralyzed by a lack of action, preventing us from getting things done. However, when the elephant is motivated, he will give you the grit of Tom Brady during the NFL playoffs.

Chip and Dan Heath's wonderful book on organizational change, *Switch*, adds another dimension to Jonathan Haidt's metaphor of the elephant and the rider—the path.[3] Sometimes, it is not the rider or the elephant that is the obstacle, but the situation or environment.Television shows like *The Dog Whisperer* and *Supernanny* are intriguing because we can see firsthand the power of an environment on dogs and kids. Outsiders who establish a new environment or path of discipline achieve radically different outcomes in a short period of time: unruly dogs are no longer vicious, and children are no longer mini-terrorists.

Having a clear path means creating environments or situations with a steep downhill slope so that we only need a slight push to get where we want to go. When the path has many clear signs, indicating that we are making progress, and is clear of debris, progress is much easier. A person's environment often shapes human behavior more than motivation.

---

3. Chip Heath and Dan Heath, *Switch: How to Change Things When Change is Hard.* (New York: Broadway Books, 2010).

ATOMIC HABITS

Although he doesn't use this language, my favorite book on creating a clear path is James Clear's *Atomic Habits.*[4] Most people approach self-improvement (whether in health, finances, or spirituality) by setting ambitious goals. However, Clear suggests that if we carve out a clear path—or better systems and practices—it will naturally take us to our desired destination over time.

Here is an oversimplified summary of James Clear's process to cut a clear path for the elephant and rider:

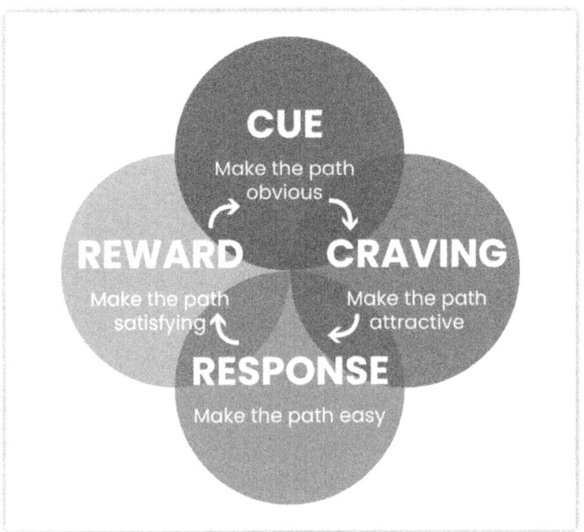

CUE–Make the Path Obvious

According to James Clear, adopting a new practice is much easier if it is noticeable in your environment. Habit stacking is putting a new practice

4. I loved this book so much that I bought a copy for my daughter and told her, "I wish I had this book when I was in my 20s. It would have changed my life." While James Clear doesn't use the language of the path, the book's basic premise is that rather than focusing on setting goals, one should create better systems (or paths). Cf. James Clear, *Atomic Habits: Tiny Changes, Remarkable Results.* (New York: Penguin Random House, 2018).

on top of an existing practice. For example, "After [current practice], I will [new practice]." In my journey, I knew that if I wanted a serious meditation practice, I needed to meditate at the same time and place every day, not only when I was inspired. So now, my morning ritual after coffee, but before checking any messages on my phone, is to meditate at the same location. Strategies like visual cues, setting reminders, or placing related items in a prominent location are helpful. I used this concept to help with physical exercise by putting out my exercise clothes as a mental prompt.

CRAVING—Make the Path Attractive

I spoke so much in this book about awe, wonder, and beauty because practices like Internet Sabbath and Treating Hurry Sickness are not appealing unless there is a positive benefit or positive emotion as a tradeoff. New practices are more likely to stick if we associate them with positive emotions and benefits. This could mean attaching a new practice with something you enjoy, joining a community of like-minded people, or reframing the practice as an opportunity for growth.

RESPONSE—Make the Path Easy

Oreo cookies are not allowed in my house for a simple reason: avoiding temptation is easier than resisting it. If you have a similar Oreo Cookie Rule in your house, you can recognize how avoidance makes the path easier. I have a friend who asks their partner to reset their social media password on Monday and then reveal it on Saturday morning so they don't have to resist the temptation of doom scrolling. Good practices can be made easier when we automate them or prepare our environments to do the practice easily. James Clear calls this "reducing friction." For example, I have a standing Thursday night workout with a workout partner. It makes the path easy because I don't have to think about it, and I don't want to disappoint them by not showing up.

REWARD—Make the Path Satisfying

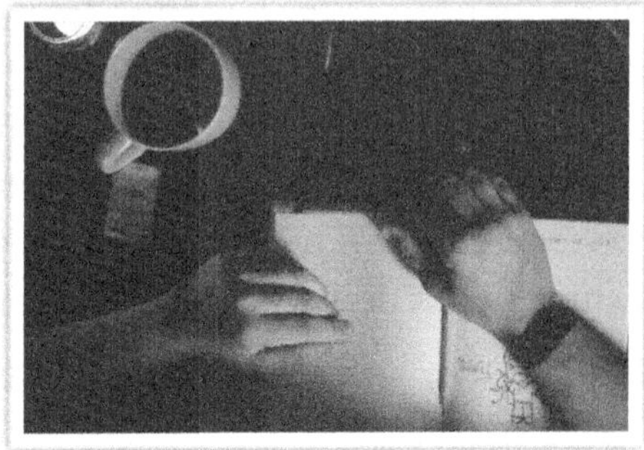

Immediate gratification reinforces a new practice. Apps that can track our progress or celebrations of small wins are reminders to ourselves of why this new practice is important. Many of the practices I have suggested in the book require a lot of quiet reflection and thought (The Five Whys, Marie Condo It, Face Your Fears, etc.). I have journaled (albeit sometimes inconsistently) for over 30 years. I harvest my journal twice a year by reading it, summarizing what I have learned and patterns I observed, and celebrating growth. Like all things organic, measuring your spiritual growth in a short time is hard, but growth is more evident and satisfying over time.

THE FIRST TRACK

You may find all this talk about starting new practices paralyzing and overwhelming. It may be difficult for many to find a good starting place. I have found comfort in Boyd Varty's book, *The Lion Trackers Guide to Life.* The book is a memoir of a lion tracker who grew up in the bush of South Africa, living the life and practices our ancient ancestors once used on the African Savannah. It's about the lost art of using our instincts, paying attention, and finding what we are really looking for.

Varty recounts how his mentor, Ren, reminded him not to look too far down the path but to instead work with what he has now, in *this* moment:

> "Track. Track. Track," Ren has said to me at other times. I understood him to mean find the first track, then the next first track, then the one after that. He does not set out into the unlikely chance of finding a lion in the future. He works with what he has now, in the moment. Joseph Campbell said, "If you can see

your whole life's path laid out then it's not your life's path." In the bush and in life, we don't get trails fully laid out. We get tremendous unknowns and, if we are lucky, first tracks. Then next first tracks…

I remembered a man I had met in a workshop I was facilitating in the Utah mountains. In our conversation, he told me he was burned-out with work and family life. He said he wanted to find his way to a more peaceful place inside himself. The workshop was full of talk but he wanted action, he said, he wanted to be transformed. It's common to think that if we can get the external metrics right everything will be okay. But that does not always leave us the room to learn about ourselves.

I asked him to be quiet for a moment. "What do you need?" I asked.

He immediately started into a story. "I don't get to ask that. I have responsibilities, it's not about me!"

"I know that story," I said. "Go deeper. What do you need?"

He sat for a long moment, then, annoyed, looked at me and said, "I need to be alone for a while. I need some time completely alone. But then what?"

"Don't jump to then what," I replied. "You have a first track. If you go and get some of what you need, you might get a second first track."

The journey to transformation is a series of first tracks. I don't know where I'm going but I know exactly how to get there.[5]

I have no idea where your spiritual journey will take you. However, I can promise you this: at times, it will be overwhelming and, at times, terrifying—not unlike tracking a lion. I can also promise you that it will be worth it. Follow that first track. I don't know exactly where your path will take you, but this book has been my attempt to help you get there.

---

5. Boyd Varty, *The Lion Tracker's Guide to Life.* (New York: Random House, 2019), 45-46. Emphasis mine.

CONCLUSION

The Urgency of The Quest

Why Thin Places Are Essential

"So at the moment the situation appears grim.
And yet there are plenty of reasons to feel hopeful
about the future. To name just a few:
[NOTE TO EDITOR – Please insert some reasons to feel
hopeful about the future, if you can think of any.]"

–Dave Barry–
(Writer and comedian)

"I don't know the future. I didn't come here to tell you how
this is going to end. I came here to tell you how it's going to
begin. I'm going to hang up this phone, and then I'm going
to show these people what you don't want them to see.
I'm going to show them a world without you.
A world without rules and controls,
without borders or boundaries.
A world where anything is possible.
Where we go from there is a choice I leave to you."

–Keanu Reeves as Neo–
(from the closing scene of the film, *The Matrix*)

Larry Laudan, a professor of philosophy at the University of Hawaii, has written a book about risk and devotes one whole chapter to dangers in your household. Some of them are what you'd expect:

- 460,000 people every year are injured by kitchen knives.
- 100,000 people every year are injured by manual and power saws—power tools.
- Every year, twenty people in America are strangled to death on drapery cords.
- Every year, some 4,000 of us seriously injure ourselves on pillows.[1]

But the most dangerous object around your house is not what Larry Laudan would think. It's probably not what you would think, either. Here is what I believe is the most dangerous object in your house:

We usually don't buy couches or chairs for their beauty but for their comfort. The number one best-selling chair in America is La-Z-Boy®. It's not "Risky Boy," not "Adventure Boy," but "La-Z-Boy."

1. Larry Laudan, *The Book of Risks: Fascinating Facts About the Chances We Take Every Day.* (Hoboken: Wiley Publishing, 1994).

What is dangerous about this couch is not what you will do but what you won't do when you are comfortable. It's the places you never go. It's the people you never meet. It's the beauty that you let pass before your eyes unnoticed. It's the gifts you never give or receive. It's the struggles you never endure. It's the tears you never weep. It's the opportunities you never seize.

Scientists did a study years ago with an amoeba in an ideal environment. It was a great life for the amoeba: it had the ideal temperature, humidity, light, water, and food conditions (not unlike that guy on that couch). The amoeba had no stress, no problems, and no challenges. And the amoeba died. Too much comfort can be lethal. Too much comfort can destroy your body, of course. But it can also kill your soul.

Our world has a framing story that says comfort and security are the path to happiness. I have never met you, but I'm confident of this: in your better moments, the deepest desire of your soul, that "thing beneath the thing," is a desire for wonder, awe, and beauty. That is why that couch is the most dangerous thing in your home. Those things are not usually found on couches as we passively watch the world go by.

When I think of the deepest longings of the human soul, I often think of Robin Williams' character, Mr. Keating, in the film, *Dead Poet's Society*, and his introduction to poetry speech. I think one can easily replace the word *poetry* with *thin places*:

> We don't read and write poetry because it's cute. We read and write poetry because we are members of the human race. And the human race is filled with passion. And medicine, law, business, engineering, these are noble pursuits and necessary to sustain life. But poetry, beauty, romance, love, these are what we stay alive for. To quote from Whitman,

"O me! O life!...
of the questions of these recurring;
of the endless trains of the faithless...
of cities filled with the foolish;
what good amid these,
O me, O life?"

Answer: That you are here—that life exists, and identity; that the powerful play goes on and you may contribute a verse.

That the powerful play *goes on* and you may contribute a verse.

What will your verse be?[2]

THE URGENCY OF THE QUEST

As I wrote this book, my day job consisted of working for a nonprofit whose mission is to alleviate poverty in the county that I live in. The underlying idea is that almost all social problems society wants to eradicate find their roots in poverty. A colossal dent could be put in issues like domestic violence, chemical dependency, homelessness, hunger, lack of healthcare, etc., if people simply had the skills and resources to climb out of poverty.

At times, while writing this book, it has felt like an excessive luxury to write about things like awe, wonder, and transcendence on the weekends, while during the week dealing with people in my community who were only concerned with putting food on the table, making the rent payment, or recovering from debilitating traumatic experiences.

Moreover, I am aware that the planet I live on is becoming more difficult to inhabit. An X (formerly Twitter) post from Professor Mark Maslin from University College in London lives rent-free in my mind:

2. Peter Weir, director. 1989.*Dead Poets Society.* Touchstone Pictures.

This clip can be viewed in its entirety at: https://www.youtube.com/watch?v=-7OE6bDfM2M&ab_channel=AcademiaLiteraria

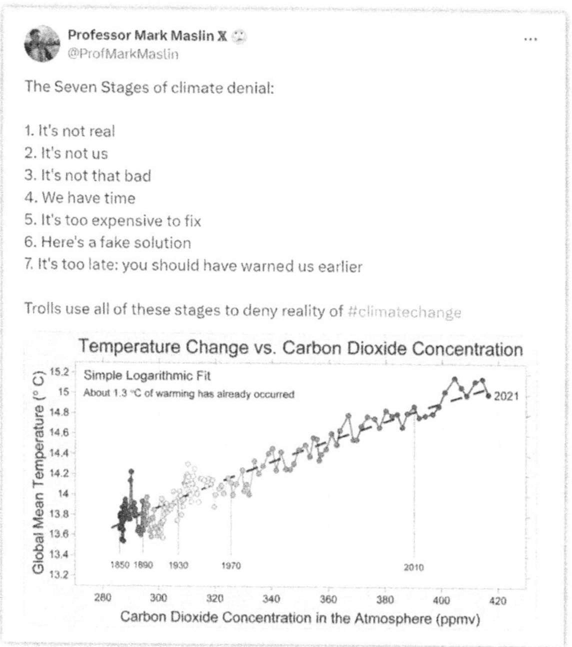

If I think about all this too much, it can overwhelm me. I can also empathize with people who use the term *woke* in a pejorative way—sometimes, sleepy ignorance feels blissful to me. It's deadly, no doubt, but blissful.

With all that is wrong with the world, why spend so much time discussing how to find spirituality after deconstruction? Is the quest for thin places a "weapon of mass distraction" from the more critical issues of the world?

Gus Speth, co-founder of the Natural Resources Defense Council, said:

> I used to think the top environmental problems were biodiversity loss, ecosystem collapse, and climate change. But I was wrong. The top environmental problems are selfishness, greed, and apathy. To deal with those issues we need a spiritual and cultural transformation—and we scientists do not know how to do that."[3]

3. Gregory E. Sterling, "From the Dean's Desk: Reflections." Yale.edu. https://reflections.yale.edu/article/crucified-creation-green-faith-rising/dean-s-desk, accessed June 15, 2024.

We face some enormous challenges as a species. While science and technology may be tools that can help, if we use the Five Whys exercise in this book, we quickly discover that the "thing beneath the thing" at the root of many of our challenges is our lack of spirituality.

To compound our challenges, the religious systems that we have inherited are ill-equipped to provide us with a usable spiritual path forward. In some ways, it is not their fault. As discussed in Chapter 20, large institutions whose primary motivation is self-survival find it difficult to act in ways that enable the common good. In the US, our need is not for "The popular and domesticated Jesus, who has become little more than a chrome-plated hood ornament on the guzzling Hummer of Western Civilization."[4]

WHY THIN PLACES ARE ESSENTIAL

Evolutionary psychologists remind us that we are here as a species because we have learned to do one essential task over millions of years: survive and procreate. The human mind was designed by natural selection to deceive us and enslave us to ensure that we survive and procreate. As a result, most of us are trapped in a prison that we cannot smell, taste, or touch—a prison for our minds. Centering the self above all else is hard-wired into us. Selfishness, greed, and apathy come naturally to us.

But it doesn't have to be that way. The quest for the thin places where The Divine and our world intersect is the search for awe, wonder, beauty, and transcendence. The poet Ralph Waldo Emerson famously said, "Beauty is its own excuse for Being,"[5] but I think beauty has a pur-

4. Brian D. McLaren, *Everything Must Change: Jesus, Global Crisis, and a Revolution of Hope* (Nashville: Thomas Nelson, 2007), 6.

5. Ralph Waldo Emerson, *The Essential Writings of Ralph Waldo Emerson.* Ed. Brooks Atkinson (New York: Modern Library, 2020), 689.

pose. The Russian novelist Dostoevsky contended that beauty points us to something beyond ourselves and will "save the world."[6]

It is possible to get off the couch and "take the red pill" to see the world as it is. We can see beyond our deeply held impulse to survive and procreate. We can let go of framing stories that cause us to suffer. We can turn toward what we are afraid to feel. We can let go of the fears that drive us to act without regard for the common good.

Even more profoundly, we can escape the trick mirror of rugged individualism and know that we are all interconnected and that there is no such thing as "them." We are all swimming in the same pool. There is no isolated "me" apart from "you."

These thin places where The Divine and our world intersect can make us more generous, empathetic, and compassionate toward all living things. Other people's suffering becomes our suffering. Harming other people is the same as hurting ourselves. Our planet's plight becomes our plight. Albert Einstein, reflecting in the wake of World War Two on our place in the universe, said:

> A human being is a part of the whole called by us 'universe,' a part limited in time and space. He experiences himself, his thoughts and feelings as something separated from the rest, a kind of optical delusion of his consciousness. This delusion is a kind of prison for us, restricting us to our personal desires and to affection for a few persons nearest to us. Our task must be to free ourselves from this prison by widening our circle of compassion to embrace all living creatures and the whole of nature in its beauty.[7]

---

6. Fyodor Dostoevsky, *The Idiot*, trans. Constance Garnett (Hertfordshire, UK: Wordsworth Classics, 1996), 356.

7. Walter Sullivan, "The Einstein Papers. A Man of Many Parts." The New York Times. March 29, 1972. https://www.nytimes.com/1972/03/29/archives/the-einstein-papers-a-man-of-many-parts-the-einstein-papers-man-of.html. Gender-exclusive language is *sic erat scriptum* from its original context.

I can appreciate that the lure of comfort and security can be seductive. I own a couch, also. Beyond that, I know you have things to do—bills to pay, kids to pick up from school, laundry to fold, etc. I get it. I feel it, too. But Gus Speth is right: our planet's greatest challenges are not scientific and technological but spiritual. Your quest for thin places is bigger than you and me. It is not an exaggeration to say that it can save the world.

APPENDIX A

Training Your Puppy

Some Meditations on Meditation

When it comes to meditation, I know enough to know that I don't know very much. In the Dunning-Kruger scale, I am at the low point of confidence, which may mean that I know just enough to be dangerous. With that disclaimer, here are some very basic instructions to get your meditation practice started:

- Find a quiet, comfortable place where you won't be disturbed. Sit in a relaxed position, cross-legged on the floor or in a chair with your feet flat on the ground. Keep your back straight but not tense.
- Close your eyes and take a few deep breaths to settle yourself.
- Allow your breathing to return to its natural rhythm. Focus your attention on your breath, noticing the sensation of air moving in and out of your body.
- As you meditate, your mind will inevitably wander. This is normal and very common. When you notice your thoughts drifting, gently bring your attention back to your breath without judgment.
- Start with short sessions, perhaps 5–10 minutes, and gradually increase the duration as you become more comfortable with the practice.
- Consistency is vital, so try meditating daily, even for a few minutes.

One of my favorite explanations of meditation comes from Jack Kornfield's book, *A Path with Heart.* His comparison of training one's mind to training a puppy was beneficial to me:

> In this way, meditation is very much like training a puppy. You put the puppy down and say, "Stay." Does the puppy listen? It gets up and it runs away. You sit the puppy back down again. "Stay." And the puppy runs away over and over again. Sometimes the puppy jumps up, runs over, and pees in the corner or makes some other mess. Our minds are much the same as the puppy, only they create even bigger messes. In training the mind, or the puppy, we have to start over and over again.
>
> When you undertake a spiritual discipline, frustration comes with the territory. Nothing in our culture or our schooling has taught us to steady and calm our attention. One psychologist has called us a society of attentional spastics. Finding it difficult to concentrate, many people respond by forcing their attention on their breath or mantra or prayer with tense irritation and self-judgment, or worse. Is this the way you would train a puppy? Does it really help to beat it? Concentration is never a matter of force or coercion. You simply pick up the puppy again and return to reconnect with the here and now.[1]

BOOKS TO GET YOU STARTED

There are thousands of books written on meditation, most of whose authors know a lot more about it than I do. So, to avoid malpractice on my part, I'll give you a brief annotated bibliography of some introductory resources that may be helpful. Keep in mind that there are many types of meditation. Experiment to find what works best for you. Also, remember,

---

1. Jack Kornfield, *A Path with Heart: A Guide Through the Perils and Promises of Spiritual Life* (New York: Bantam Books, 1993), 59.

there's no right way to meditate—the goal is to cultivate awareness and presence.

1. Bhante Henepola Gunaratana, *Mindfulness in Plain English* (Boston: Wisdom Publications, 1991).

This book is a highly regarded and accessible guide to Vipassana meditation, written by Theravada Buddhist monk Bhante Gunaratana. It offers a clear, practical, and in-depth exploration of mindfulness meditation, making it valuable for beginners and experienced practitioners. The author addresses common misconceptions about meditation and then provides detailed instructions on posture, breathing, and mindfulness practice. His writing style is direct and often humorous, making potentially dry subject matter engaging and relatable. While rooted in traditional Buddhist teachings, the book presents meditation in a secular context, making it accessible to readers of various backgrounds. It has been particularly influential in introducing Vipassana meditation to Western audiences and is often recommended as a foundational text for those interested in mindfulness practice.

2. Thich Nhat Hanh, trans. Mobi Ho, *The Miracle of Mindfulness: An Introduction to the Practice of Meditation* (Boston: Beacon Press, 2016).

Originally written as a long letter to his colleagues in Vietnam during the Vietnam War, this book has become a classic guide to mindfulness practice. Thich Nhat Hanh is a Vietnamese Zen Buddhist monk and peace activist. He presents mindfulness not just as a formal meditation practice but as a way of life, encouraging readers to find mindfulness in everyday activities such as washing dishes, drinking tea, or walking. The book includes practical exercises and anecdotes illustrating how to cultivate mindfulness in various situations. Hanh emphasizes the interconnectedness of all things and the importance of living fully in the present moment. While rooted in Buddhist tradition, the book's teachings are presented in a way that resonates with people of all backgrounds. This book has been particularly impactful in demonstrating how mindfulness can be applied to promote inner peace and social change.

3. Dan Harris, *10% Happier: How I Tamed the Voice in My Head, Reduced Stress Without Losing My Edge, and Found Self-Help That Actually Works—A True Story* (New York: It Books, 2014).

In this book, ABC News anchor Dan Harris recounts his journey from skeptic to meditation advocate. The book begins with Harris's on-air panic attack in 2004, which catalyzed his exploration of mindfulness and meditation. He takes readers through his encounters with self-help gurus, religious figures, and neuroscientists, as he searches for ways to quiet his inner voice and reduce stress. Harris argues that meditation can lead to being "10% happier," a modest but meaningful improvement in one's life. The book blends memoir, scientific inquiry, and practical advice, making it accessible to readers new to meditation.

4. Andy Puddicombe, *The Headspace Guide to Meditation & Mindfulness* (New York: St. Martin's Griffin, 2016).

Andy Puddicombe is the co-founder of the popular *Headspace* meditation app. This book offers a practical and accessible introduction to meditation and mindfulness practices. Drawing from his decade of experience as a Buddhist monk and his subsequent work bringing meditation to a wider audience, he presents meditation techniques in a secular, science-based context. The book is structured to guide readers through a 10-minute daily meditation practice over ten days, with each day focusing on a different aspect of mindfulness. Puddicombe combines clear instructions with relatable anecdotes and metaphors, making complex concepts easy to understand for beginners. He addresses common obstacles to meditation and provides strategies for incorporating mindfulness into daily life. While the book is meant to be a companion to the

Headspace app, it can stand alone as a comprehensive guide to starting a meditation practice.

5. Robert Wright. *Why Buddhism Is True: The Science and Philosophy of Meditation and Enlightenment* (New York: Simon & Schuster, 2017).

This book is less of a "how to meditate" and more of a good intellectual jumping-off point. In the book, Robert Wright explores the intersection of Buddhist philosophy and modern scientific understanding, particularly in evolutionary psychology and neuroscience. He focuses on how Buddhist practices, especially mindfulness meditation, can help individuals overcome the psychological challenges inherent in our evolutionary heritage. The book examines concepts such as the illusory nature of the self, the role of natural selection in shaping our perceptions and emotions, and how meditation can lead to a more accurate and beneficial understanding of reality. Wright draws on his personal experiences with meditation retreats to illustrate these ideas, making the book part philosophical argument, part scientific exploration, and part memoir.

MEDITATION APPS

Many people, including myself, find meditation apps helpful in their meditation practice. The two big players in the meditation app business are Headspace and Calm. I've used both but currently use Headspace.

Currently, both cost about $70/year for all the bells and whistles, but for basic functions, they are free. The paid version will get you many guided meditations, teachings, courses, and meditations for particular solutions (i.e., pre-interview jitters).

Early in my meditation journey, I paid the annual subscription and used many of the guided meditations. Now, however, I just use the timer and background ambiance, which are free.

APPENDIX B

A Brief History of Technologies of the Sacred In the Western World

Because of my academic background in Christianity, I found the Eleusinian mysteries in Greece fascinating. While largely ignored or minimized by Western historians, these rituals and spiritual experiences enormously impacted Greek culture and, by proxy, western civilization. Among its initiates were a who's who of ancient celebrities: Plato, Aristotle, Epictetus, Sophocles, and Cicero,[1] to name a few.

Exactly what mind-altering substances were used at these rituals remains unknown. (Hence the name, "Mystery Religions.") Some scholars, however, speculated that the potion was a mixture of alkaloids of ergot, similar to LSD.[2] What is clear is that the carrier of this "technology of the sacred" was wine, served during a ritualized meal. The effects of this wine on its participants were profound enough to keep the rituals alive for almost 2,000 years.

Two years of studying the Koine Greek language were part of the core curriculum of my academic training, because both early Christianity and the New Testament were profoundly influenced by Greek culture (Hellenism) and these Mystery Religions. The two religions share similarities in

1. In his book *De Legibus,* Cicero spelled out his experiences with mystical technologies and their effects on ancient civilization. Cf. Marcus Tullius Cicero, *De Legibus*, trans. Clinton Walker Keyes (Cambridge, MA: Harvard University Press, 1928).

2. R. Gordon Wasson, Albert Hofmann, and Carl A.P. Ruck, *The Road to Eleusis: Unveiling the Secret of the Mysteries* (New York: Harcourt Brace Jovanovich, 1978).

Painting of Dionysus, the Greek god of wine, by Caravaggio

metaphors: death/rebirth, eating symbolic meals, and, most notably, wine in the Dionysian Mysteries.[3] A parallel reading of John's Gospel and *The Bacchae* (an ancient Greek tragedy written by Euripides that describes the rituals of the Mystery Religions) reveals eerily similar scenes and vocabulary. While they appear in different contexts, words common in the Mystery Religions, like *mystery* (μυστήριο) and *learned secret* (μυέω), also appear in other parts of the New Testament.

The scholarship of Brian C. Muraresku argues that the earliest Greek-speaking Christians used the wine of the Eucharist (Holy Communion) similarly to their Greek ancestors: as a technology of the sacred with psychedelic substances. In his controversial book, *The Immortality Key*, he wrote:

> I sat down with the government ministers, curators, and archivists whose mission is to guard precious relics that rarely see the light of day. I grilled the excavators, archaeobotanists, and archaeochemists who are in the field and laboratory right now, unearthing fresh evidence of our ancestor's ritualistic use of drugs and subjecting it to a battery of high-tech instrumentation. And I trekked through time with the classicists, historians, and Biblical scholars who are trying to make sense of it all.

3. The rejection of Gnosticism at the Council of Nicaea (325 AD) was a clear repudiation of the Mystery Religions. However, for the first couple hundred years, the Christians were deeply influenced by the Hellenistic culture that dominated the world at that time and very likely benefited from the spiritual technologies that were commonly in use.

This investigation has led me to conclusions I never could have anticipated twelve years ago. Not only is there evidence of psychedelic beer and wine at the heart of the Greek and Christian Mysteries, but also evidence of their suppression by the religious authorities.[4]

Despite the Christian church's aversion to "technologies of the sacred" through the centuries, there remained a thread of people who were much more interested in the mystical and spiritual aspects of its founder rather than the political and institutional baggage. From the Jesus Prayer in Eastern Orthodoxy (Hesychasm) to the exercises of Ignatius of Loyola, technologies of the sacred have always been a part of the Christian tradition in the Western world, although it has often been an almost trivial thread.[5]

A MODERN RENAISSANCE

Humanity's longing for transcendence and spirituality runs so deep in the human soul that it emerges in unexpected places when it can't find expression in religious institutions. On April 16, 1943, the Swiss chemist Albert Hofmann worked at the Sandoz Laboratories in Basel, Switzerland. He was conducting research into the medicinal value of lysergic acid compounds derived from ergot, a fungus that grows on rye and other grains. While re-synthesizing LSD-25 (the 25th compound in the lysergic acid series he had produced), he accidentally absorbed a tiny amount of the drug through his fingertips.

Later that day, Hofmann began experiencing strange symptoms like dizziness, anxiety, visual distortions, and an altered perception of reality.

---

4. Brian C. Muraresku, *The Immortality Key*, 20.

5. As noted by scholars like Phillip Jenkins, Christianity in the global South (the non-Western world) is, unlike the global North, thriving. One reason (among many) for this is that its expression is much more charismatic and mystical. Africa, Asia, and Latin America have very different expressions of Christianity than what we are used to in the US. Cf. Philip Jenkins, *The Next Christendom: The Coming of Global Christianity* (Oxford: Oxford University Press, 2002).

Dr. Albert Hoffman

He noted unusual sensations and perceptions that were unlike any other known drugs at the time. At first, Hofmann was unsure of what caused these bizarre effects. It wasn't until a few days later, when he intentionally ingested a small dose of LSD, that he could confirm it was the source of his psychedelic experience.

At the same time, Freudian psychology and behaviorism were beginning to fall out of favor, with psychiatrists and researchers looking for new models of treatment for mental illness. Hoffmann's serendipitous discovery became the basis for our pharmacological understanding of the brain's workings. One physician recalled:

> In the 1950s and 1960s, psychedelics were the "wonder drugs" of psychiatry. They lifted psychiatry off the psychoanalytic couch and into the brain, ushering in the new discipline of psychopharmacology—how drug effects on brain chemistry change our consciousness. While antipsychotic and antidepressant medications also appeared at this time, psychedelics promised the greatest revolution in mental health care. Their allure included providing psychedelic—assisted psychotherapy for intractable emotional and addictive disorders, keys to unlock the secrets of psychosis, training aids to enhance empathy in psychotherapists, and a shortcut to creativity and spiritual enlightenment.[6]

6. Rick Strassman, *The Psychedelic Handbook* (Berkeley, CA: Ulysses Press, 2022), 7.

Twelve years after Hofmann's discovery, a Manhattan banker and amateur mycologist named R. Gordon Wasson and his pediatrician wife, Valentia, stumbled upon a religious ceremony of the Mazatec Indigenous people in the town of Huautla de Jiménez in the southern Mexican state of Oaxaca. A couple of years later, Wasson wrote an article for Life Magazine describing the "mushrooms that cause strange visions."[7]

Life Magazine in 1957 with the story of the "mushrooms that cause strange visions."

The impact of Western science's discovery of these two molecules is hard to overstate. Michael Pollen reflected:

> In time, [psychedelics] would change the course of social, political, and cultural history, as well as the personal histories of the millions of people who would eventually introduce them to their brains. As it happened, the arrival of these disruptive chemistries coincided with another world historical explosion—that of the atomic bomb. There were people who compared the two events and made much of the cosmic synchronicity. Extraordinary new energies had been loosed upon the world; things would never be quite the same.[8]

As is the case with powerful new technologies of any kind, humanity's ability to understand psychedelic's impact and create healthy boundaries around it could not keep pace with its popularity. The Baby Boomers

7. R. Gordon Wasson, "Seeking the Magic Mushroom." Life. May 13, 1957, 100–120.
8. Michael Pollen, *How to Change Your Mind,* 3.

were coming of age, and part of their countercultural movements of the 1960s meant experimenting with psychedelics recreationally for the first time. Timothy Leary's promotion of psychedelics at Harvard University included catchphrases like "Turn on, tune in, drop out," which encouraged illegal drug use and an anti-establishment counterculture.

By 1965, all the optimism created by the advent of these "wonder drugs" had been replaced by sheer panic in the broader culture, as fears of bad trips, psychotic breaks, flashbacks, and suicides made their way into the public consciousness. By the end of the 1960s, psychedelic drugs became illegal and were forced underground. Timothy Leary's salesmanship and self-promotion overshadowed the science, leading to a backlash that halted academic research for decades.

In 1971, there was a raging war in Vietnam, and America's young people were growing increasingly unwilling to fight it, because some of their psychedelic experiences had so profoundly changed the way they saw the world. Murdering people in another part of the world on behalf of a social construct like a nation-state suddenly seemed absurd. So, President Richard Nixon declared Timothy Leary "The most dangerous man in America," and the Nixon administration worked to "blunt the counterculture by attacking its neurochemical infrastructure."[9]

Timothy Leary in 1969.

Historically speaking, psychedelic experiences can be so profound and life-altering that political and religious hierarchical structures, whether Spanish missionaries in Mexico or the US

9. Michael Pollen, *How to Change Your Mind*, 58.

President Richard Nixon, are threatened by them. Unsurprisingly, they were pushed underground in the Western world for over 40 years.

NEW PSYCHEDELIC RESEARCH

After almost 40 years of virtually no progress on the academic front, there slowly began to emerge a renaissance of psychedelic research at major academic institutions. During the past 20–25 years, scientists have been rigorously investigating the therapeutic potential of compounds like psilocybin (Magic Mushrooms), LSD, and MDMA (Molly or Ecstasy) for conditions like depression, post-traumatic stress disorder, obsessive compulsive disorder, eating disorders, addiction, and end-of-life anxiety. Studies at places like Johns Hopkins, NYU, and Imperial College London have shown that psilocybin can produce lasting reductions in depression and anxiety when given in a supportive setting.

Meanwhile, because of its overwhelmingly positive results in clinical trials, any day now, MDMA is expected to be fully approved by the Food and Drug Administration as an assisted psychotherapy for treating PTSD.[10]

Religious statues involving Psilocybe Mushrooms

At other places, research into the neurological mechanisms behind psychedelics' consciousness-altering effects is also advancing our understanding of brain circuitry and perception. Newer molecules inspired by psychedelics' structures, like psilocybin derivative compounds, are being explored as next-generation therapeutic psychedelics. While

10. Let me temper these assertions with the observation that since the days of Timothy Leary, there is often an irrational exuberance around psychedelic research. I don't believe that these molecules are a panacea for whatever mental health affliction ails us. For a variety of reasons, my prediction is that the current enthusiasm will eventually give way to a more modest assessment of their potential.

much work remains, this research is knocking over past stigmas by generating evidence-based data on powerful neuropsychiatric treatments.

Psychedelics are powerful chemical compounds. In the broadest sense of the word, they are drugs: they can have intended physiological effects when administered to diagnose, treat, or alter the body's systems and functions in some way. But psychedelics are qualitatively different from the way that most Western medicine has thought of drugs. For example, your sense of consciousness probably won't be altered if you take a high blood pressure medicine or an allergy pill.

The recreational use of psychedelics is also different than other recreational drugs. While there is no danger of addiction with psychedelics,[11] its careless usage by inexperienced guides can sometimes create terrifying and mind-altering "bad trips." The use of Magic Mushrooms by Baby Boomers in the 1960s and 1970s, for example, was not supplemented by the centuries-old rituals designed by the indigenous people of Mexico that made it into a transformative technology of the sacred. They failed to recognize that some things are just bigger than us and demand our respect. Not surprisingly, casually playing with a nuclear bomb for one's brain can be hazardous.[12]

---

11. Multiple peer-reviewed studies and literature reviews from credible research institutions have consistently shown that psychedelics are very safe for humans. They are non-addictive, and it is virtually impossible to die from an overdose of them. Cf. Yasmin Schmid, Alistair A. Gasser, Daniela Gasser, Matthias E. Liechti, and Ferdinand Aaltonena, "Repeated Low Doses of LSD In Healthy Adults: A Placebo-Controlled, Dose-Response Study." Psychopharmacology. 237, no. 4 (2020): 1135–1152. Their non-addictive nature is considered one of their advantages as potential therapeutics.

12. Unlike many Millennials, I am not asserting that Baby Boomers have ruined *everything*. However, it is undeniable that they set back important psychedelic research by decades.

APPENDIX C

Magic Mushrooms

Some Practical Considerations

DISCLAIMER:

As you read this appendix, please keep in mind that despite the potentially beneficial effects of altering consciousness with psychedelics, I do not condone any illegal activity. In most of the world, it is unlawful to possess psychedelics such as mescaline, DMT, LSD, and psilocybin. Additionally, always seek the advice of your doctor or other qualified health provider before using any new chemical substance.

Like the Appendix on meditation, I confess that I am far from an expert on psilocybin or other chemical technologies of the sacred. As a practical matter, I have found Rick Strassman's book, *The Psychedelic Handbook*[1] an invaluable resource. Dr. Strassman is a clinical associate professor of psychiatry at the University of New Mexico School of Medicine. He has dedicated his academic life to the study of psychedelics and is both credible and measured in his guidance. Please read his book

1. Rick Strassman, *The Psychedelic Handbook: A Practical Guide to Psilocybin, LSD, Ketamine, MDMA, and DMT/Ayahuasca* (Berkeley: Ulysses Press, 2022).

before experimenting with any psychedelic medicine, including Magic Mushrooms.

That being said, here are the main things I have learned in my psychedelic journeys.

SET AND SETTING

Undoubtedly, you have heard horror stories of bad psychedelic trips. Magic Mushrooms and other psychedelics are not like most medications that are prescribed to alter the biological processes in our bodies. Psychedelics affect our brains in powerful ways. As a result, our psychological mindset when we take the medicine matters greatly. This is why the exact dosage of the same drug can have drastically different responses in different people. Psychedelics do not automatically generate mystical or spiritual experiences. What is paramount is what researchers call "set" and "setting."

"Set" refers to the person taking the drug: their physical health, their mental health, the other medications they are taking, their diet, other substances they are taking (including alcohol and opioids), their sleep patterns, their stress level, the presence or absence of supportive social structures, their previous experiences (if any) with psychedelics, etc.

Additionally, "set" includes a person's intentions and expectations. Do they want it to be a recreational, "trippy" experience? Or are they looking for healing or a spiritual experience? What are their goals, if any?

Beyond that, what are their beliefs about the psychedelics themselves? What do they expect to happen?

"Setting" has to do with the physical space in which a person experiences the drug: indoors or outdoors; in a clinical research context or at a rave party; alone or with friends; with an experienced guide or with novices; in silence or with music; eyes opened or blindfolded?

As you can see, the infinite variations in set and setting creates unlimited possible outcomes.

DOSAGE OF PSILOCYBIN

Usually, psilocybin is taken orally as a mixture in tea or chocolate. The effects of Magic Mushrooms begin about 30 minutes after ingestion, peak at one to two hours, plateau for about two hours, and are mostly gone after six to eight hours.

Dailing in the exact dosage of psilocybin you desire can be tricky for several reasons. Unlike the prescriptions you pick up at your local pharmacy, Magic Mushrooms do not have laboratory standards or a government agency overseeing them. As a result, their quality and potency vary greatly. Additionally, because Magic Mushrooms are organic fungi, particular strands can differ significantly in their potency of psilocybin from region to region and grower to grower. Finally, like any mind or body-altering chemical, legal or illegal, people's responses vary. What has a mild effect on some people has a powerful impact on others.

GUIDES

If you are considering using magic mushrooms as a technology of the sacred in your spiritual journey, I would strongly encourage you to find an experienced guide to help you find a good set, setting, and dosage to optimize your experience. I wouldn't trust anyone who hasn't already helped guide at least 50-100 people. I am partial to Mexico and the indigenous healers there, because I don't worry about law enforcement and psilocybin-healing rituals have existed there for centuries. I'm sure other places are great, but I am unfamiliar with them.

Moreover, knowing what you want from the experience will help you pick a good guide. Are you looking primarily for a spiritual experience or a healing experience? Different guides have different "specialties."

If you decide to venture out to a spiritual or healing ceremony, I would love to hear about your experience. Please send me an email!

PICTURE CREDITS

INTRODUCTION

Image #1 – Gungor, Michael (@michaelgungor) "Thread: The typical stages of religious deconstruction are a journey that many of us have been on. Here are some thoughts on each stage:" Twitter, May 31, 2023, 3:36 PM. http://twitter.com

Image #2 – Dana Hicks. "Michael Gungor's Stages of Deconstruction." Digital Image.

Image #3 – Dana Hicks. "The Deconstruction/Reconstruction Cycle." Digital Image.

CHAPTER 1

Image #1 – "Bishop William Willamon." Digital Image. Crackers and Grape Juice Podcast. October 23, 2023. https://crackersandgrapejuice.com/dont-look-back/.

Image #2 – Pixabay. "Grayscale Photography of Bottles on Top of Table." Digital Image. Pexels. January 27, 2024. https://www.pexels.com/photo/grayscale-photography-of-bottles-on-top-of-table-274192/.

Image #3 – Jia Tolentino sitting on a box. Digital Image. Jai Tolentino's Blog. November 16, 2023. https://jia.blog/.

Image #4 – Mennenga, Mason (@masonmennenga) "I'm grateful evangelicals introduced me to jesus because I probably wouldn't have left evangelicalism if they hadn't" Twitter, October 18, 2023, 3:08 PM. http://twitter.com.

CHAPTER 2

Image #1 – Kevin Malik. "A Person Removing a Jenga Piece." Digital Image. Pexels. June 17, 2024. https://www.pexels.com/photo/a-person-removing-a-jenga-piece-8762363/

Image #2 – Alexandra (@alexbilbs) "*in hell* Me: excuse me I was told there would be a special place for me here?" Twitter, September 22, 2023. http://twitter.com

CHAPTER 3

Image #1 – Pixabay. "Person Leaning on a Wall." Digital Image. Pexels. June 17, 2024. https://www.pexels.com/photo/person-leaning-on-wall-236151/

Image #2 – Dana Hicks. "The Bridge Across the Colorado River from Nevada to Arizona." Digital Image.

Image #3 – Dana Hicks. "Somewhere in the Jungle of Quintana Roo, Mexico." Digital Image.

CHAPTER 4

Image #1 – Asher Perlman (@asherperlmanalexbilbs) "I mean, I can throw it a third time." Twitter, April 19, 2023. 5:05 PM. http://twitter.com

Image #2 – Pixabay. "Abraham Lincoln Statue." Digital Image. Pexels. June 17, 2024. https://www.pexels.com/photo/abraham-lincolcn-statue-161892/

CHAPTER 5

Image #1 – "Three Tiered Universe." Digital Image. Quora. February 28, 2022. https://www.quora.com/Does-the-Earth-really-have-a-firmament-over-it

Image #2 – Domenico Feti. "Moses before the Burning Bush" Digital Image. Web Gallery of Art. https://www.wga.hu/html_m/f/feti/moses.html

Image #3 – Nextvoyage. "Grayscale Low Angle Photo of High Rise Buildings." Digital Image. Pexels. June 17, 2024. https://www.pexels.com/photo/grayscale-low-angle-photo-of-high-rise-buildings-2019546/

Image #4 – Paul Jones. "Irish rock band U2 performing at The O2 in London, England on October 24, 2018 on their Experience + Innocence Tour." Wikimedia Commons. October 24, 2018. https://commons.wikimedia.org/wiki/File:U2_performing_on_Experience_and_Innocence_Tour_in_London_10-24-18_(3).jpg

CHAPTER 6

Image #1 – "Plato's Cave." Digital Image. Trimble Construction. June 11, 2021. https://constructible.trimble.com/construction-industry/how-bim-software-turned-into-platos-cave.

Image #2 – "Dacher Keltner." Digital Image. Berkleyside. July 26, 2017. https://www.berkeleyside.org/2017/07/26/dacher-keltner-pursues-happiness-things-greater-good-science-center.

Image #3 – Flyingdebris (@flyingdebrisguy) "any sufficiently large organization/institution, if pressed will almost invariably…" Twitter, June 8, 2023, 5:59 PM. https://twitter.com.

Image #4 – Vinícius Vieira. "Man in White Button-up Shirt." Digital Image. Pexels. July 17, 2024. https://www.pexels.com/photo/man-in-white-button-up-shirt-3155367/

CHAPTER 7

Image #1 – Enes Akdemir. "David of Michelangelo Sculpture in Florence." Digital Image. Pexels. July 19, 2024. https://www.pexels.com/photo/david-of-michelangelo-sculpture-in-florence-16970086/

Image #2 – "Meister Eckhart." Digital Image. Peter Rollins.com. July 17, 2024. https://peterrollins.com/miester-eckhart

Image #3 – "Marie Kondo." Digital Image. Facebook. February 6, 2019. https://www.facebook.com/photo.php?fbid=10216469438463316&set=t.100044465468175&type=3

Image #4 – Brandi, Her Royal Duckship (@ItsTheBrandi). "Marie Kondo: …so then you just get rid of everything that doesn't spark joy." Twitter, May 8, 2020, 10:38 PM. https://twitter.com

Image #5 – "St. Paul's Monastery on Mount Athos." Digital Image. Greek City Times. September 21, 2020. https://greekcitytimes.com/2020/09/21/st-paul-monastery-on-mount-athos-in-lockdown-after-11-cases-of-covid-19-detected/

CHAPTER 8

Image #1 – Abby Heugel (@AbbyHasIssues). "I get annoyed when it takes longer than five seconds for a website to load on my phone…" Twitter, March 10, 2024, 4:43 PM. https://twitter.com

Image #2 – Loren Kerns. "Dallas Willard giving a Ministry in Contemporary Culture Seminar at the George Fox Evangelical Seminary in Portland, Oregon in 2008." Digital Image. Wikimedia Commons. September 26, 2008. https://commons.wikimedia.org/wiki/File:Dallas_Willard.jpg

Image #3 – Erin. "Joe Looking at The Moon." Digital Image. ERIN PAINTS STICKS. February 6, 2013. https://anamateursview.weebly.com/someplacemagic/joe-versus-the-volcano

Image #4 – "Ixodes holocyclus before and after feeding." Digital Image. Wikipedia. July 19, 2024. https://en.wikipedia.org/wiki/Ixodes_holocyclus

Image #5 – Jon Guinn. "Sound of Metal Exposes Our Unhealthy Dependence on Technology." Digital Image. Medium. September 26, 2021. https://medium.com/jonguinn/sound-of-metal-exposes-our-unhealthy-dependence-on-technology-37df57b55d09

CHAPTER 9

Image #1 – Owl! At the Library (@SketchesbyBoze). "kids today are like 'so what did ya'll do before the internet?'" Twitter, July 26, 2022, 9:14 AM. http://twitter.com

Image #2 – Michael Erhardsson. "Grayscale Photo of a Train." Digital Image. Pexels. July 19, 2024. https://www.pexels.com/photo/grayscale-photo-of-a-train-5265138/

Image #3 – Dan Byles. "Technology, disruption, the Internet of Things…and you." Digital Image. LinkedIn, January 26, 2016. https://www.linkedin.com/pulse/technology-disruption-internet-things-you-dan-byles/

Image #4 – Emo Philips (@EmoPhilips). "To the chimp I laughed at in a psychology textbook that was addicted to flushing a toilet again & again…'" Twitter, February 12, 2016, 1:25 PM. http://twitter.com

Image #5 – Roman Odintsov. "Couple Hugging and Using Smartphone Near Sea On Sunset." Digital Image. Pexels. July 19, 2024. https://www.pexels.com/photo/couple-hugging-and-using-smartphone-near-sea-on-sunset-4555321/

Image #6 – Tima Miroshnichenko. "Grayscale Photo of People Sitting on the Chairs." Digital Image. Pexels. July 19, 2024. https://www.pexels.com/photo/grayscale-photo-of-people-sitting-on-the-chairs-5711022/

CHAPTER 10

Figure #1 – Dana Hicks. "Quincy 'Wiggle Butt' Hicks." Digital Image.

Figure #2 – David Sheff. "M. Scott Peck." Digital Image. DavidSheff.com. March, 1992. https://www.davidsheff.com/m-scott-peck

Figure #3 – Dibakar Roy. "Grayscale Photo of a Man Wearing Turban." Digital Image. Pexels. July 19, 2024.https://www.pexels.com/photo/grayscale-photo-of-man-wearing-turban-5598616/

CHAPTER 11

Image #1 –Pixabay. "Close Up of Zipper of Blue Denim Bottoms." Digital Image. Pexels. July 19, 2024. https://www.pexels.com/photo/close-up-of-zipper-of-blue-denim-bottoms-206365/

Image #2 – Samuel Perry (@profsamperry). "The human capacity to delude ourselves, as individuals and in groups, never ceases to astound this social scientist." Twitter, November 23, 2022, 4:36 AM. http://twitter.com

Image #3 – New York World-Telegram and the Sun Newspaper Photograph Collection (Library of Congress). "Lenny Bruce, head-and-shoulders portrait, facing left." Digital Image. Wikimedia Commons. October 15, 2020. 2008. https://commons.wikimedia.org/wiki/File:Lenny_Bruce_1961.jpg

Image #4 – Jason Adam Katzenstein. "Let me interrupt your expertise with my confidence." Digital Image. Facebook. August 8, 2020. https://www.facebook.com/newyorker/photos/a.430906773868/10157721925768869/?type=3

Image #5 – Historic Vids (@historyinmemes). "McArthur Wheeler wearing the lemon juice." Digital Image. Twitter. August 22, 2023. https://x.com/historyinmemes/status/1693897564557324767

Image #6 – 7804j. "Satirical diagram inspired by the XY scatter plot representation of data from the original Dunning and Kruger study and illustrating a subject's self-report during skill acquisition." Digital Image. Wikimedia Commons. February 14, 2022. https://commons.wikimedia.org/wiki/File:Dunning%E2%80%93Kruger_effect_chart.svg

Image #7 – Ted Lasso Lassoism (@TedLassoism). "If they were curious, they would've asked questions." Digital Image. Twitter. August 20, 2023. https://x.com/TedLassoism/status/1693314340659839368

CHAPTER 12

Image #1 – Samantha Bereson. "Keanu Reeves in 'The Matrix' screenshot." Digital Image. IndieWire. March 7, 2023. https://www.indiewire.com/features/general/keanu-reeves-still-has-matrix-red-pill-1999-movie-1234816681/

Image #2 – AurélienPierre. "Donald Hoffman. Under-exposed picture taken from https://en.wikipedia.org/wiki/Donald_D._Hoffman#/media/File:DonaldHoffman.jpg and retouched for better clarity." Digital Image. Wikimedia Commons. July 19, 2015. https://commons.wikimedia.org/wiki/File:Donald_Hoffman.jpg

Image #3 – Designecologist. "Silver iMac Turned on Displaying Different Photos." Digital Image. Pexels. July 19, 2024. https://www.pexels.com/photo/silver-imac-turned-on-displaying-different-photos-1999463/

Image #4 – Pixabay. "Bengal Tiger Laying in Green Grass at Daytime." Digital Image. Pexels. July 19, 2024. https://www.pexels.com/photo/bengal-tiger-laying-in-green-grass-at-daytime-68134/

CHAPTER 13

Image #1 – Freepik "Portrait Person with Visual Metaphor Memory." Digital Image. Freepik. July 5, 2024. https://www.freepik.com/free-ai-image/portrait-person-with-visual-metaphor-memory_138701776.

Image #2 – jcomp. "One Hiking Lifestyle Summer Yoga." Digital Image. Freepik. July 19, 2024. https://www.freepik.com/free-photo/one-hiking-lifestyle-summer-yoga_1088161.htm

Image #3 – Katrin Bolovtsova. "Brain Shape Eraser and a Paper Clip." Digital Image. Pexels. July 19, 2024. https://www.pexels.com/photo/brain-shape-eraser-and-a-paper-clip-6192326/

Image #4 – Valeriia Miller. "Converse All Star Low Top Sneakers on Brown Wooden Surface." Digital Image. Pexels. July 19, 2024. https://www.pexels.com/photo/converse-all-star-low-top-sneakers-on-brown-wooden-surface-2530912/

Image #5 – methodwriter85. "Let me show you the most beautiful thing I've ever seen....*cut to floating plastic bag*." Digital Image. Reddit. https://www.reddit.com/r/Xennials/comments/npjoom/let_me_show_you_the_most_beautiful_thing_ive_ever/

Image #6 – WikiPedant. "Chuck Yeager next to experimental aircraft Bell X-1 #1 Glamorous Glennis." Digital Image. Wikimedia Commons. May 30, 2017. https://commons.wikimedia.org/wiki/File:Chuck_Yeager.jpg

CHAPTER 14

Image #1 – Spindled. "A solid tone image of the first card in the Rorschach inkblot test." Digital Image. Wikimedia Commons. October 19, 2006. https://commons.wikimedia.org/wiki/File:Inkblot_svg.svg

Image #2 – nuraghies. "Wooden table with a blurry wine shelf backdrop." Digital Image. Freepik. July 19, 2024. https://www.freepik.com/free-ai-image/wooden-table-with-blurry-wine-shelf-backdrop_84736883.htm

Image #3 – DreamStudio. "Road Rage." AI-generated Image. FreePik. July 5, 2024.

Image #4 – Beao. "Bill Maher attending a ceremony to receive a star on the Hollywood Walk of Fame." Digital Image. Wikimedia Commons. September 14, 2010. https://commons.wikimedia.org/wiki/File:BillMaherSept10.jpg

Image #5 – Jonnmann. "Ciclo de conferências do filósofo francês Michel Foucault, no Hospital das Clínicas da Universidade do Estado da Guanabara (UEG)." Digital Image. Wikimedia Commons. October 13, 1974. https://commons.wikimedia.org/wiki/File:Michel_Foucault_1974_Brasil.jpg

Image #6 – Pixabay. "Man in Water." Digital Image. Pexels. July 19, 2024. https://www.pexels.com/photo/man-in-water-247616/

Image #7 – Mikhail Nilov. "Man Practicing Meditation on Sports Mat." Digital Image. Pexels. July 19, 2024. https://www.pexels.com/photo/man-practicing-meditation-on-sports-mat-6945094/

CHAPTER 15

Image #1 – Remitamine. "Alexis de Tocqueville" Digital Image. Wikimedia Commons. September 28, 2020. https://commons.wikimedia.org/wiki/File:Alexis_de_Tocqueville_(Th%C3%A9odore_Chass%C3%A9riau_-_Versailles).jpg

Image #2 – Max Flinterman. "Silhouette of a Man Standing under a Lamp Post." Digital Image. Pexels. July 19, 2024. https://www.pexels.com/photo/silhouette-of-man-standing-under-lamp-post-715425/

Image #3 – Stable Diffusion. "Fecal Matter in The Pool Sign." AI-generated image. Canva. March 28, 2024.

Image #4 – Pittigrilli. "Steve Jobs at the WWDC 07." Digital Image. Wikimedia Commons. June 17, 2007. https://commons.wikimedia.org/wiki/File:Steve_Jobs_WWDC07_(cropped).jpg

Image #5 – Patton Oswalt (@pattonoswalt). "There is no 'Them.'" Digital Image. Twitter. April 1, 2022. https://twitter.com

CHAPTER 16

Image #1 – "Ramadan Will Officially Begin on March 23rd." Digital Image. Scenenow. March 13, 2023. https://scenenow.com/Buzz/Ramadan-Will-Officially-Begin-on-March-23rd

Image #2 – Stable Diffusion. "Oneness Symbol." AI-generated image. Canva. March 28, 2024.

Image #3 – Stable Diffusion. "Deconstructed Toyota Tacoma." AI-generated image. Canva. March 28, 2024.

Image #4 – Matanya (usurped). "Harvard University image of Whitehead, circa 1924." Digital Image. Wikimedia Commons. May 10, 2007. https://commons.wikimedia.org/wiki/File:ANWhitehead.jpg

Image #5 – Nathalie Robin Justice Gravel (@welcomewords). "If a monkey hoarded more bananas that it could eat, while most of the other monkeys starved…" Digital Image. Twitter. February 2, 2021. https://twitter.com

CHAPTER 17

Image #1 – kjpargeter. "Male Medical Figure with Brain Highlighted." Digital Image. FreePik. July 19, 2024. https://www.freepik.com/free-photo/3d-male-medical-figure-with-brain-highlighted_2800856.htm

Image #2 – "Prof. Dr. Roland Griffiths." Digital Image. Insight Conference. https://insight-conference.eu/speaker/roland-griffiths/

Image #3 - Stable Diffusion. "Plunging into Water." AI-generated image. Canva. March 28, 2024.

Image #4 – "The Saturday Evening Post." Digital Image. The Saturday Evening Post. October 18, 1958.

Image #5 – 45154james. "Robin Carhart-Harris during meeting at the Centre for Psychedelic Research. Imperial Centre for Psychedelic Research, London.

Photograph by Thomas Angus, Imperial College London." Digital Image. Wikimedia Commons. July 23, 2019. https://commons.wikimedia.org/wiki/File:190723_Robin_Carhart-Harris,_Centre_for_Psychedelic_Research_meeting_(cropped).jpg

Image #6 – Dana Hicks. "The Sliders." Digital Image.

CHAPTER 18

Image #1 – Dana Hicks. "Nine Perfect Strangers in Playa del Carmen." Digital Media.

Image #2 – Dana Hicks. "Receiving a Blessing from the Mayan Shaman." Digital Media.

Image #3 – Dana Hicks. "Sunset over The Pacific Ocen in Puerto Vallarta." Digital Media.

CHAPTER 19

Image #1 – Stable Diffusion. "Chaos." AI-generated image. Canva. March 28, 2024.

Image #2 – Dana Hicks. "The Deconstruction/Reconstruction Cycle." Digital Image.

Image #3 – Gruban. "Stanford Psychology professor and author Carol Dweck speaking for the documentary Innovation: Where Creativity and Technology Meet, http://www.innovationmovie.com." Digital Image. Wikimedia Commons. July 13, 2015. https://commons.wikimedia.org/wiki/File:Carol_Dweck_for_Innovation_documentary.jpg

Image #4 – Akil Mazumder. "Person Holding a Green Plant." Digital Image. Pexels. July 19, 2024. https://www.pexels.com/photo/person-holding-a-green-plant-1072824/

CHAPTER 20

Image #1 – Nehrams2020. "Joseph Gordon-Levitt and Zooey Deschanel at a premiere for (500) Days of Summer in March 2009." Digital Image. Wikimedia Commons. March 22, 2009. https://commons.wikimedia.org/wiki/File:Joseph Gordon-LevittZooeyDeschanel500DaysMar09.jpg

Image #2 – Chiquo. "A pyramid chart with examples of the categories." Digital Image. Wikimedia Commons. April 10, 2019. https://commons.wikimedia.org/wiki/File:Maslow%27s_Hierarchy_of_Needs.jpg

Image #3 – Chattrapal (Shitij) Singh."Photo Of Crowd Of People Gathering Near Jama Masjid, Delhi." Digital Image. Pexels. July 19, 2024. https://www.pexels.com/photo/photo-of-crowd-of-people-gathering-near-jama-masjid-delhi-2989625/

Image #4 – JMGRACIA100. "Bayaka people in the Dzanga Sangha Ndoki reserve. Central African Republic rainforest." Digital Image. Wikimedia Commons. August 10, 2014. https://commons.wikimedia.org/w/index.php?curid=52373514

Image #5 – FreePik. "Gender Violence Concept." Digital Image. FreePik. July 19, 2024. https://www.freepik.com/free-vector/gender-violence-concept_8967837.htm

Image #6 – Courtneyperry. "Phyllis Tickle." Digital Image. Wikimedia Commons. October 9, 2009. https://commons.wikimedia.org/wiki/File:Phyllis_Tickle.jpg

Image #7 – Ron Lach. "Smiling Girls in a Small Group of Teenagers on Walk on Forrest Footpath." Digital Image. Pexels. July 18, 2024. https://www.pexels.com/photo/smiling-girls-in-small-group-of-teenagers-on-walk-on-forest-footpath-10484693/

CHAPTER 21

Image #1 –FreePik. "Door Leading to a Magical World." Digital Image. FreePik. July 19, 2024. https://www.freepik.com/free-ai-image/door-leading-magical-world_94542042.htm

Image #2 – Apprehensive-Listen6. "Ketchup and Carp Meme." Digital Image. Reddit. July 19, 2024. https://www.reddit.com/r/memes/comments/oxvadn/true_d_d/

Image #3 – Tara Winstead. "Drawing on Chalkboard." Digital Image. Pexels. July 19, 2024. https://www.pexels.com/photo/adhd-drawing-on-chalkboard-8378736/

Image #4 – Dana Hicks. "Starbucks Mug." Digital Image.

Image #5 – Allie Feeley. "Paper Card on Tree Bark." Digital Image. Pexels. July 19, 2024. https://www.pexels.com/photo/paper-card-on-tree-bark-20671757/

CHAPTER 22

Image #1 – Merson. "Brady and Stidham in 2019." Digital Image. Wikimedia Commons. October 6, 2019. https://commons.wikimedia.org/wiki/File:Tom_Brady_2019.jpg

Image #2 – Kent Zhong. "Man Riding an Elephant." Digital Image. Pexels. Jun 25, 2024. https://www.pexels.com/photo/man-riding-an-elephant-9206628/

Image #3 – Dana Hicks. "Summary of James Clear's Atomic Habits." Digital Image.

Image #4 – Isaac Taylor. "Person Holding Notebook Beside Ceramic Cup." Digital Image. Pexels. June 28, 2024. https://www.pexels.com/photo/person-holding-notebook-beside-ceramic-cup-1541216/

CONCLUSION

Image #1 – Freepik "Robot Vacuum Cleaning Floor" Digital Image. Freepik. July 5, 2024. https://www.freepik.com/free-ai-image/robot-vacuum-cleaning-floor_150959022.htm

Image #2 – DreamStudio. "Robin Williams in Dead Poets Society" AI-generated Image. FreePik. July 5, 2024.

Image #3 – Maslin, Mark (@ProfMarkMaslin) "The Seven Stages of climate denial:" Twitter, March 28, 2024, 1:31 AM. https://twitter.com/ProfMarkMaslin/status/1773266583663624234

APPENDIX B

Image #1 – Commonists. "Dionysus in Bacchus by Caravaggio." Digital Image. Wikimedia Commons. August 1, 2021. https://commons.wikimedia.org/wiki/File:Bacchus_by_Caravaggio_1.jpg

Image #2 – "Albert Hofmann" Digital Image. Lapham's Quarterly. https://www.laphamsquarterly.org/contributors/hofmann

Image #3 – "Life Magazine." Digital Image. May 13, 1957.

Image #4 – PascalHD. "Tim Leary, antique pot head of the world, press conference in the Federal Building after testifying in the conspiracy trial." Digital

Media. Wikimedia Commons. December 19, 1969. https://commons.wikimedia.org/wiki/File:Timothy_Leary_(1969_press_photo).jpg

Image #5 – Thenub314. "Religious statues involving Psilocybe Mushrooms." Digital Image. Wikimedia Commons. September 30, 2003. https://commons.wikimedia.org/w/index.php?curid=10869478

Made in the USA
Coppell, TX
01 March 2026

72666724R00173